Poletown

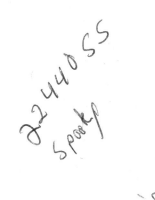

Poletown
Community Betrayed

Jeanie Wylie

with a Foreword by
Ralph Nader

and Photographs by
David C. Turnley

University of Illinois Press
Urbana and Chicago

Illini Books edition, 1990
© 1989 by the Corporate Accountability Research Group
Manufactured in the United States of America
P 5 4 3 2

This book is printed on acid-free paper.

Library of Congress Cataloging-in-Publication Data

Wylie, Jeanie, 1956–
    Poletown : community betrayed / Jeanie Wylie.
      p.   cm.
    ISBN 0-252-06153-5 (alk. paper)
    1. General Motors Corporation. 2. Automobile industry
and trade—Social aspects—Michigan—Detroit. 3. Factories—
Location—Social aspects—Michigan—Detroit. 4. Poletown
(Detroit, Michigan)
    I. Title.
    HD9710.U54G4758   1989
    323.4'6—dc20   89-32070
                                                               CIP

Previously published in a cloth edition (ISBN 0-252-01624-6)
by the University of Illinois Press.

To Samuel and Beatrice Wylie,
in thanksgiving for their faith and joy,

and to Bill Kellermann,
who has made my life complete.

Contents

Foreword
Ralph Nader

This is the story of the spirited, integrated, lower-middle-class urban community in Detroit that refused to die until the bulldozers of corporate socialism destroyed its physical being. The story has an epic
quality that speaks to the future as well as the past. The sovereign power
of the world's largest automobile manufacturer—General Motors—
sighted the community's 465 acres—hundreds of homes, schools,
churches, retail stores, small producers, and a hospital. Its imperious
demands for city hall to exercise eminent domain over the area for an
automated luxury-car factory were conveyed. A former socialist and
civil rights advocate, Mayor Coleman Young moved to condemn the
neighborhood under the state's new "quick take" law. Over $350 million
of local, state, and federal subsidies were placed on the sovereign's table
as an enticement for the plant's construction within Detroit's city limits
instead of at a nearby location that would have saved Poletown with its
4,200 residents. The corporate sovereign told the political bureaucracy to
move quickly to flatten, clear, and prepare the area or risk losing the
factory to other jurisdictions. Negotiations and arrangements, even
those in writing between city hall and General Motors, were concealed.
All necessary city council approvals and permits were secured in record
time. Epidemics of arson began breaking out in Poletown, adding fire to
the combined power of the corporate state.

The people of Poletown were at first plainly stunned. These were
avowedly patriotic Americans whose sons fought in World War I and
World War II and later police actions in Asia. They were devout church-
goers, as the twelve churches testified. They were community people
helping and consoling and enjoying each other up and down and across

the streets. Poletown had a sense of history—the late-nineteenth-century settlement by Eastern European immigrants, their important role in the sit-down strikes leading to the creation of the United Auto Workers Union, the sober adjustment to an integrated neighborhood without disruption, and the neighborly rituals and communal projects going back decades—that gave spice and remembrance to everyday talk on porches, between windows of close-by homes, and in the neat gardens and sidewalks that spelled a comfortable familiarity with roots.

Then suddenly, as if issued from the guns of Fort Sumter, the news imploded on them. General Motors wanted their homeland and the news came not from the GM Building but from city hall. The first hearing brought disbelief, but the reality of the planned demolition was conveyed to them by the emissaries of condemnation who invaded the neighborhood in the early fall of 1980. It was urgent that Poletowners reach out for help, but there was no extended hand. Other citizen groups, muzzled by the grants machine that Washington provided city governments, looked the other way. The UAW chose its priority—the factory—and declined to credit the claims that both factory and community could co-exist with some acreage and local adjustments. The Catholic archdiocese saw an opportunity to sell its churches and consolidate its patronage, diminishing due to outward immigration of a younger generation to the suburbs. The lawyers were ridden with the conflict between their desire to retain more lucrative clients and their concern not to offend the establishment and thus curtail their careers, while Poletown's representative, George Crockett, and senators Donald Reigle and Carl Levin refused even to meet with them, much less represent their pleas for help in any way. Poletown was a community abandoned to its lonely fate of extinction. Even the courts became a mirror image of the power structure that wanted what Rome warranted for Carthage—*delenda est* Poletown. In perhaps the most extreme judicial sanction behind corporate power against individual property rights, a majority of the judges deciding the Poletown cases up to the Michigan Supreme Court ruled that a city government could take private property by eminent domain and transfer it to a profit-making corporation. Such is the extension of the "public purpose" rationale for eminent domain that General Motors' proposal was defined as a "public purpose."

The destruction of Poletown took place during an auto industry recession brought about by the now widely acknowledged inefficiency, waste, and mismangement of its leadership that led foreign competitors with more fuel-efficient cars to expand their market share. The top executives did not resign, but many autoworkers were laid off in the Detroit region. As the auto companies became temporarily weaker economically, they became stronger politically. Their demands on governments for abatements, lenient enforcement, and direct subsidies became commands meekly accepted. Michigan Supreme Court justices Fitzgerald and Ryan wrote in their dissent: "Eminent domain is an attribute of sovereignty. When individual citizens are forced to suffer great social dislocation to permit private corporations to construct plants where they deem it most profitable, one is left to wonder who the sovereign is." Assailing the majority's opinion that pronounced lawful the taking of Poletown by the City of Detroit for General Motors, the dissenters wrote that "there is virtually no limit to the use of condemnation to aid private businesses. . . . . No homeowner's, merchant's, or manufacturer's property, however productive or valuable to its owner, is immune from condemnation for the benefit of other private interests that will put it to a 'higher use.'"

Almost unmentioned in the discourses over the Poletown controversy was the fact that taxpayers inside and outside that enclave were also paying for the direct and indirect subsidies woven together by the mayor and handed to the giant automaker. Thus GM took, and made their victims pay, an added premium on top.

Writ large, Poletown becomes a metaphor for the politics of abandonment, where the rule of power in an economic recession rides roughshod over the rule of law with scarcely a murmur of protest from a clutch of countervailing constituencies that society was entitled to rely upon in a crunch. It becomes a metaphor for institutionalized deceit, prevarication, and betrayal as the ballooning costs of subsidizing GM continue to pile on the City of Detroit while an ineffective robotic factory limps along with a work force less than half that promised by the company as a key inducement to the city's demolition power and its corporate welfare package. In fact, one industry insider said that the Poletown plant was the "single worst implementation of computer-integrated manufacturing in the United States."

There will be more to the Poletown story as the insiders and participators begin to unencumber their consciences and speak about the machinations. Perhaps the media, which reported the personal tragedies of Poletown but ducked the hard investigative job of going behind the visuals to the backroom powerplays and exchanges, will take a retrospective and prospective look at the demolition decision now nearing its tenth anniversary. At least, they may pay factual tribute to the survivors of Poletown, whose warnings have borne truth, and to those martyrs, such as Father Joseph Karasiewicz, of their beloved community who lost their breath of life when the set fires, the bulldozers, the steel ball pulverized the place where they lived, worked, played, and prayed from their childhood to older age. Someday, too, a plaintiff will pursue Michigan's "quick-take" law to the Supreme Court of the United States as an unconstitutional taking of one's private property for another private property's profit and benefit.

The end of the physical Poletown, where now a parking lot and shrubbery surround a factory that occupies only one-sixth of the total seized acreage, does not end its lesson for future corporate–city hall aggressions. Before going down it showed that a defenseless but stalwart community can jolt a city and a corporate giant to their heels and demonstrated that much can be learned from its loss: the next communities who choose survival over servility will be more likely to prevail.

In this book Jeanie Wylie provides the text and context for the Poletown saga that only an on-the-spot observer with an acute eye can offer. The growing interest by professors in this clash between corporation and community made the documentary film *Poletown Lives!* a popular presentation in classrooms around the country, and this volume will be a welcome literary addition to that award-winning portrayal of character in a community beset by the soulless juggernauts of mercantilism.

Preface

The first time I stepped foot in Poletown, the neighborhood had already been condemned by the City of Detroit. It was a dark night, but even so I could tell that the neighborhood was much like my own—wood-frame homes, brick churches, well kept but poor.

The Poletown Neighborhood Council was meeting in the basement of the Immaculate Conception Church. An American flag was tacked above the clock, a piano stood at the side of the stage, and 150 people sat at long tables. The room was comfortable. The people seemed solid. It would be a good place for a Shrove Tuesday dinner or a Polish dance.

But the air was tense. Older women and mothers with children sat upright, listening keenly, trying to sort through the laws and regulations that were mowing down their hopes of staying in their community. The city's plan was to clear the land for a new GM Cadillac plant.

"I got the deed to my house, how can they say my house doesn't belong to me?" one woman asked. "I haven't signed anything."

"I wrote a letter to the president," another woman began. "They said the president doesn't answer mail and they referred me to the HUD office downtown."

These were people who believed in the system. People who wore flags on their union jackets. People who had paid their dues in the factories and in their homes. People whose children couldn't afford college but were willing to join the Service.

I was struck by their integrity and stricken by their vulnerabilty.

I wrote articles for the *Village Voice*, the *Progressive*, and the *San Francisco Chronicle*, explaining that, while Detroit needed jobs, taking

Poletown away from the people who had built it violated civil rights. I outlined the alternatives that some architects believed could allow the neighborhood and the new plant to co-exist. I tried to help by being present. When the church was seized by the city's Special Weapons Attack Team, I went to jail in the company of four elderly women.

The last months of the demolition in Poletown were excruciating. I remember a Saturday afternoon when three homes were burning. A woman stood on the street in tears because teenagers had just broken in the basement window of her landlady's home. Word came to the church that three elderly people had died during the trauma of relocation. Residents complained that they couldn't breath because of the smoke and demolition dust that filled the air.

I was overwhelmed by the injustice. And I was constantly shocked by the media reports that somehow made the whole enterprise palatable.

After the neighborhood had been bulldozed and the lives of 4,200 people uprooted, I coproduced *Poletown Lives!* a documentary that contrasts the faith of the residents with the arrogance of those who considered them expendable. But I still felt that the story remained largely untold: the powers which coalesced to force the demolition of Poletown were unexposed. And I believe that at the heart of this story is something critical to democracy in America.

Detroit was nearly bankrupt when it made the decision to level Poletown in order to accommodate GM's new Cadillac plant. Times were extremely hard for city residents. Businesses had been fleeing Detroit for some time. Certainly something had to be done, but I question whether the solution was for General Motors and the City of Detroit (and the union, the church, and the media) to coalesce to displace 4,200 people.

In Europe in the 1940s the economic climate was foreboding and the middle class was suffering. Many nations opted then for fascism. Getting the trains to run on time became a symbol, but the price was sacrificing democracy to the primacy of business, government, and labor.

Felix Rohatyn, an American corporatist, suggests that democracy works only in times of prosperity. When the pie is shrinking, he says, the public won't make voluntary sacrifices. The decisions must be made by those who know best. Coalition groups involving politicians, corporate executives, and union officials are so credible. They are professional. They have money to spend. Their public relations experts can take the wrinkles out of anything. They have the resources to make things happen, and the media nearly always heralds their aptitude and benevolence.

This book shares the experience of a community shattered by a decision made by a corporation, a city, a union, a church, and an unquestioning public. It shows how Poletown's residents studied the specifics involved, proposed their own alternatives, aggressively sought media attention, and did everything in their power to demand redress. From the beginning, Poletown's residents said their fight was waged for America, for freedom, and for the future.

Their courage, their insistence that things be explained to them and that they be heard, gives all of us an opportunity to see into the brutal mechanics of betrayal. But their struggle is in no way parochial. It is a betrayal that is being acted out in cities around the nation, where poor neighborhoods are routinely sacrificed for commercial development projects. It is acted out in the Midwest, where family farms and whole towns are being swept out of existence.

Acknowledgments

First thanks go to Bill Kellermann for believing in the book and in what it stands for. Secondly, I'd like to thank Rich Feldman for insisting that the manuscript be published and Peter Stine for his merciless editing.

I am fundamentally endebted to Sandy Livingston, who worked in Poletown during the struggle and later organized a great deal of data for this book, writing a chronology and drawing together composites of many Poletown residents. Despite working under frustrating conditions, Sandy was able to put together a major contribution to this book.

Special thanks to David Turnley for making so many of his exquisite photographs available. While working for the *Detroit Free Press*, David spent a great deal of time in Poletown, documenting the character of the neighborhood. In the process, he clearly learned to know and care for its very spirit.

For comments and suggestions, I am indebted to Grace Boggs; Rich Feldman; Jane Slaughter; Pat Barszenski; Bernice Kaczynski; Carol Dockery; Don Martin; Mel Hall; and Gordon Judd.

A number of people provided clippings, memos, and files. Thanks to Clark and Helen Cunningham, George Corsetti, Pat Barszenski, Bernice and Harold Kaczynski, Henry Stokes, Michael Betzold, Dave Crummy, Liz Walters, and the Corporate Accountability Research Group.

Coordinating use of a word processor gave rise to more problems than I care to remember, but I am very grateful to Deb and John Ferris for lending me their home computer and for continuing to help even after their system was stolen from my house. I am grateful to Laura Markham for liberating my disks from a computer transfer center and to Kevin Bentley for his technical help.

Essential Information Inc. provided a grant for the continuation of this project. Carol Bernstein-Ferry and W. H. Ferry also offered support.

I'm indebted to Gary and Mildred Kellermann and Kim Conwell for occasionally keeping Lydia Wylie-Kellermann out from under foot and to Lydia herself for finding the world worth exploring.

Poletown

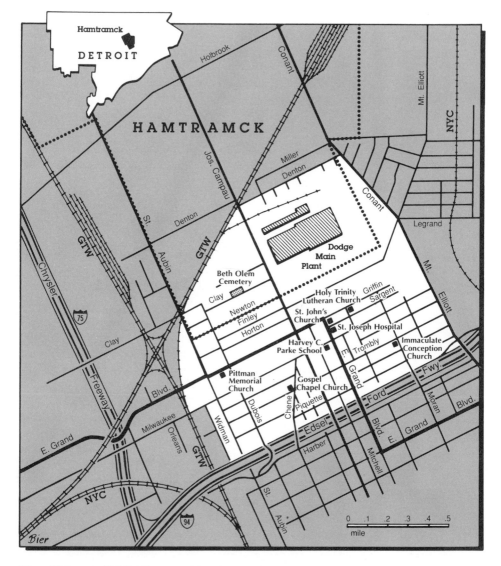

Map of Poletown, highlighting area claimed for the Poletown Cadillac plant

1

The Assembly Line, the Old Country, the Church

It was what you'd expect of the early days of urban areas—all of us foreign-born people. The little cobbler that came over, the little hole in the wall. He'd say, "That's where my shoe store's going to be." And the little guy that took a couple bolts of cloth and says, "That's going to be my dry-goods store...." They took a chance with their lives. They couldn't speak English, yet they could open up a tinsmith's shop, a blacksmith's shop.... In the morning you would get up and you could feel the ground breathing under your feet. It was like a symphony in music the way it played and hummed. You could almost set your clock by the trucks—at the way the trucks started going by in the morning, the milk man and this one and that one. You could feel the rhythm.

—Carl Fisher, owner of Poletown's Famous Bar-B-Q Restaurant

As early as the 1880s, there was a thriving immigrant neighborhood in Detroit known as Poletown. The area was a lower-income, working-class community, crowded with Polish shops and well-kept wood-frame houses. The immigrants, who came from areas in occupied Poland under German, Austrian, or Russian domination, were united in a common religious heritage, and within four decades six Polish Catholic churches were dedicated in the neighborhood. Predictably, old-world prejudices were maintained in the new world, and Poles, who were following German immigrants to Detroit's east side, were held at arm's length by their neighbors.

As early as 1893 Poles rioted for jobs, an act which historian John Bukowczyk says may have been prompted by their belief that "they possessed a social right to have work."[1] The following year, Poles engaged in a major riot over low piece rates at the Conner Creek water main construction site. One Detroit Pole who agonized over the poverty and inhumane working conditions was Leon Czolgosz. In 1901 Czolgosz, a self-described socialist and anarchist, shot and killed President William McKinley. His confession has disappeared, but newspaper reports indicate that his grievance was that "McKinley was going around the country shouting prosperity when there was no prosperity for the poor man."[2]

By the turn of the century, 48,000 Poles had settled in Poletown, in an area between two rail lines where farm land soon gave way to an industrial corridor. The men found work in heavy metal industries; the women, in cigar and match factories. Five cigar companies located plants right in Poletown. A number of manufacturers, including the American Radiator Company, Russel Wheel and Foundry Company, and Acme White and Color Works, located in Hamtramck, an independent German town of 3,500 north of Poletown. Men also found work in Detroit manufacturing stoves, ships, steam engines, iron and steel, and doing unskilled construction.[3]

In 1910 the Dodge Brothers built their massive, eight-story auto-parts plant in Hamtramck. Tens of thousands of Poletown residents walked to work at "Dodge Main," stopping in the bars and shops that grew up around the edges of the plant property. Employment at the Dodge plant drew 45,000 new residents to the two-square-mile village of Hamtramck; it incorporated as an independent city in 1922 and yielded control of its government to the Poles, who were then an 80 percent majority. Dodge Main drew other auto-parts and assembly plants into the area, which eventually housed a Detroit Electric Car plant, three Cadillac plants, a Packard plant, a Studebaker plant, a Hudson auto plant, and Hupp Motor Car.[4]

Poletown's men had the lowest echelon of heavy industry jobs and were often the first laid off during a recession. New immigrant arrivals, including some drawn from Pennsylvania's factories and coal fields, were surprised to have to face the contempt always reserved in this country for the most recent arrivals. Signs in storefronts read, "Poles don't need to apply." The Germans building St. Joseph's Church said the Poles could help pay to build the church but would have to sit in a segregated balcony. Company managers assigned Poles to the dirtiest and most dangerous factory jobs, forcing them to work ten- to twelve-hour days, six days a week.[5]

Polish political loyalties at the turn of the century were complex. When Woodrow Wilson called for volunteers for World War I, 40 percent of the first 100,000 to respond were Polish. However, in 1920, during Eugene Debs's candidacy for president, many Poles chose not to vote Democrat and voted Socialist. Such a great proportion of the Socialist voters in 1918 were foreign-born that Detroit auto manufacturer William Brush referred to them as the "alien threat" and the "enemy in our midst." He proposed "the total extermination of such monstrosities in human form." The American Protective League assigned 4,000 Detroit volunteers to keep watch on the Motor City's foreigners and radicals.[6]

In 1920, during the Palmer Raids when the federal government ordered the simultaneous arrests of labor activists around the country, some of the socialist literature collected was illegible to the authorities because it was in Polish.[7] And a decade later, when labor strikes began to sweep the country, Poles played key roles. Detroit's first, largest, and longest sit-down strikes all took place in Poletown's steel, auto, and cigar factories. It was an era when nearly 130 Detroit shops, plants, and offices were occupied by workers, an era when 200 shoppers at Woolworth's, surprised by an unexpected sit-in, chose to stay inside with the strikers after management was locked out.[8] Fighting for the right to unionize became a community occupation that won the support of some Roman Catholic clergy and the government of Hamtramck.[9]

The old order in Detroit—the Protestants who controlled the factories, the newspapers, the court system, and city hall—consistently viewed these people as a threat and went to work both to cut off immigration and to pressure immigrants into conforming to their standards. In an article titled "Who Shall Rule?" the *Patriotic American* editorialized that "we are now simply the waste-house of Europe and the receptacle of its refuse and scum" and that these "semi-barbarous" elements would overwhelm the United States and ruin "the perfectly free, modern country that it is, or used to be, 40 or 50 years ago."[10]

This attitude on the part of the elite in the Motor City had two effects. It contributed to the politicization of immigrants who quickly perceived themselves as part of an unwelcome class and therefore were more willing to challenge management and form unions. And second, it strengthened the Polish communities' tendency to turn inward, resisting any semblance of assimilation. For example, in graduation ceremonies at the Ford English School, an Americanization program run by the Ford Motor Company in 1918, all the participants descended from a boat, crossed a gang plank, and stepped into a fifteen-foot-wide "melting pot." The director, Clinton C. DeWitt, explained the pageant that followed: "Six teachers, three on either side, stir the pot with ten-foot ladles, representing nine months of teaching in the school. Into the pot fifty-two nationalities with their foreign clothes and baggage go, and out of the pot after a vigorous stirring by the teachers comes one nationality."[11]

The Poles were singularly uninterested in surrendering their "foreign clothes and baggage." Teaching their children the language, culture, and history of Poland was primary, and they were willing to make considerable sacrifices in order to build parochial schools that would stress these things. They came to look upon the Catholic church as the embodiment of their heritage, since Catholicism was a constant thread throughout a thousand years of their history.

Poletown residents made considerable sacrifices in order to build St. Albertus Church, which was, in 1885, the largest church in the city.[12] And each of the subsequent five churches built by Poletown residents required similar sacrifices, especially during the Depression, which hit the community hard. Tensions developed when it became clear that the archdiocese expected immigrant communities to pay for church construction and their priests' salaries—while not allowing them to keep the title to the building or choose their own clergy.[13]

These issues were exacerbated by the fact that archdiocesan officials were not Polish; in most cases they were Irish. Moreover, the Roman Catholic hierarchy stressed assimilation. Consequently, despite the centrality of the Catholic church to the lives of Poletown residents, they were often at war with their ecclesiastical leaders. Fist fights, arrests, and even shootings took place in early Poletown when Bishop Caspar Borgess attempted to interfere with the residents' right to expand their schools, retain their own priests, or own the deeds to the new churches they had financed.[14]

Poletown was composed of cheap, two-story frame houses that were famous for being scrupulously tidy. Merchants, who often lived above their businesses, established themselves on Chene Street, a north-south artery linking Poletown with Hamtramck. Chene Street had a street-car line which brought people to the area's bakeries, meat markets, and clothing stores. At Ferry Street, toward the southern end of Poletown, was the Chene-Ferry farmers' market. Poletown also had Polish funeral homes, a Polish newspaper, the first Polish vaudeville theater in the United States, and even a Polish seminary. In this respect nothing had changed since the *Detroit News* wrote in 1883 that the residents of Poletown "live and retain their customs to such an extent that the whole region more nearly resembles a fraction of Poland than a part of a city in the heart of America."[15]

But Poletown was American and its residents helped determine what urban America would be. Like the rest of the nation, the

The Poletown neighborhood included all the homes from the bottom of the photo through the line that cuts diagonally across the top of the photo (the diagonal is Interstate 94). The church at the center is the Immaculate Conception Church, which hosted the resistance to GM's project.

DAVID C. TURNLEY

DAVID C. TURNLEY

Little things, like the survival of home milk deliveries in Poletown, made the community exceptional.

Walter Duda, a life-long resident of
Poletown, fought the labor-union battles
of the thirties and joined the
Poletown struggle of the eighties.
Photo by Sandy Livingston.

community sent its sons to fight and die in World War I; it fought equally hard during the epic labor struggles of the 1930s and saw that momentum undercut by government red scares and the outbreak of World War II; it lived through the early cold war and the McCarthy era. Poletown suffered in the 1950s when federal monies sponsored the development of the suburbs by subsidizing freeways that ripped through inner-city neighborhoods; it endured the influx of new immigrants and U.S. refugees from other low-income neighborhoods bulldozed for freeways; it witnessed Detroit's 1967 riots.

Poletown felt the effects of all these changes as it began to age and lose its population. But even as late as 1980, the community was known for its sound housing stock, its low rents, its good access to shops and services, and its tolerance for divergent ethnic groups and religious denominations. There were some black and white neighbors who had shared a block for fifty years, and a study done by the University of Michigan in 1980 suggested that "this area may be one of the most continuously racially integrated areas in Michigan."[16]

Poletown residents whose roots stretched back to the turn of the century remember the vitality of the area. They speak easily of the excitement and hardships of a people struggling with America's language and culture. They recount the risks taken by craftspeople who worked overtime to keep little shops open and they sometimes laugh and sometimes grow angry as they recollect the real and costly battles between workers and private and public police. The story of Poletown, its history through 1980, is best told by them.

By 1980, Walter Duda had lived sixty-six years in Poletown, working at Midland Steel and later at Chrysler's Dodge Main. He was a key organizer for the United Auto Workers in the 1930s, participating in the largest sit-down strike in the auto industry.

Duda's family life overlapped and meshed with his work life. His sister, Ann, worked in one of Poletown's five cigar factories. He stood side by side with his neighbors at work. Everyone shared the pain implicit when the Motor City endured 30 percent unemployment in the mid-1930s.[17] Union struggles were community struggles: mothers, fathers, and children banded together to help shut down plants, protect picketers from the police, and fend off company goons and vigilante groups. During World War II many of Duda's friends' sisters took the places of the men at the auto and tank plants.

Duda smiles, his lips hidden by his waxed handlebar mustache, when he recalls how he got to know his wife:

> "Did you see that little cement-block church over there at the corner of Chene and Trombly? Well, that used to be Sam and Hymie's fruit stand

and I used to work there. I used to sweep the floors. I used to hide all the rotten apples and oranges under the top of the pile. . . . I worked there until I started work at Midland Steel; it was a part-time job. Wouldn't pay any wages that would amount to shit anyhow. I don't remember how many times I quit on him. He'd come down to here banging on the door. "Where is Walter?" "Walter's not home." "Tell him I've got a job for him." So, I'd come home, Mother would get on me. "Why aren't you working?" And I'd say, "Well, he doesn't pay me enough." "You want a raise? Tell him fifty-cents-a-day raise for sweeping that sidewalk."

I was up to a dollar a day and then around the holidays—like Thanksgiving or Christmas—he would hire extra help. And she was one of the girls that came in there. She worked there for about two weeks. That's where I got to know her. When we got married, we moved in with her folks. But that didn't last long—I couldn't get along with her mother. I went and talked to my Dad. He says, "Yeah, come on, we got plenty of room here." We grabbed one of the rooms upstairs. So I called one of my friends and we loaded my mattress up on top of his car and brought it down here. That's how I started out.

Duda left Midland Steel in 1935. He complained that, even though it paid better than the grocery store, the conditions were too dangerous. Molten metal would spill haphazardly from buckets. Duda was "glad to get the hell out of there." Midland Steel was unionized, but Duda complained that the Mechanics Educational Society of America wasn't "even a paper tiger."

A year later 1200 Midland Steel workers began the first sit-down strike in the state, demanding recognition of the UAW as their bargaining agent and a ten-cent-an-hour wage increase. The sit-down both prevented the management from merely shipping strikebreakers through the picket lines and helped build morale and cohesion among the workers, who spent eight days together playing cards and doing calisthenics. Less than a week later Ford and Chrysler laid off 100,000 workers because their production was being slowed down by the shortage of Midland Steel body frames. On the eighth day Midland Steel consented to the strikers' demands.[18]

A wave of sit-down strikes spread through Detroit and up to Flint during the months that followed. By February 1937 five of Poletown's cigar factories were struck, with Polish women bearing the brunt of the strike duties and police attacks. During those two months, 35,000 workers held control of more than 100 factories, stores, and offices in Detroit alone. Newspapers estimated 100,000 people marched in supportive picket lines. Interestingly, the strikers held tight to American flags and imposed pretty strict standards prohibiting drunkenness and stealing inside the shops.[19]

Walter Duda was drawn into the cigar workers' strike when he learned on March 16 that the police were trying to evict 150 women from the Bernard Schwartz plant. By the time Duda got there, 500 strike sympathizers were gathered outside the plant. Inside, thirty women were trying to fend off the police with heavy wooden cigar molds. "They were dragging these women out by their legs," he recalls, "and by their arms, by their hair—wherever they could grab and just dragging them out into the street. We got into a confrontation with the cops, and we were doing pretty good; we were holding our own until the horse cops came. I don't know if you've ever seen the nightstick a horse cop carries, but it can almost reach down to the ground from his saddle. I got that twice in the back. I don't remember how many fences I jumped, but, boy, I jumped plenty to get away from that horse cop. It was wild. It was wild that night because we really harassed the hell out of them."[20]

By the end of the night thirty women and eight men were taken into custody. But within five weeks three of the five companies agreed to recognize the union and the women took to the streets. "The triumph of Local 22 of the Cigar Makers Union was very much a Polish affair," writes University of Michigan historian James Anderson. "When the early victories were won in March, 1937, 1,000 women celebrated with a march up Joseph Campeau to the cheers of the Dodge Main Workers."[21]

One of the Dodge Main workers cheering the women was Walter Duda. Three weeks later these same workers learned that Chrysler had blacklisted 3,000 of them for supporting the fledgling United Auto Workers Union. Ten thousand workers turned off their machines and sat down. Within hours 17,000 workers had taken over nine other Chrysler plants in Detroit.

Dodge Main was one of the biggest single employers in Detroit.[22] The facility, designed by Detroit architect Albert Kahn, was constructed of reinforced concrete, steel rods, and twelve-inch-thick cement floors and was touted for being flexible for production changeovers. It was the first American auto plant able to produce an entire automobile under one roof. When Chrysler closed the facility in 1980, it contained thirty-seven miles of conveyor belts.[23]

"You got to remember that all these manufacturers were 100 percent against any union organization," Duda explained. "They had their spy centers. We used to hold our meetings in anybody's basement. . . . Prior to the unions, job security depended on how your supervisor felt about you. In order to stay in good with him during the summertime, guys would go off and paint his house. In the wintertime, they'd haul ashes out. These kind of things—wash his car on Sunday, take him out to a picnic, bring him a jug for Christmas. That was tough to break." Duda added that when persuasion didn't yield solidarity, they'd "use other methods, whatever came to mind—intimidate them."

When the sit-down strike began, Duda recalled,

> The word went through the plant like wildfire. Everybody just laid down their tools and just sat down and that's it. Won't touch no buttons, no line, don't do anything—that was just like a mortal sin. . . . The foreman, the supervisor tried to get us back on the job. And we picked up a broom and started to clean up around there. He said, "What are you doing?" And we said: "Just trying to make it neat so that when you people leave, you won't blame us for all this garbage and trash laying around."
>
> About 4 P.M. all the supervisors were told to leave. They left the plant and we wouldn't come out. People that came into work the second shift saw that we had a bonafide picket line. We'd welded the gates shut. Nobody could come in; nobody could go out. So the afternoon shift just threw our lunches over the fence and a week later they [the union] hired a catering firm to bring in the stuff.
>
> Inside we had a number of chores. We had to organize a maintenance outfit to keep the boiler going so we wouldn't freeze. We had to organize a sheriff's department. When the highlow batteries run down, we had to run some stuff up on the roof, in case they were going to break down the gates. We were going to bombard them from the top floor with some heavy objects—like starter motors and stuff. We weren't aware what they were going to do, we just prepared for it.

After sleeping on car seats for a week, the strikers learned that a circuit court injunction had been issued ordering them to vacate by March 17, despite the UAW's argument that Chrysler was violating the Wagner Act by refusing to recognize the majority's preferred bargaining agent. On that morning of March 17, more than 10,000 picketers turned out. The people inside the plant armed themselves with scrap metal and fire hoses. But the police failed to move on the plant, and Governor Frank Murphy, formerly a welfare-rights mayor in Detroit, refused to send in the National Guard.

On March 23 the UAW and the Wayne County AFL (American Federation of Labor) called for a rally at Cadillac Square to protest the police evictions of strikers at smaller plants in the city. One hundred thousand people turned out for the demonstration and cheered union activist Frank Martel when he said they would soon elect "a police commissioner who put human rights above property rights." On March 25 Chrysler signed a truce with the UAW. The strikers, having the governor's word that he would seal the plants shut pending the results of negotiations between the union and management, walked out of

Dodge Main and the other occupied Chrysler plants. On April 7 Chrysler officially recognized the union.[24]

During the strike the city of Hamtramck supported the strikers. Neighboring bar owners agreed to stop selling alcohol so that the strike wouldn't be contaminated by somebody getting drunk and causing an incident. Chrysler was unable to splinter community support at Dodge Main because of the strong ethnic allegiance of the people in Hamtramck and Poletown. When the American Legion threatened to attack the "Bolshevik" union members, workers were able to put out a call through the neighborhood. "If they had to, they'd run from house to house," Duda recalled. "They knew where every one of us lived." Duda eventually became a member of the UAW's "flying squadron," a group of union members who would take their expertise from plant to plant. In April 1937 the UAW picked up 245,000 members, many of them in Poletown's Chrysler, Briggs, and Hudson Motor plants.[25]

Ann Duda, Walter's sister, her strong face framed by thick white hair, remembers dancing outside and singing out loud as a child in Poletown on Christmas Eve. In the background the sound of church bells blended with the clang of metal against metal in the nearby factories.

"It was like the place was full of miracles," she recalled. "We were poor but my father bought some wood and built a manger with wise men and camels, angels, a star, and a baby. It was wonderful. Christmas. A real Christmas spirit."

Ann and Walter Duda's father supported all eleven of his children by working at Ford Motor Company. The family had moved to Detroit from Pennsylvania, because it was too hard to find work there. The Duda's home, like most of the homes in Poletown, was not lavish. It was a two-story frame house that stood on wooden stiles, the same home at Harper and Grandy streets that Walter Duda had returned to with his new bride.

Ann met Andy Giannini through a friend. "That's when all the trouble started," Ann laughs. The couple settled on East Milwaukee Street, where they lived for thirty-six years. In 1936 the Detroit Gasket Company went on strike, and Andy was out of work for two years. "He worked at the baseball park," Ann said. "He used to sell peanuts and everything. And then he was WPA and then he got a job at Montgomery Wards. He got recalled to Detroit Gasket in 1939, and he stayed there until 1966, when the company moved to Tennessee."

Ann worked days at General Cigar and R.G. Dunn, while her mother watched the children. Ann remembers standing out in front of

R.G. Dunn during the strike. "I ran away though," she said. "I had two little kids. I would bring the girls food and blankets and pillows." She remembered that during that period her brother Walter had bullet holes in his car windows and used to sleep in garages to keep away from company police and goons.

During World War II Ann worked at Dodge Main, building tank parts. But when the war was over she settled in to raise their six children and, in the summer, to tend her roses. Andy devoted himself to the corn, pepper, bean, lettuce, radish, and carrot plants. In 1954 he opened a pool hall called Hupps Billiards and Snookers on Chene Street, just down the block from the Famous Bar-B-Q Restaurant. At night a metal, accordion-style door stretched across the opening, but by day it was open and patrons could step downstairs into the semidark of the old-fashioned pool hall. A half dozen tables filled the hall, the old heavy-legged kind with woven leather pockets. Point counters hung on wires across the wall and individual lamps hung over each table. Andy or his son Don served up racked balls or soda pop and candy bars from behind the wood-and-glass candy counter at the front.

By 1980 the Gianninis' youngest son, John, had a law degree and was working for Alan Ackerman, one of the condemnation lawyers who helped draft the condemnation law that would soon threaten Poletown.

For nearly forty years, the Famous Bar-B-Q Restaurant faced onto Chene Street, its red neon sign hanging inside a row of dingy windows. Inside, an old Wurlitzer stood backed against the window, just a few feet from the rib cooker in the corner. A counter lined one wall and a row of booths the other. Each booth had a small jukebox selector offering five plays for a quarter. Small American flags and statues of soldiers stood amidst plastic flowers on the countertops.

Carl Fisher, a small, wiry man, worked at the stove, happy to keep a steady running commentary on most anything. It was the kind of place that drew the same crowd again and again. One Detroit police officer lunched there daily for ten years.

Fisher recalled that when he opened the Famous just after World War II the Chene Strip was "very downtownish. Every store was going. As a matter of fact, I think there was business here when the business was letting up someplace else. There was religion here. There was people from all walks of life."

Fisher's father came to Detroit from Greece and impressed upon his son that in America every child could afford to wear shoes. The Fisher family was proud to be American, even though Carl's mother

DAVID C. TURNLEY

The Famous Bar-B-Q Restaurant was one of many small businesses on the Chene Street strip that some had hoped to renovate into a Poletown that could rival the city's Greektown area. Poletown's businesses employed 1,000.

Carl Fisher, owner of the Famous Bar-B-Q Restaurant, claimed the heartbeat of the city depends on the work of small businesspeople and the rhythm of communities.

Poletown's bars drew a lively crowd.

had to repeatedly endure the humiliation of being refused apartments because her family was Greek. "But in Poletown, you could be anything you wanted," Fisher said. "There were a lot of Italians, a lot of other nationalities, a lot of Jewish. They got along good."

Fisher worked in Poletown through the 1950s, when a freeway intersected the neighborhood and first forced dislocation. He stayed through the early 1960s and watched more than fourteen ethnic groups settle into the area. More significantly, he stayed through the 1967 riots. Fisher was impressed by how well Poletown's residents stuck together during those times—times when many neighborhoods were destroyed by people fleeing to the suburbs.

"It's a shame I didn't have a tape recorder," he said. "You could have heard all the different groups of people calling in to help me. You know, black people calling me, 'Do you want me to sit in your place with a shotgun all night, Carl?'"

Fisher's gentle eyes peered out through black-frame glasses. His hands, swollen by arthritis, flew over the grill—one copper bracelet on each wrist. "I grew up in the city," he said. "But like I say, the city has lost the rhythm. It was like a fluttering heart beat wanting to come alive again. They lost it some place along the line."

Now when Fisher goes downtown and looks over the new multimillion-dollar hotel and retail construction projects that are touted as the harbingers of a renaissance, he's disappointed. "I don't believe it comes about that way. As long as we see profit-grabbing at the expense of a person's life, a person's pride, or whatever that person holds dear to, they will never rebuild an area—because all it is is the buck— money, money, money. . . . This area here, though, it still has a bakery shop. You know it's funny, we don't have bakery shops in many busy sections. To me, it's a rare achievement for a bakery shop to remain."

Josephine and Walter Jakubowski lived on the second floor of a white frame house on Kanter Street for forty-six years of their married life. Walter had been raised in that home and had brought his bride to live there. The apartment was not large. It had three small bedrooms, a living room crowded with comfortable furniture, and pictures of the family and of the pope. People tended to congregate in the kitchen, which was large and usually full of activity. Walter's niece lived with her family in the first floor flat.

By 1980 Josephine was white-haired and plump, with wire-rimmed glasses. She spoke enthusiastically in a high-pitched voice, calling everyone "honey." For years she had served on nearly every committee at the Immaculate Conception Church, so she was well known to most of the Catholics in the neighborhood and most had eaten her excellent Polish food at church fundraisers. Walter, a retiree from Chrysler, often wore a suit, tie, and hat. He was slight and graceful, with grey hair and a studious glance. He was less active at the church than his wife, but he was a member of a local community organization and a part of a citizens-band-radio neighborhood patrol.

After retiring the Jakubowskis picked out a home in suburban Westland, a nearly all-white suburb that is advertised as safer than the inner city. The house was nice. The neighborhood, by many people's standards, was an improvement. But when it came time to move, the Jakubowskis decided not to leave. They liked living in the home Walter had been raised in. They liked the area. And for Josephine, there was the Immaculate Conception Church.

The Immaculate Conception Church, which lay to the north when freeway construction tore the area in two, became known in 1980 as a center of neighborhood resistance to relocation. But its original claim to fame was its beauty. Founded in 1919, the church was originally housed in a corner grocery store, but by 1928 parishioners had raised enough money to start construction of the deep-red brick building that was completed in 1935. The fifty-two-year-old church sufficiently impressed the people who drafted the Environmental Impact Statement (which was a necessary first step to demolition plans) that they wrote: "The exterior is but scant preparation for the overwhelming wealth of detail found within. Colorful tile flooring, dark stained wood pews, elaborate case metal railings, stenciled and gold leaf plastering—all combine to form a richness that is truly unique."[26] In the center of the sanctuary stood a white marble statue of the Virgin Mary. On each side, the walls were covered with frescoes of angels cradling lilies in their arms. Three separate frescoes were attached to the ceiling, running from back to front. Since the church was moderate in size and unobstructed by pillars, the paintings dominated the interior.

Construction of the church, the accompanying school, and the convent was costly. Some neighborhood residents went so far as to mortgage their homes, because they considered the construction of Polish Catholic churches, where they could maintain their traditions and teach their children, tantamount to survival. In the process strong lay leadership and a new spirit of self-determination evolved which was more typical of Protestantism.[27] This new lay independence resulted in volatile parish relations throughout the country.

Between 1919 and the early 1950s the Immaculate Conception

DAVID C. TURNLEY

The paintings that graced the ceilings and walls of the Immaculate Conception Church could not be removed because the original artisans had attached them with a glue of wheat and black-strap molasses. No one then imagined that the building itself would be torn down.

Poletown's Albanian community worshipped at the Immaculate Conception Church. Here, a young bride is entering into an arranged marriage with a groom she has never met.

Henry Michalski, one of the last people to leave Poletown, hung the Last Supper next to a photo of himself during his military service. Religious faith, military service, patriotism, and union membership were strong elements in many Poletown lives prior to the community's betrayal by the church, the government, and the union.

Church ministered almost entirely to Polish immigrants. However, during the next fifteen years, fourteen different nationalities moved into the neighborhood and, to a lesser extent, the parish. These new immigrants were Ukrainian, Cuban, Irish, Scotch, Albanian, Lithuanian, French, English, Turkish, Egyptian, Yugoslavian, Lebanese, Portuguese, and Afro-American. Monsignor Alexander Cendrowski, who was raised in Poletown and later served as the rector at the Immaculate Conception Church for twenty years, claims that the new immigrants were well received. His parishioners supplied furniture and household supplies from their attics. With the help of the Felician sisters, the parish sponsored night classes in English and in citizenship.

"We had to furnish school; that's where the big expense came from," Cendrowski said.

> Immaculate Conception parish paid totally out of their own funds for all of these programs. We prepared people for citizenship so that they were able to read and get accustomed to the American way of life. Some of them were just like children. They would go in the middle of the street and play in the sand. They didn't sleep in homes; they slept outside. The children would get all bitten up by mosquitos. They didn't all know the use of soap.
>
> The people of Immaculate Conception parish, they were not just ordinary people. They were people who loved community life. It made no difference to them whether you were German, Polish, or black. During the [1967] riots, we had absolutely no problem, not even one incident. We lived together as neighbors. We helped each other. They helped us. We helped them. If someone got stuck with a car, they'd come and pull you out. We had excellent relationships.

Interstate-94 was the first freeway to divide the community. It cut east-west through the center of Poletown, taking with it hundreds of homes, including the Dudas' first family home. An estimated 1,400 families had to be resettled between 1953 and 1955. The freeway intersected the commercial strip on Chene Street, diminishing the flow of foot traffic. It also separated some of ICC's parishioners from the church, reducing membership. Cendrowski was able to persuade city officials to build foot bridges over the freeway so that ICC school children in the southern section of Poletown could still attend class.

At about the same time a spur of I-75, a north-south freeway, was rolling over an all-black, center-city neighborhood known as Black Bottom. Nearly 3,000 housing units were destroyed. One man who saw his father's tailor shop decimated for the freeway project was Coleman Young, who later became the city's first black mayor and the man who would oversee the Poletown project. Hundreds of families evicted from Black Bottom flowed over into Poletown, which had been only modestly integrated in the 1950s.

By the 1960s Poletown had entered a period of decline that most people attributed to the freeway construction. The new federal highways gave people easy access to the suburbs and enticed many to move, but they also took their toll on the integrity of Detroit neighborhoods by ripping them into ragged sections. Chene Street merchants found it harder to get insurance after I-94 split their trade route and in the ensuing years store-front vacancies were common. Poletown's commercial strip suffered from a combination of problems that plagued nearly all retail strips in the city. White flight to the suburbs, the construction of shopping malls, insurance redlining, and the reduction of city services combined to cripple the Chene Street merchants.

During the late 1960s, when much of the city went up in flames, Poletown was unscathed. Some speculate that this was because Poles and blacks both shared a bottom-level economic standing and did not perceive each other as the enemy. In fact, most of the property damage that occurred during the 1967 riots took place in areas where the majority of housing units were owned by absentee suburban landlords. This does not mean there was no racial tension in Poletown. Racially based fears and complaints were prevalent, but the tension remained low-level and the neighborhood stayed cohesive.[28] Ten years later, after thousands of white Detroiters had moved to the Motor City's bloated and energy-inefficient suburbs, Poles would stand out as the ethnic group least likely to abandon Detroit.[29]

In May of 1968 workers at Dodge Main, which had been declared a fire hazard in 1948, staged a wildcat strike. The walkout was supported by 4,000 black and white workers who were angry about line speed-ups, but it was in direct violation of a Chrysler-UAW agreement made the previous year. Chrysler responded to the strike by singling out black workers for punishment, which swelled the ranks of the newly formed Dodge Revolutionary Union Movement (DRUM).[30]

Polish workers and Poletown residents could hardly be said to have stood in solidarity with DRUM or what eventually became known as the League of Revolutionary Black Workers.[31] During the 1950s, when Chrysler started integrating the assembly lines, white workers sat down in protest. Having officially supported the Dodge Main strike in the 1930s, the City of Hamtramck sent police to intimidate the 1968 demonstrators.[32] However, some of DRUM's criticisms of the UAW were shared by white workers. Many workers felt unprotected by the union. By the early 1970s there was a series of wildcat strikes, more often than not over safety issues.[34] During the same period, the auto companies were painting pictures of affluent workers which the union did little to combat.

Although Poletown had entered a period of decline by the late 1960s and was no longer the bustling immigrant community it had once been, new people continued to move into it and some invested their lives there. Bernice and Harold Kaczynski brought their six children to Poletown in 1965. They left behind a rented home, which they hadn't moved out of voluntarily. They were chased out when their landlord decided to sell it to General Motors, which had plans to expand the parking lot at its Chevrolet Gear and Axle Plant.

"I went all over the place to rent a place," Bernice explained later. "I wasn't going to buy and with little kids—they slammed the door in your face. I'd go home and cry. I'd say, 'Where are we going to go? General Motors wants the house. The landlord has sold it. And what are we going to do?'"

The Kaczynskis found a house on Mitchell Street, which they planned to rent with an option to buy. The upstairs was stained dark with smoke and the toilet was broken. The former tenants had knocked holes in the walls, but it had four bedrooms and they figured they could make it over into a home. "I used to work for a contractor," Harry said. "That came in handy. The water tanks were upstairs for upstairs and downstairs were in the kitchen. I took them out and put them in the basement. I put in all new pipes, new sinks, new water basins, toilets. We planned to stay."

Poletown had a good feel to Bernice and Harry. Harry's parents had lived there, on Horton Street, and Harry had driven a delivery truck in the area in the 1930s. Both their mothers had worked in the cigar factories.

"You should have seen the Boulevard," Harry recalled. "When I got out of high school back in the thirties, you couldn't drive down the Boulevard. I used to drive a truck. They used to stop you and take your number, then they allowed you just so far to deliver your coal. Lawns and everything there was strictly high society. You should have seen some of those houses and that. They were beautiful. They were immaculate, built like, you know, Grosse Pointe [one of Detroit's oldest and most affluent suburbs.] That's how them ones were, beautiful. If you stopped because you had a flat tire, boy, the cops would be on your ass right away."

The Kaczynskis quickly got to know the Crosbys, the Dockerys, the Watsons, and others. Bernice, a quick energetic woman who sometimes seemed to live on caffeine and cigarettes, kept coffee on the burner constantly and was always prepared to spend time with her neighbors. By 1980 she was as much a relative to three-year-old Brian Dockery as his own grandmother, Louise Crosby.

"People watched out for one another in Poletown," Bernice explained. "If you were on ADC, you were on ADC. Who cared, as long as you got along with your neighbor? If your husband went out and made more money than the other guy, nobody asked. Nobody cared. And if I went and bought something new, that didn't mean the other one was going to do it because they wanted to keep up. In the suburbs it's 'keep up with the Joneses.' Over here, nobody cared. You were friends. You were neighbors."

"Every time I went on vacation," Harry interjected, "we wouldn't have to worry about somebody breaking into the house or stealing anything; we watch our own neighborhood over here. You don't have no baloney going on."

The last Kaczynski child graduated from high school in 1976. By then most of them had married or joined the service. Harry was looking forward to retiring but was also frustrated that his employment at Hanson Wheel and Grinding was on again, off again. He and Bernice made the best of it by traveling east and west to visit their new grandchildren and by pursuing their hobbies. Bernice had a music box collection and liked to make her own dolls. Harry enjoyed making balsa wood airplanes for his grandchildren and fixing up a sixteen-foot boat he had on blocks in the garage.

In 1979, Ben and Ethel Feagan, a black couple, bought a thirty-four-year-old lawn mower repair and blade-sharpening shop on the eastern border of Poletown from its white Polish owner. It was a dream come true for Ben and a sign of the respect that the former owner had for Ben. The two men were able to work out a land contract arrangement which allowed Ben to take over the shop when the owner retired.

The shop was a large, single-story building on the corner of I-94 and Mount Elliott. Its small windows were barred and the customer entrance was locked even when the shop was open for business. Inside the shop was dark and oil stained. The walls were lined with tools and appliances, accessible only to those who knew them well. The little office with its vinyl-covered furniture was usually smoke-filled since both Ethel and Ben smoked packs and packs of Kool cigarettes. If it wasn't busy, they were likely to be in the office, drinking sixteen-ounce Pepsis and talking to each other over the television.

On good summer days, Ethel was often out front tending an oil barrel barbecue. If he were free, Willy might be playing blues on his guitar. Both were heavy-set and wore glasses. They were quick to spar with each other verbally and loved the visitors who often stopped by to pass time with them. Their thirteen-year-old granddaughter, Tiny, moved quietly around them, shyly beginning conversations, gaining attention edgewise, which was the only way possible, given the over-flowing conversation of her grandparents.

The shop wasn't terribly profitable, but it made enough to pay the land payment and to support the Feagans. Customers came from around the area, as well as off the freeway. The Feagans were proud that they could often repair something for elderly neighbors for cost or less.

"Some people come in here and you know they're on fixed in-comes," Ben said. "So, you say, 'That's going to run you four bucks.' You know it's going to cost you seven or eight, but when people are older and they can't go somewhere else. . . . " Feagan shrugged. "I'm my own man."[33]

In January of 1980, Chrysler announced that it would close Dodge Main by spring. Chrysler was trying to streamline its production and bail itself out of bankruptcy with a $1.5 billion government loan guar-antee. More than 3,000 workers and family members rallied in Ham-tramck to protest the closing. The plant was Hamtramck's greatest tax payer, contributing $3 million annually to the city's coffers.

Within five months two government task forces released studies recommending alternate uses for the Dodge Main site. A consulting firm in Washington, D.C., published a five-volume study. The most popular option, within county government circles, was to convert the factory into a state prison which would house between 400 and 500 people who could be contracted out to the auto companies "with some compensation given to the UAW," according to Christian Gallio of the Wayne County Economic Development Corporation. No one noted the irony of converting a plant that had been central to worker-rights battles into a prison where convicts would do auto work for negligible pay.

By 1980 Poletown's homes were selling for an average of $9,000, among the cheapest in Detroit. Half the area's residents were young, black families, the majority of whom were renters. Most of Poletown's black families had incomes below $6,000 a year. Only one-half of the area's white residents still owned their own homes.[34] Poletown was .being undermined by a lack of employment, an aging population, crime, the increasing poverty of people on fixed incomes, a decline in private and public services, and deteriorating housing stock. Nearly

DAVID C. TURNLEY

Half the residents of Poletown were black, and although many of the black residents were not homeowners, later surveys indicated a real reluctance among most of them to leave Poletown.

Ethel and Ben Feagan (center) were raising their granddaughter, Tiny, and employing several people at their lawn-mower sharpening shop. The barrel barbeque grill to the right was put to frequent use. Friends were always welcome.

Stella Barowski ran a store in Poletown for decades, often welcoming friends into the back room for a white russian cocktail.

two-thirds of the people living in northern Poletown moved out during the 1970s.[35]

Yet despite the changes in the neighborhood the community was still recognized as one in which there were strong emotional attachments, affordable housing, exceptionally good access to public transportation, and good health care at St. Joseph's Hospital. In June 1980 the *Detroit Free Press* ran a glowing story about Poletown's chance of making a comeback. Patricia Chargot noted the area's Polish flavor and continuing old-world feel. She visited the farmers' market at Ferry and Chene, which was still open on Wednesdays and Saturdays, and noted the prevalence of older women wearing colorful babushkas pulling little red wagons full of groceries. She found residents who saw indications of new life returning to the area.

One such was Wlodzimierz Nowalkowski, who had recently returned from several years in Poland. "I think now this is better," he said. "In 1976, it was more tough. I am only back ten days, but I know— it's better. This area is very good to live in, very comfortable, but it needs a renaissance. I wouldn't want to live in the suburbs. There it's quiet, like village life. People live too much by themselves, separately. I think people who are living here have more communication."[36]

At least two neighborhood residents were trying to organize the merchants for an ethnically based comeback. One was Tom Olechowski, who lived in southern Poletown and worked for a state senator, and the other was Richard Hodas, an urban studies graduate and small landlord in northern Poletown.

Hodas's interest in the area, where his mother had operated a dress store since 1945, was sparked by the Near East Side Community Organization (NESCO), a community group spawned by the Roman Catholic Archdiocese. In 1977 he bought a house on East Grand Boulevard and started buying up other vacant homes and stores. Hodas started working with merchants on the Chene strip to organize promotional programs and a neighborhood newspaper. Before Christmas in 1977 NESCO organized a fair at the Chene-Ferry Market at which a number of church choirs sang and dance troupes performed.

At about the same time, Hodas's activity in Poletown caught the attention of Olechowski, who had plans to renovate the area exclusively along Polish lines and initially considered Hodas an interloper. Olechowski complained that Hodas didn't have the political connections or inside knowledge to pursue revitalization. "He said he knew all the politicians and that we had to have Mayor Young's approval for anything or we'd never get anywhere," Hodas said. "He said he'd known Mayor Young for years and began to fill me in on his political contacts. And I said, 'Okay, that makes sense to me. This guy seems to know what he's talking about, I'll go along with it.'"

Olechowski, a Lech Walesa look-alike, usually wore a blue blazer with a Solidarity button pinned to his lapel. Olechowski spoke confidently and commandingly but played his cards close to his chest. It was hard for people to assess the real nature of his political links.

By 1978 Olechowski did manage to persuade Emmett Moten, the head of the city's Community and Economic Development Department (CEDD), to take a tour of Poletown. Moten, a former high school sports coach, was an extremely valued part of the Young administration. It was widely presumed that Moten's contacts with the Carter administration could help Mayor Young secure the lion's share of the available HUD monies for Detroit's development projects. (Moten's political career had been launched by Carter secretary of HUD Moon Landrieu.)

"When he (Moten) first came to Detroit, this was the first neighborhood he saw," Hodas said.

> Tom Olechowski drove him around the neighborhood. Shortly thereafter I met with him and we had several discussions on the possibilities for the neighborhood, the character of the housing stock, the shape of the business strip, the types of programs that the city had that would fit with the type of program we were putting together.
>
> The last meeting we had with Moten was in March of 1980. We met specifically to discuss the coordination of the preservation work we were doing with the expertise that C&EDD had available, to discuss the setting up of the neighborhood strategy area which is a necessity to implement a number of government low-interest loans and grants, the setting up of a commercial revitalization district which would make tax breaks available to the merchants along the street, and to deal with the coordination of all these things.
>
> Moten told us that he would work with us all the way in revitalizing this neighborhood, that it had excellent potential, that neighborhoods like this, Detroit needs. His attitude at the time seemed to be that this was the kind of thing that they were looking for, for neighborhoods in Detroit to initiate programs and to work with them and coordinate them with the city.

Olechowski and Hodas persuaded the city council, with the mayor's approval, to allocate $100,000 of Neighborhood Opportunity Funds for the rehabilitation of senior-citizen housing in Poletown. They also persuaded Detroit Renaissance, a private business roundtable of Detroit's chief executives, to match up to $15,000 for an analysis of the potential of the nineteen-block Chene Street commercial strip.

Olechowski and Hodas raised $10,000 from the Chene merchants for the feasibility study. Then they got a $5,000 grant from the National

Bank of Detroit and a smaller grant from the Detroit Economic Growth Corporation, a quasi-private development group whose board is also composed of ranking corporate executives. Olechowski organized the Polish Interparish Council in January 1979. This group brought together the rectors of the six Polish Catholic parishes in Poletown and gave Olechowski frequent contact with Fr. Francis Skalski of St. Hyacinth's. The hope was to enhance the ethnic identity of the area and to work together to address social needs.

It appeared that Poletown was on a roll. Nowalkowski's optimism upon his return from Poland seemed well-founded. There was promise that Poletown might be a "better area" with a full-fledged renaissance. What Olechowski and Hodas didn't know was that there was another group of people examining the potential of Poletown. These others, some of them Detroit's prime power brokers, were not interested in the community's history, ethnic character, or retail possibilities. They saw its proximity to rail lines, to the Detroit river, to freeways, and to a pool of unemployed, skilled workers. They considered it prime for industrial development.

These power brokers were free to lay plans for Poletown without consulting any of its residents or any of the task forces compiling data on Dodge Main. There was an understanding between the city administration and corporate executives that assured them privacy in their negotiations and priority in implementation of their projects. The little merchants, the tailors and bakers that Carl Fisher at the Famous Bar-B-Q said made up the heart beat of the city and set its rhythm in the 1940s, were no longer considered a major asset in the city of Detroit. And the communities that grew up around the Motor City's plants, complete with schools and churches, were considered expendable. The memories of generations baptized and buried, of neighborhood men and women putting their bodies between the police and strikers, and of the sound of Christmas bells blending with industrial churnings could be counted as nothing and swept away in corporate board rooms and city offices.

2

Detroit's Back to the Wall

The eighties are going to be a very exciting decade. I feel that government, labor, and industry and management must really all get together to
take on the challenges that face us. And I see that happening.

—GM president F. James McDonald
University of Detroit address, April 4, 1981

In 1980 Detroit was in the crest of a wave of economic depression.
Unemployment had reached 15 percent; major industrial employers
reported record losses and gave bleak forecasts. City officials were
afraid. Violent crime, thwarted in the mid-seventies by Detroit's award-
winning community and police patrol program, was rising again.[1] The
elderly were frightened. Recipients of social welfare were cynical. Headlines announcing the closing of yet another city shop hit the streets with
a disturbing and steady rhythm.

In 1979 Warner-Lambert Company fired 2,000 people when it
closed its Parke-Davis pharmaceutical plant. In 1980 Uniroyal shut
down its riverfront tire-making plant, putting 5,000 people out of work,
and moved its research offices to suburban Troy. Scores of auto-related
shops closed or moved during these years, throwing more than 100,000
out of work.[2] Uniroyal left behind the mammoth, three-dimensional
tire it had erected as an advertisement on Interstate 94. Hudson's
downtown department store, which was second only to New York's
Macy's in the 1950s, reduced its retail space in 1982 and started moving
its white-collar staff to other locations. Headlines reported that Hudson's
had hired a consulting firm to counsel its employees who were going to
be laid off. The fee was $12,000 a head. The store closed in 1983.[3]

The trend that started the demise of downtown Detroit was set by the federal government when it made monies available for highway construction and suburban development. "Washington has done a lot to the town (Detroit) in the past, all of it bad," wrote Walter Guzzardi, Jr., for *Fortune* magazine. "It was Washington that paid for those freeways that crisscross and ring Detroit, stripping it of its urban richness and of public transport—highway robbery that gave everyone in the Motor City the means to leave town. At the same time government loans helped build the housing and shopping centers in the suburbs, which have been constantly sucking dollars out of Detroit." [4]

The numbers of dollars drawn out to the suburbs are hard to estimate, but we do know that between 1954 and 1977 Detroit lost 11,137 retail stores—a loss of 59,706 jobs—while the surrounding suburbs picked up 76,760 retail jobs.[5] In addition, between 1970 and 1980 so many corporate offices moved from the city to the suburbs that the number of income tax returns filed for businesses within the city limits dropped by one-third.[6] During the same decade Detroit's property tax base dropped from $5.3 billion to $5.2 billion. Meanwhile, suburban Oakland County experienced a boom that raised its property tax base by 500 percent to $14 billion.[7] The changing business climate made new investors and insurance companies reluctant to invest in the city— adding to the cycle of disinvestment.

The Detroit Urban League estimated that unemployment exceeded the Michigan Employment Security Commission's estimates by a multiple of 2.5. Everyone agreed that unemployment for minorities was more than 26 percent, while at least 54 percent of Detroit's black teenagers were out of work. The extent of the trauma in the city became clear when 2,000 people lined up for 200 minimum-wage jobs advertised at a fast-food outlet and another 1,000 lined up for six openings at a cable television station. Even temporary agencies had no work for secretaries, telephone surveyors, or delivery drivers. City morale suffered a special blow when laid-off union members lined up to scab at struck shops.

The only booming industry in Detroit in 1980 was military recruitment. Over the first nine months of 1980, 20,000 Michigan residents enlisted. They provided one-third of the quota usually drawn from twelve Midwestern states. Army Sergeant Millard Hill told the Associated Press that he tells applicants that "this is the one job you'll never be laid off from. And now, when high school people come in, I tell them to look around and they'll see that if people out of college are getting laid off, your chances of getting a good job aren't that great."

All three of Detroit's major car companies were reporting record losses in the late 1970s. Analysts nation-wide tolled doom for the nation's "frostbelt," saying that the steel, glass, and auto companies would never provide adequate employment for the industrial north again. U.S. car production fell 32 percent. At that time, one in every six workers in the nation worked in auto-related industries. A collapse of Detroit's Big Three–General Motors, Ford, or Chrysler Corporation— could cripple the country.[8]

By 1980 nearly one out of three Americans buying cars chose imports. Belatedly, the American automakers decided that to be competitive they were going to have to produce small, fuel-efficient cars. Previously, American auto makers had counted on the strong profits made on big-car sales to more than compensate for foreign competition in the small-car market.[9] "The U.S. auto industry is in very bad shape right now," complained Harley Shaiken, a technology expert at M.I.T. "It is not selling cars. That, however, is not a function of the productivity of its manufacturing plants and design staffs. It's a function of having the wrong product to sell at the wrong time."[10]

By 1980 the Big Three were willing to concede that they had to retool for small, front-wheel-drive car production, but they didn't have the capital on hand to convert their plants. One industry analyst told *Business Week* that "Detroit's dilemma is that it must sell cars that no one wants to get the cash to make the cars that people will buy."[11] The car makers themselves complained that union wages, taxes, and regulations were combining to do them in.[12] In either case, the tight money policy initiated under President Jimmy Carter in 1980 and continued under Ronald Reagan's administration created a shortage of investment capital and drove up interest rates to 18 percent.

But the editors of *Business Week* wrote in 1980 that despite corporate complaints against taxes, imports, and environmental regulations, the real problems in frostbelt industries, like steel, included "poor management, parochialism, and accounting methods and financial decisions that have made steel companies appear to perform better than they did." The problem of capital, the editors added, was that it was being spent on acquisitions rather than new development—speculation, real estate exchanges, and futures.[13]

Critics from the other end of the spectrum reached the same conclusion. William Winpisinger, president of the International Association of Machinists, complained that it was typical now for corporations to take funds gained from tax incentives designed to encourage them "to refurbish plant equipment and to rebuild our competitive posture in the world" and invest them instead "in acquisitions, mergers, amalgamations, conglomerations—you name it. In all of those transactions, not one single job is created for the American workers."[14]

The Detroit media generally steered clear of critical analyses, focusing instead on the "short-sightedness" of both Americans who bought foreign cars and the unions which, they claimed, had driven wage rates up so high that American companies couldn't stay competitive.[15]

A radical trend toward concession bargaining began, despite worker advocates' complaints that corporations were making union laborers pay for management's errors. In some corners policymakers did start discussing the possibilities of legislation which would make it harder for corporations to arbitrarily close shops or move overseas.

Just how severe was the crisis among the Big Three and how did they respond to the crisis?

General Motors reported a record after-tax profit of $1,257 million during the first quarter of 1979 but saw that figure drop 85 percent during the next two years. By 1980 GM reported a net loss of $763 million, the first loss the company had experienced since 1921.[16] Between the first quarters in 1979 and 1981 car production fell 32 percent and GM dropped 14 percent of its workforce.[17] In 1980 GM announced that it would invest several hundred million dollars in two assembly and two engine plants in Mexico and probably close its Clark Cadillac and Fisher Body plants in Detroit, since both contributed to the production of rear-wheel-drive luxury cars.[18] These two Detroit plants had employed 15,000 people. By 1982 GM threatened to close four more plants and opened UAW negotiations with a demand for a $5-an-hour wage and benefit reduction.[19]

Ford Motor Company lost $1 billion on its North American operations in 1979. In the first quarter of 1981 the corporation reported its sixth successive after-tax quarterly loss. This $439 million loss was two and half times higher than that of the same quarter the previous year.[20] In 1981 Ford announced that it would close its Michigan Casting Center in Flat Rock, which would idle 2,500.[21] A 1980 *Detroit Free Press* story indicated Ford was investing $42 million in a Mexican car assembly plant.[22]

By 1980 Chrysler Corporation reported a $760 million loss. During the first quarter of 1981, the corporation lost another $298 million— the ninth consecutive quarterly loss, bringing its total decline during that time to $3.1 billion. Chrysler, apparently hanging by a thread, appealed to Congress to bail out the corporation by guaranteeing a loan that would allow Chrysler to streamline itself and invest in more modern and competitive equipment. The loan guarantee was arranged and finally ratified after UAW employees agreed to make wage and benefit concessions valued at more than one billion dollars.

In early 1980 Detroit's mayor, Coleman Young, had been in office for six years and headed a powerful political machine, but the city appeared to be heading for bankruptcy. Detroit had lost more than 25 percent of its income-tax-paying residents. Even the number of suburban residents who worked in Detroit and were therefore assessed city income taxes dropped by one-sixth.[23]

At the same time, a vehement tax rebellion erupted throughout the state. Several legislators who had helped pass a state income tax increase for new Democratic Governor James Blanchard were recalled. State legislators began to protest all money outlays, particularly those to the city of Detroit. Citizens began passing petitions to put a radical tax-cut amendment on the ballot. The mayor described this trend as racist, and he was probably correct.

Mayor Young warned that the city was going to fall into receivership to the state, thus ensuring that white politicians would control it. He suggested that this would eventually force the state to default on its debts, possibly beginning a domino of financial failures across the nation. In 1980 he laid off 690 police officers—an act which altered the racial balance of the department, removing many of the lower-seniority black and female officers that Young had put on the force during his first term.

The mood in the city was tense. Thousands of Detroiters, laid off after years of high-wage employment, had depleted their unemployment benefits. Many had lost their health insurance. The prevailing wisdom was that the auto industry would never make a comeback that would restore employment to previous levels. Some people began to move home to their parents' houses. Most resorted to social welfare checks, and some even began taking their children to the city's soup kitchens for meals.

Bizarre incidents made headlines—stories of unemployed men who barricaded themselves in their homes with shotguns and refused to come out, fathers who killed their families and themselves. A mother with a four-month-old baby and a shotgun in her arms arrived at Detroit Edison to complain that when they shut off her electricity they also shut down her furnace and hot-water heater because they had electric ignitions. Newspaper specials were written on child, spouse, and alcohol abuse. The state department of public health reported that enrollment in substance abuse programs in 1979 rose 12 percent and that by 1980 suicide was the tenth leading cause of death in the state.[24]

The trends that were apparent in 1980 pushed the mayor to declare a state of emergency in 1981 and to create a city hotline. Within the first five days, 1,100 people called requesting help. Many churches began dispensing cereal, dried milk, and canned goods. Church leaders circulated a letter instructing churches to make heated space available during the day so that neighborhood residents whose heat had been shut off wouldn't freeze.[25] Even General Motors and the United Auto Workers began food drives to provide for city residents.

In 1980 welfare dependency was at an all-time high and the state would have to borrow money from the federal government to meet its unemployment compensation payments. The media was extremely attentive to the shifts in the welfare of the middle class, but the effects of inadequate food and heat took a disproportionate private toll on poorer Detroit residents.[26] The Detroit City Health Department reported that due to malnourishment of pregnant mothers infant mortality was increasing. By 1982 the mortality rate for black infants was two-and-a-half times as high as that for white babies.

Detroit area clergy reported that they noticed transient newcomers, who moved often to avoid bills. A community organizer on the city's northwest side welcomed an elderly woman who arrived terrified because someone had come to her door offering to torch her home in exchange for half her fire insurance.

As the quality of life deteriorated for Detroiters, so did the city itself. The streets were rutted with deep potholes, which residents joked about except when their tire was flattened and their rim bent by the impact. One woman actually sued the city when she stepped from a cab into a puddle and found herself neck deep in water. Likewise, the cars that passed over Detroit's freeways became more and more disabled. Motor City residents know cars and baby their own vehicles. Yet cars with heavy rust, missing fenders, wooden bumpers, roped-down trunks became a familiar sight. A *Detroit News* columnist spoofed the cars on Detroit's roads, complaining that there were six million pieces of "junk" on the road, which in more affluent days would have been retired.

Commercial strips in the city become increasingly garish. Occupied storefronts, mixed in among others that were boarded over, advertised that they accepted food stamps and sold liquor and lottery tickets. Many of these same stores also sold dream books and magic candles that promised extrasensory aid to win the lottery. The city's homes—and there was a time when Detroit boasted that it had the largest percentage of family-owned housing units in the country—fell increasingly into disrepair. Six thousand homes a year fell into city ownership. Abandoned and boarded-over houses appeared in every neighborhood. In some areas the population density was cut in half when abandoned homes were bulldozed.

Not all Detroit residents despaired during this time of decline. People protected their homes with guns and dogs, but they also welcomed home their adult children and put energy into repairs and projects they had no time for previously. Increasingly people exchanged thie skills and goods for trade rather than for money. The pride of survival mingled with a cynical appraisal of the powers-that-be.

Economic conditions throughout the country—except perhaps in the Southwest sunbelt—were bleak, but one body of people in the nation found the creeping economic depression of 1980 cause for optimism. Representatives of big business and finacial analysts saw the economic downtown as an opportunity to preach to the public and to the government. They anticipated, rightly, that people, watching their standard of living eroded by unemployment or the threat of it, would be amenable to wage and benefit concessions. And they predicted that the public might be ripe for a corporate attack on poluution and labor safety legislation, if executives could claim the change would create jobs. The governemtn might also be prevailed on for tax abatements and even outright grants.

"It will be a hard pill for many Americans to swallow—the idea of doing with less so that big business can have more," Business Week editors surmised. "Nothing that this nation, or any other nation has done in modern economic history compares in difficulty with the selling job that must be done to make people accept this new reality."[27]

"Selling" the belief that American citizens would have to finance corporate growth required business leaders to paint a very dismal portrait of the future, since people wouldn't surrender wages and health regulations to ward off a brief economic slump. In Michigan the prevailing word from the corporate leaders was that the state was a very poor place to do business—despite the fact that Michigan offered unlimited fresh water, good railroad and highway infrastructure, and an excellent labor pool. The Chamber of Commerce, corporate executives, and business round tables took turns lamenting that Michgan's taxes were too high, its unions too demanding, and its unemployment and worker injury compensation laws crippling to the industry.

But within business circles the word was considerably different. At a University of Detroit business conference GM president F. James

McDonald boasted that the 1980s were going to be a "very exciting decade." McDonald outlined the ways in which labor and government were yielding concessions. While GM claimed to the public to be staggering under record losses, *Business Week* reported that the corporation was actually streamlining itself and would emerge stronger and more profitable than it had ever been.[28] GM used its reported losses to lobby hard for tax breaks and the easing of government regulations. It put intense pressure on city governments around the country, threatening each that the corporation might move out of state in pursuit of a "better business climate." And it intimidated both unionized workers and nonunion white-collar workers by cutting back large numbers of its personnel.

Chrysler chief Lee Iacocca explained how the Big Three managed to play crises for subsidies: "Ford, when I was there, General Motors, Chrysler, all over the world, we would pit Ohio versus Michigan. We'd pit Canada versus the U.S. We'd get outright grants and subsidies in Spain, in Mexico, in Brazil—all kinds of grants. With my former employer (Ford), one of the last things I did was, on the threat of losing 2,000 jobs in Windsor, I got $73 million outright to convert an engine plant. . . . I've had great experience in this. I have played Spain versus France and England so long I'm tired of it, and I have played the states against each other over here. . . . You could give a litany of these kinds of things."[29]

The trend toward corporatism—the collusion of business, government, and labor—clearly was exciting to some. It was exciting to corporate executives when their profitability was made such a community priority that cities were prepared to turn over public funds and workers were willing to concede their wages. The logic used to sell the concept was that the region's most powerful institutions had to make a coordinated effort if the area's resources were to be salvaged. Corporatism is generally an easy thing to promote. Channeling the expertise of officials in business, government, and labor toward solutions acceptable to all parties sounds like a sane alternative to adversarial bickering. Generally the rhetoric surrounding corporatist projects suggests that each sector makes a sacrifice on behalf of the whole.

Critics, however, question whether the sacrifices are made equally, and they question the process that is used to determine who will be required to sacrifice. They point out that, in most cases, businesses have the advantage in terms of capital, public relations finesse, and power to compel since they can hoist the flag of jobs whenever they feel embattled. Sidney Lens, editor of *The Progressive* magazine, predicted that, at best, the corporatist trends of the 1980s would "—create a kind of riskless capitalism that would impose new burdens on the working class, further reduce the power of the unions, lower living standards, and introduce a new era of repression."[30]

It's symptomatic of the popularity of corporatism that big business is given considerable ink for its cries of excessive taxation, even though corporations have contributed a continuously smaller portion of the national revenue for years. Corporatism allowed President Ronald Reagan's first secretary of the interior, James Watt, to virtually give away the nation's coal and oil supply, to expand uranium mining rights, to violate national park lands and wildlife preserves. The assumption is that corporate profitability is more important than clean air and water.

Felix Rohatyn, a New York financial analyst who popularized corporatism in many circles, concedes that the concept is not democratic. When he masterminded New York City's bailout plan in the late 1970s, he ran into opposition from Mayor Abraham Beame. So he appealed to the legislature, which created a superboard that essentially usurped the city budget. "Whether [democracy] can work during a time of shrinking resources, when it has to allocate pain instead of surpluses, is something I seriously question." Rohatyn acknowledged.[31]

Of course, the unanswered questions are: Who has the power? Who is responsible for enforcing corporatist agreements? If workers trade their standard of living and the public forfeits tax revenues and a healthy environment for economic growth, who ensures that the companies in question actually hire the projected number of workers? In the worst case, who intercedes when a corporation has taken advantage of every tax break, gorged itself on natural resources, spewed out its pollution, marketed its product, and banked the proceeds? Does the public get enforceable assurances that the corporation will maintain employment in the area even if two years down the line Taiwan offers a tempting alternate site for the plant?

Yet, even though there is no mechanism in place obligating corporate responsibility in exchange for public sacrifices, the announcement of new development projects is nonetheless heralded as a sign of new life in a community. Media reports are accompanied by pictures of smiling entrepreneurs, politicians, and labor representatives—all of them lauded for saving the community from economic collapse. Meanwhile, corporatist coalition groups are brainstorming and removing obstacles from the path of potential projects even before they're made public and subjected to debate.

*　　*　　*

Detroit's first black mayor, who was able to hang onto the office for an unprecedented four terms, seemed an unlikely candidate for corporatist alliances. At the outset Young seemed to be the same outspoken, racially sensitive leader he had proved himself to be during World War II, when he did time in the stockade for challenging the Air Force's racist policies. When he was first elected, Young told *Ebony* magazine that his priorities were to reform and integrate the police department, convert HUD housing for the poor, and improve mass transit.[32] He soon became the one elected official all city residents looked to for city services and economic recovery during a time when the city bordered on bankruptcy.

The mayor's style was confident and gutsy. He was prone to obscenities which amused city residents and gave them the impression their mayor was a streetfighter who was giving the white power structure a licking. Young's popularity with city residents made the city's council members timid. Occasional flurries of rebellion against the mayor were always quelled when he won the vote and the council apologized. Under the Carter administration Young had significant national influence; some thought he was looking for a position in the federal government. Young rallied black voter support for Carter and, in exchange, was given federal financial support. Detroit routinely took the lion's share of federal grants, including $75 million in Urban Development Action Grants during the first three-year period of the program's existence.

Between 1974 and 1980 Young entrenched himself with a million-dollar-plus war chest, his own appointees in nearly every position of influence, and a first string of Baptist pastors who were available to front off opposition. Young won the lasting support of black city residents by integrating the Detroit police department and abolishing a unit called STRESS (Stop the Robberies, Enjoy Safe Streets).[33] Young appointed the city's first black police chief, William Hart, and established an independent police commission under the directorship of Doug Fraser, who later became the president of the UAW. By 1980, 39 percent of the city's police force was black.

City residents who had been impressed by Coleman Young's exchanges with the U.S. House Un-American Activities Committee during the Red Scare in the 1950s felt his first actions in office were consistent with his courageous, if not belligerent, posture then. When many victims of the House Un-American Activities Committee were scrambling to obscure or deny their political beliefs, Young was outspoken.[34] But by 1980 the mayor was prepared to mend fences with the city's power elite, his aggressive rhetoric and former union activity notwithstanding.

Young became friends with Lawrence Doss, who headed New Detroit, a civic association set up by the city's power brokers to quell the social unrest of the times. Doss paved the way for a meeting with Henry Ford II, who seemed pleased with Young. "We saw eye-to-eye on a lot of things," Ford said later. "He's sensible and knows what he wants to do. You don't get any kooky ideas, and he doesn't ask you to do things that are unreasonable."[35]

While Ford's surprise that a black mayor wasn't full of "kooky ideas" may have been uncomfortably transparent, others registered surprise and disappointment at the warmth of Young's response to Ford. (These same people would be further surprised when Young indefinitely delayed the release of the city police "Red Squad" files, which had been kept on over 100,000 activists since the turn of the century, despite a 1976 Circuit Court order demanding their release. In the early 1980s Young would also veto a city council ordinance which would have restricted political spying in Detroit.)

Soon after Henry Ford gave Young his stamp of approval, Detroit's first black mayor was embraced by financier Max Fisher, UAW president Leonard Woodcock, Joe Hudson, Jr. (of department store fame), Republican Governor William Milliken, as well as local clergy and academics. For the most part Young also retained the allegiance of the Motor City's Leftists, who were continually grateful that he had not denounced them during the 1950s. At best, a politically astute and outspoken black mayor had found a working relationship with the powers that, like it or not, were in a position to dominate the city. At worst, the ruling elite had found the perfect solution to the racial and class tension that culminated in the 1967 riots: they had a radical black mayor to front for their profit-making ventures in the city.

Young's administration successfully engendered and buttressed a black middle class by instituting an affirmaive action policy for city contracts. A fierce loyalty to the mayor developed in these circles. When the mayor had to take an issue to the public, his media campaigns were funded by some of his employees, a large number of whom made $500 contributions to his campaign fund. But he also received support from the Big Three auto makers, the utilities, and the banks.[36]

Young even seemed willing to put up with the paternalism of his allies. "We've got a black mayor who has done a great job. He supports the business community." This statement was made by the chief execu-

tive officer of Detroit Edison in a twenty-seven-page advertising spread
put together by the city's public relations department and run in *Fortune* magazine.[37] The same spread boasted that Detroit would provide
businesses interested in locating in Detroit with public grants, loan
guarantees, tax-exempt bonds, property tax abatements, and tax credits. And these weren't idle offers. In 1979 alone Detroit provided corporate tax abatements valued at $14.2 million. Chrysler received $3.1
million worth of these.[38] In 1979 *National Geographic* published a spread
titled "Detroit Outgrows Its Past," which included a photograph of
Young standing beside Henry Ford II and shaking hands with David
Rockefeller. The cutline rejoiced that "Detroit's struggle for self-respect
includes allies that might have seemed unlikely a decade ago."[39]

At about the same time, the National Bank of Detroit decided to
suppress a study that it had conducted, because it might be damaging
to the mayor's reputation. The survey results indicated that the poorer
and blacker a neighborhood was, the less likely it was that the city
administration had even contacted it, let alone come to its aid.[40]

Much of the groundwork for Detroit's corporatist alliances was
laid just after the riots. The Detroit News noted that the city's "historically powerful" were put on notice by the riots. "What the city needed,
experts agreed, was a forum to put rich power together with street
power."[41]

The first coalition group was New Detroit, Inc., organized and
chaired by multimillionaire Max Fisher. New Detroit was set up to give
poor and/or black residents an arena in which they could expect to
have their concerns listened to. Even though New Detroit, which was
financed by corporations, served the business community well by defusing sentiment around volatile issues and by purporting to represent
community interests on expeditions to Washington, business leaders
soon abandoned it.

By 1971 the power elite had formed a new and more exclusive
coalition group called Detroit Renaissance. "Detroit Renaissance is a
businessman's dream," the *Detroit News* explained. "It builds
things. It makes things happen. Discussions are matter-of-fact. Henry
Ford II, Max Fisher, builder-developer A. Alfred Taubman and its
president Robert McCabe run the show. No substitutes are allowed.
Either chief executives come, or no one does. And there's less
hostility from blacks who 'don't understand the problems of
business,' to paraphrase many."[42]

The third really consequential coalition group to surface was the

Detroit Economic Growth Corporation (DEGC), which was formed in 1978 to promote economic development. The organization's founding members were the chairman of Michigan Consolidated Gas Company and auto executives James Roche and Lynn Townsend. The DEGC is a private organization which selects the city's development projects, although two-thirds of its budget comes from government funds. It shares office space and staff with the Economic Development Corporation (EDC), a smaller "public" agency through which all public monies for such projects have to flow.

Not surprisingly, some of the most costly projects undertaken by the DEGC have been sponsored by corporations which have members on the DEGC's board. GM chairman Thomas Murphy chaired the DEGC when it agreed to pour hundreds of millions of public dollars into two GM development projects, while the DEGC vice chairman, a ranking executive at the American Natural Resources Company, a major gas supplier, started channeling DEGC funds into his corporation's plans to build a specialty mall in the riverfront warehouse district.

What has been the record of these corporatist projects?

Lauded as a civically responsible coalition group but unencumbered by vocal blacks "who don't understand business," Detroit Renaissance exercised a heavy hand in Detroit. With Henry Ford II as prime mover it spawned the Detroit Renaissance Center development on the riverfront.

The "Ren Cen" was labeled the "Spirit of Detroit" and touted as the seed that would lead to the growth of all kinds of retail, office, and hotel development. It's rarely mentioned that at the same time that Ford sponsored this project, he also sparked the construction of Fairlane, a huge mall complex in suburban Dearborn with three times the retail space afforded in the Ren-Cen. Fairlane actually sucked business offices out of Detroit at the time when the Ren Cen was supposed to attract them. Managers of the Ren Cen found that to get office tenants they had to lure businesses out of existing downtown office buildings. Triple-A decided to move into the new space but abandoned the Guardian Building in the process. That multistory building was promptly boarded over.

The glittering cylindrical towers didn't gain full occupancy. Since the specialty restaurants and boutiques outpriced most Detroiters, its clientele was largely suburban. City residents noted that the building was constructed like a fortress and everyone knew that plainclothes detectives supplemented the visible security guards. A series of outdoor, free, rock concerts on the riverfront was abruptly canceled after several hundred teenagers, primarily black, wandered over to the neighboring Ren Cen. The kids made headlines when they complained that the Ren Cen management locked the doors to keep them out.

Within several years the Ren Cen fell into default and was sold to a Chicago developer, which led to jokes about the Spirit of Detroit being owned by Chicago. But less than one year later, the Chicago owner forfeited the Ren Cen to its mortgage holders.

Another large-scale corporatist development project was the creation of the New Center Commons, an upper-income residential neighborhood adjacent to General Motors' world headquarters. Although GM designed the project, which required the eviction of lower-income neighborhood residents, two-thirds of the cost was borne by the public. The other third was financed by a private sector coalition, which included a Ford Motor Company property subsidiary, the city's three largest banks, all the major utility companies, and the Hudson department store chain.[43] Slick, multi-colored brochures advertised the successfully gentrified area, which once housed black families, elderly whites, and single people, as "your new neighborhood. . . which has been returned as nearly as possible to its turn-of-the-century elegance." The brochure welcomed "people of all ages, all races, all religious beliefs," adding that "there is only one real qualification for potential buyers: a sincere desire to make the New Center Commons one of the finest neighborhoods anywhere."

The brochure neglected to mention that the area's 175 apartments, which once averaged $120-a-month, now rented for up to $600. Likewise, the 125 homes which once sold for a top price of $30,000 now sold for between $75,000 and $118,000. Area residents who were displaced by the New Center Commons were promised first option to buy after the homes were renovated but were not able to afford the new prices.

Frank Pospisil was one of those evicted to make room for the gentrification of the area. He found all his possessions on the sidewalk one winter afternoon in 1981. The fifty-five-year-old economics professor, who had fled Stalinist Czechoslovakia twenty-five years previously, was bitter about his eviction. "I never imagined in my dreams that in twenty years I would've jumped from the frying pan into the fire," Pospisil complained.

Until that afternoon, he had lived in an apartment in the New Center area for $80-a-month, which he paid out of his monthly $265 disability check. Because he knew that he would be forced to leave, Pospisil had found another apartment, renting for $195-a-month, but he couldn't move right away because the plumbing there was damaged. He claimed that he had failed to appear at an eviction hearing that morning because he hadn't received the notice.[44]

According to Sgt. Robert McClary, an arson investigator, the New Center area's development was plagued with fires and vandalism which drove the old tenants out, helping to make rehabilitation possible sooner.[45]

"It was a power struggle for land," according to Richard Martzolf, a Lutheran pastor just north of the project area. Martzolf said he got involved in the fight against the project when it became clear that the "interests of the poor and the powerless" weren't being considered. He said he also worried that the plans for gentrification would push into his parish area, displacing his largely black congregation. He was sure that GM's staff would show no more consideration in his neighborhood than they had in the New Center. "They were genuinely surprised when people in the neighborhood said 'What are you doing to us?' I think they really thought people were going to be grateful for it."[46]

One former resident who said she was glad for the development project was Donna Redden, a thirty-year-old mother of two. She lost her home but was able to get a Comprehensive Employment Training Act job which allowed her the privilege of rehabbing the neighborhood she had been displaced from for minimum wage.[47] Years after their completion many of the New Center homes stood empty, possibly because they were ringed by low-income neighborhoods—a little island of luxury in a city without fat. Security concerns dictated that all the streets in the area be rerouted so that they faced into quick turns and dead-ends.

Other heavily subsidized projects initiated under the Young administration included luxury apartment buildings and a boat marina by the river, as well as the construction of the $71 million Millender Center complex, which includes luxury hotel, apartment, and office space right opposite the still-partially-vacant Renaissance Center. Only one-tenth of the cost of the project, which was to employ 200 people, was slated to be picked up by private developers. Private interests, converting a refitted rail ferry into a luxury riverfront restaurant, benefited from $2.2 million in city bonds and arranged that if they were unable to gross $2 million within the second year, they had the right to move their restaurant to a dock in the city of their choice. [48]

When the city appeared to be teetering on the verge of bankruptcy, Coleman Young enlisted the services of Felix Rohatyn. Rohatyn's corporatist views that public services be reduced and public money be made available to the private sector were winning acclaim in the Democratic party. Although sometimes characterized as a liberal, he was quite popular in the frostbelt business community. At a Detroit Economic Club luncheon, Rohatyn reviewed the causes of the frostbelt's industrial crisis: foreign competition, inadequate capital for modernization, "ill-advised" government regulations, "weak" management, "short-sighted" unions, poor education, and "an ethical culture lionizing rock stars." Rohatyn put very little emphasis on corporate mismanagement.[49]

Rohatyn's critics on the Left and the Right complained that he used taxpayers' money for big business bail-outs. They also complained that his methods were often brutal and undemocratic. In New York City, where Rohatyn salvaged the Big Apple by going over the mayor's head, the economy did recover from its brush with bankruptcy. But increasingly Manhattan has become a haven for the rich, with the poor being displaced by gentrification. In a matter of a few years, economic forces drove thousands of people out of Manhattan and into the South Bronx and Newark. Even middle-class burroughs outside Manhattan began to complain that they were pinched by the withdrawal of city services.

"Everyone paid a price," Rohatyn told the Detroit Economic Club. He pointed to frozen wages and reduction of municipal jobs, increased school tuition, higher mass transit fares, and increases in credit offers from banks. Missing from the list of "everyone" are those whose income continued to increase because they worked for private corporations or reaped the benefits from their investments. These New Yorkers, of course, weren't likely to ride mass transit or to notice the increased fares.

Rohatyn proposed a three-point plan for Detroit. It required the freezing of municipal wages, an increase in the city income tax, and the floating of $100 million worth of long-term bonds. The two most difficult parts of the package were persuading the city's unions to make concessions and arranging for the tax increase. Detroit's 2 percent income tax was already at the maximum level allowed by state law and, in addition, the issue couldn't be revised on the ballot in time to keep with Rohatyn's schedule unless the legislature allowed for an emergency election.

The city had to convince the electorate that the crisis was acute and also not the mayor's fault. To this end, a twenty-five-member blue-ribbon panel of business experts was created. Under the guidance of former Ford Motor Company executive Fred Secrest, the panel studied the city's economic situation and periodically released reports that confirmed and buttressed everything the mayor was saying. The mayor approached the legislature to request permission for a special election, but Young's "abrasive manner and unsubtle arm-twisting" alienated legislators, according to the *Detroit Free Press*. So GM's Thomas Murphy and the UAW's Doug Fraser stepped in and persuaded the legislators to allow the election.[50]

To pass the income tax increase the mayor did two things. First, he cast the issue to the electorate as one of racial control. Although the Detroit rescue plan had been designed, aided, and funded by the city's corporate elite, the mayor saw fit to convene his loyal conference of black pastors and ask: "Are we willing to see that the city's destiny remains in our hands? Or will we do what thousands of bigots hope we do—vote no and let the state take us over?"[51] Second, he spent $427,000 on the campaign. More than half the money was contributed by the city's largest corporations and banks. GM contributed $40,000; the UAW donated $37,500; Ford Motor Company gave $20,000, and, Michigan Bell, American Natural Resources, Detroit Edison, and the National Bank of Detroit each contributed $16,000. [52]

Some of Young's advisors were concerned when he portrayed the tax question in racial terms, but it worked. The Detroit Police Officers Association agreed to the wage freeze on the eve of the election, and the municipal workers union followed suit even though city workers had previously foregone cost-of-living increases. "The city of Detroit is like the mayor's personal pinball machine," one of Rohatyn's associates remarked after the election. "He gets an endless free game."[53]

The bonds were sold—one half to local banks, the other half to city pension funds. The plan was in place and Coleman Young had done the impossible. In the process, of course, he had acted very much like his antagonist, Ronald Reagan. He had balanced the city budget on the shoulders of those least able to afford it. He had raised taxes, forced union concessions, and cut city services. All this with the cooperation of, if not at the behest of, the most powerful members of Detroit's business community.

Young's style of implementing plans for the City of Detroit was not without its critics. One member of the City Planning Department, who requested anonymity, complained that the department learned of Detroit's major development projects only by reading the newspaper. "It's not clear who runs the city," the employee said. "It might be Detroit Renaissance. It might be Max Fisher. I don't know, but it sure isn't us."[54] A Chamber of Commerce official referred to the planning department as the "eunuch of city hall." Many small business organizations and community groups in Detroit were infuriated by the mayor's closed-door decision making with his well-financed colleagues. They criticized New Detroit, the Detroit Renaissance, the DEGC and the EDC, and the Chamber of Commerce for their overlapping membership and centralized power. "The city doesn't want to hear from the little guy down the street," complained Walter Roesler, president of a northwest-side business group. "They look to the big boys, like Detroit Renaissance. Their idea of a small business is AMC (American Motors Corporation.)"[55]

The mayor was not given to defending his actions, but his staff members would. Wallace Jackson, a project planner for the city, said people's criticism that only big businesses got attention was unfair. The mayor's office "controls the city budget and 85 percent of that money goes into the community," Jackson noted in a *Detroit News* series on small businesses. "Somewhere between 20 and 30 percent of the people in the city don't have access to private transportation. Our people need shopping facilities in their neighborhoods, plus government statistics show that 80 percent of the jobs are generated by small businesses. They're the ones that hire Suzy Q down the block. She can't go to General Motors and expect to get a job. We need our small businesses."[56]

Asked why Young's administration routinely turned over hundreds of millions of dollars earmarked by HUD for community development to big business projects, Wallace responded, "We have, at best, very little control over where that federal money is spent in our city. UDAG [Urban Development Action Grant staffers] won't even talk to you unless you're talking $25 million. The big guys get the bucks. We go to the federal government and get $25 million for Al and his Pals [builder Al Taubman and financier Max Fisher] and that's going to generate five times the private investment in the city. We think it's a good investment for the city and it doesn't cost us anything. . . . If that's what they're giving away, even if we need other things, should we pass up the money? . . . Look at the defense budget. The mayor bitched and moaned that our kids need shoes, but now that [the defense budget] is a fait accompli, he's gone out to get some of that money. I think it's grossly unfair to criticize the mayor, because this dude brings home the bacon."[57]

Young made no apologies for this. In an interview with Studs Terkel, he declared: "I realize that the profit motive is what makes things work in America. If Detroit is not to dry up, we must create a situation which allows businessmen to make a profit. That's their self-interest. Ours is jobs. The more they invest in Detroit, the more their interest becomes ours. That is the way the game is played in America today. I don't think there's gonna be a revolution tomorrow. As a young man, I thought it. I think the revolution's for someone else."[58]

The revolution *was* for someone else and in the meantime there were luxury hotels to be built, conventions to host, and a city to be marketed. There were corporate tax give-aways, special financing authorities and districts to be set up, tax-exempt bonds to be floated, city pension funds to be invested in corporate ventures. In the *Fortune* ad which boasted of all that Detroit would do for resident corporations, there was a photograph of a young white man whose face was wrapped in a $100 bill. The caption read, "How to pick up that healthy Michigan tan."[59]

Poletown Exchanged
for Cadillacs

There is a state of emergency within the city and bold, far-reaching and
innovative initiatives, beginning with the city's Central Industrial Park
Project, must be undertaken immediately to deal with the foundations of
this crisis.
> —Mayor Coleman Young, September 10, 1980, letter
> to the Council on Environmental Quality

In late June of 1980, just four months before the presidential
election, Mayor Coleman Young and General Motors chairman Thomas Murphy announced that a new $500 million Cadillac plant would
be built in the center of Detroit—on a site including the northern third
of Poletown. The Central Industrial Park Project would demonstrate
GM's fidelity to southeastern Michigan and serve as a replacement for
two older Detroit Cadillac plants that GM had announced would probably close by 1983. The two older Cadillac plants had employed 15,000
people as recently as 1979. The new one, which they said would produce 1983 Cadillac Sevilles and Eldorados, was projected to employ
6,000.

GM officials declared that they had taken a beating in 1979 and
1980 and needed to act quickly to become more competitive. To this
end they had devised a $40 billion "reindustrialization" plan, which
would call for the construction of at least a half dozen identical, highly
automated, assembly plants. GM's $40 billion plan, which allowed for
the expenditure of $32 billion domestically and $8 billion overseas, was
described as an aggressive capital gamble to make the corporation
competitive with the Japanese.

GM's proposed Detroit plant would cost the corporation $500

million and would represent a substantial chunk of its $40 billion plan. In addition, Michigan officials were well aware that GM had, just a few months earlier, broken ground for a nearly identical plant in suburban Pontiac. To some it appeared that GM's new corporate investment plan might restore Michigan to its former affluence, putting Michigan's workers back on line.

GM's announcement that it would build in Detroit was greeted with banner headlines and a spirit of festivity downtown. This factory, and the one under construction in suburban Pontiac, were, after all, the first auto plants to be built in Michigan since the 1950s. They appeared to be a promise on GM's part that it would not allow the area's industrial infrastructure to become obsolete. The Poletown plant was projected to provide 6,000 union jobs and tens of thousands of spin-off jobs for parts suppliers and service stores.

Detroit officials were delighted, even though they would have to evict 4,200 people from Poletown homes and businesses, to provide the "greenfield site" General Motors wanted. They had been trying to sell the city to corporate investors for some time. So when GM made its announcement, city officials speculated that the corporation's decision to locate a new multimillion-dollar facility in Detroit would lure other companies to do the same.

City officials boasted that GM's investment would improve the city's tax revenue both by yielding property taxes and by employing workers whose wages, whether they lived in the city or the suburbs, would be subject to a city income tax. Detroit's Community and Economic Development officials vowed to accommodate GM as thoroughly and quickly as possible. They viewed GM's construction in Detroit as a sort of test case, which they hoped they could use to illustrate to other companies that Detroit knew how to do business.

It was fortunate Detroit officials were eager to cooperate quickly with GM, because the corporation gave the city just 10 months to clear the 465-acre site. General Motors executives made it clear that if the city of Detroit could not clear the neighborhood off the site by May 1, 1981, they would locate the plant elsewhere.

The prototype plant for the reindustrialization plan was designed for semirural Oklahoma. It offered a number of corporate advantages, some of which could be construed as public advantages as well. The prototype plant was designed to meet pollution standards. (GM claimed bringing its older plants up to environmental code would cost nearly as much as building new plants.)[1] It was also designed so that it could be quickly retooled for different lines of production, increasing the corporation's ability to respond to market demand. GM boasted that its single-story design would improve the production flow inside the plant. The plant would follow the Japanese lead by arranging for all assembly to be done on-site, thus reducing handling costs. The plant would require enough rail space to accommodate railcars carrying three days' worth of production supplies, thus eliminating the need for in-plant stock inventories. In addition, the new plant would rely heavily on robots and was expected to be further automated during the next five years, cutting down labor costs and labor-dependency. (See Appendix C.)

There were perhaps two constituencies most likely to resent GM's new proposed plant. One was, of course, the homeowners who were to be displaced. The other was American auto workers. GM's increased reliance on robots in these new plants posed radically significant questions for workers and the public. Early media reports boasted that GM's new plant in Poletown would employ 6,000 people, but critics observed that one-shift production was common in the Oklahoma prototype plant. One-shift production would only employ 3,000 people who would work with over 150 robots.[2] GM officials proudly forecasted in 1981 that they hoped to triple their robot work force within ten years, which would mean that the corporation would have 14,000 robots on line.[3] "Their application," GM informed its stockholders, "contributes to improving the quality of work life by reducing the number of monotonous, tiring and undesirable jobs."[4]

There is, of course, another perspective on robotics.

At a spring 1981 auto conference in Detroit, Harley Shaiken, a technology expert at the Massachusetts Institute of Technology, pointed out that strengthening the auto industry through automation means decreasing the employment of auto workers. "The paradox is that precisely those measures that strengthen the industry will result in the greatest loss of jobs in domestic plants," Shaiken said. "In the past it was possible to say that measures strengthening General Motors might in fact stabilize or create employment, but the introduction of powerful new forms of automation make that no longer the case." Shaiken predicted that GM's new 14,000 robots would displace at least 60,000 workers.

Shaiken also noted that car production was being designed to rely on robots first and workers second. For that reason GM was able to predict in the early 1980s that its new S car would require only ten direct labor hours, while its Chevette had required eighteen hours as recently as 1979. Chrysler cars required thirty-six labor hours. As automation becomes more and more primary, workers will be increasingly confined, Shaiken said. Computer-aided factory management systems will substitute mechanized job performance review for human interaction. And the overall effect will be that skill levels required of human workers will be diminished, thus minimizing the contribution and the power of human workers.

While people like Shaiken and many union reform groups shared this analysis, the United Auto Workers and the Detroit media dismissed it, saying that if GM failed to modernize there would be no jobs at all.

The new plant design called for a massive site, something more easily arranged in semi-rural Oklahoma than in the center of Detroit. The physical plant itself covered only seventy acres, but GM argued that it needed the additional 395 acres for parking lots, landscaping, and railmarshalling. In defense of its size GM pointed to an 890-acre Japanese Honsha plant in the U.S. but neglected to mention that the ratio of land to plant size at that site is three-to-one. GM officials also neglected to mention that in Japan, where land is at a premium, the ratio of land required to actual plant size is two-to-one. GM's Poletown project required six times as much land as the physical plant would occupy.

The prototype design called for a powerhouse, a pumphouse and waste treatment complex, a truck haul-away area, and a rail marshalling yard, which would extend over 238 acres. GM required track room to store 135 multi-level railcars, capable of carrying twelve Cadillacs each. The storage area would permit a three-day accumulation of cars, since GM expected to ship out 600 cars a day. The corporation also requested storage space for 509 box cars. GM officials indicated that the southern end of the site would be used to house the plant's administrative offices.

In addition, GM planned to encircle the plant with landscaped areas, an eight-acre stormwater retention pond, and 27 acres of parking lot with a ring road. Nearly 100 acres of land had undesignated use.

No attempt was made to alter the configuration of the Poletown plant in order to accommodate the neighborhood. The land on which the Immaculate Conception Church stood was designated for shrubbery. The area on which most of the plant and the power house would stand was already designated for industrial use as it had housed Chrysler's Dodge Main factory for most of the century. (Hamtramck City officials had the title to the Dodge Main site in hand since the factory closed in January.) The only area to be spared within the Central Industrial Park Project [CIPP] was a Jewish cemetery, called the *Beth-Olem.* Ironically, the name means "Eternal Home."

To accommodate GM, Detroit officials would have to obtain title to Poletown's 1,400 homes, 144 businesses, and 16 churches which lay north of I-94 between Chene and Mount Elliott. Taking these parcels, under the auspices of the state's eminent domain law, would require the most massive and rapid relocation of citizens for a private development project in U.S. history.[5] The city of Detroit would have to pay the property owners market value plus relocation costs, bulldoze the buildings, remove any toxic wastes found in the site area, fill in all basement areas and sewage and utility tunnels, and remove all asphalt and concrete. In addition, GM demanded a twelve-year, 50-percent property tax abatement, all necessary air, water, and waste permits, rezoning of the land, city expenditures to provide the plant with adequate access to rail lines, highways, water, utilities, and sewage removal, and city-funded upgrading of the ingress and egress roads to the plant, including more street lights, in order to provide "adequate security."[6]

Initially, observers estimated that the city of Detroit was going to have to invest $240 million to satisfy GM's demands. In time, that estimate was increased to over $300 million. The burden was considerable. When the Department of Housing and Urban Development (HUD) wrote guidelines for public-private projects, it indicated a preference for projects where the private interest invested $4 for every $1 invested by the public. In the Poletown case the starting ratio was two corporate dollars for every single public dollar. As time went on, the ratio was likely to come closer to a dollar-for-dollar investment.

City officials claimed they had taken responsibility for selecting the Poletown site. Officials at the city's Community and Economic Development Department insisted they spent one month laying a transparency of GM's prototype plant over Detroit land and discovered that only Poletown could accommodate the new plant. The point is controversial, because it was generally agreed that if GM chose the land because of its proximity to the corporate world headquarters and surrounding gentrified homes (Poletown is in view of the GM chairman's office window), the availability of raillines and highway connections, immediate access to the city airport, and the limitless supply of skilled workers and fresh water then General Motors should pay a market price for the privilege of building on the land.

If, however, GM reluctantly told the city it would build within the city limits only if an appropriate site could be found and the city had ingeniously found one, then the prevailing view was that it was in the city's interest to lure GM to stay by buying the land and virtually giving it to the corporation. The public had no certain way of knowing who actually selected the site. By the time the project was announced, the city and the corporation were in agreement that the CIPP would cover the Dodge Main plant and the northern end of Poletown.

Although General Motors was rarely challenged to provide a rationale for its decision to force the City of Detroit to finance a large part of its plant construction costs, GM officials did address that question from time to time. The rationale was three-pronged, including a reproach, an offer, and a veiled threat. First, GM claimed that the government was partly responsible for the downfall of the auto industry. Second, it said the government should do whatever might be necessary to facilitate the project, because General Motors was trying to be a "good citizen" by providing jobs which the majority of citizens wanted and needed. Third, GM was a business, not a charity; if its plans couldn't be accommodated, it would have to go somewhere else.

When trying to persuade the public of this logic, officials at General Motors consistently described the new Cadillac project as a public service. They didn't stress the profitability of the plant; instead they focused on their willingness to provide jobs to a public that needed them so badly. By construing their actions as a response to the majority will, they were able to persuade the public that city politicians should be the ones to help make it possible and to deal with dissenting voices.

"In any locality where one puts up a new assembly plant, someone is inconvenienced to some degree," GM vice president David S. Potter said in an interview. "Anyone would prefer to walk into a greenfield situation where you are not going to disturb anyone—there's no demolition, nothing to worry about. In this situation that was just not possible. And we do care about the people here. We care greatly. But when you have to balance it out—what is good for Detroit—I think there is a need for employment and there's the unfortunate situation here where some homeowners will have to be relocated. This is a decision that the city fathers have to make—what is best for Detroit."[7]

Potter added that in the instances where local officials do decide to accept the plant and the dislocation that goes with it, GM has "found it advantageous" to set up task forces to help local leaders. These task forces, designed primarily to deflect criticism of the project, include public relation experts as well as representatives of industrial and governmental relations, manufacturing, plant engineering, real estate, and environmental groups. "We serve the stockholders' best interests by making dog-gonned sure that (GM) is a good citizen in the community and the country."

Presenting itself as a victim returning good for ill, a gentle giant hampered by government but still willing to provide jobs for the community, GM could hardly be accused of requesting too much when it asked the government to go some lengths to acquire the necessary land and to front off any in-coming criticism the project might provoke. After all, GM could always go elsewhere.

The City of Detroit was able to take title to all the private property in Poletown in an expeditious fashion, thanks to a piece of state legislation signed into law just two months before the Poletown project was announced. The intent behind the new law was ostensibly to streamline and make uniform Michigan's condemnation policies. Previously, various agencies authorized to condemn land did so under differing legislative restrictions and obligations. The new law liberalized and standardized the process, but some people intimately involved in the legislation later wondered whether the new legislation was not designed with the taking of Poletown in mind.

Michigan's 1980 Uniform Condemnation Act authorized the taking of private property in order to encourage commercial development. This was an important change, because previously the law allowed for land condemnation only for "public use," as in the construction of schools, or for slum clearance. Detroit officials could not have construed the forfeiting of the Poletown neighborhood for a Cadillac plant as a "public use," nor could they condemn the area as a slum because it was not sufficiently blighted. However, under this law, they could construe the construction of a GM Cadillac plant as something that would benefit the public and serve a "public purpose." (See Appendix A.)

The new law also included a "quick-take" clause, proposed by the state's utilities, which authorized the expeditious condemnation of land.[8] It permitted the state to take title to private property at once, without having to wait for the judicial resolution of legal challenges. Property owners whose land was taken could sue, but the court's efforts to determine whether owners' rights were violated would not delay the state's appropriation of their land. Any redress ordered by the courts, therefore, would follow the forfeiting of the property in question. Home and business owners could anticipate that even if they won their case in court, they would have already lost their property. The most they could hope for would be a dollar award to compensate for the state's violation of their rights.

Under the new law, a state agency could initiate condemnation by filing a complaint in circuit court. The court was obligated to presume the project's legitimacy providing the condemning agency held a public hearing on the project's necessity. Since no review of the public hearing was required, it could be entirely pro forma. However, once the hearing had been held, the court could adjudicate against the project's necessity only if it found evidence of fraud, errors of law, or abuse of discretion.[9]

As written, the law made it nearly impossible for property owners to challenge the taking of their land. As long as they were invited to a public hearing, even if their complaints were disregarded, they could not make their claims heard in court. Property owners could raise questions about the value of a project or the alternative land available only if they could prove misconduct on the part of the condemning agency.

The only requirement for application of quick take was that the court find "a reasonable need of the agency to have possession in advance." In this case the city could and did point to GM's statements that it might move out of state if the project were delayed. Logically one can see that if an appeal were finally successful, the victory would be moot, since the property in question would already have been destroyed. The Michigan legislature praised the bill for ensuring that the "settlement of cases will be quicker and more fair." The legislative analysis claimed that "land assembly for redevelopment will be facilitated and opportunities to attract industry and create jobs will be enhanced. The quick take provisions, which are not now available to all agencies, will mean that construction can commence promptly, when it must, while safeguarding the property owners' rights by escrow requirements and indemnity bonds." The legislature seemed content that property owners' only recourse would be to sue for monetary compensation.[10]

Michigan's new condemnation law passed the legislature on March 18, 1980. On April 4, Republican Governor William Milliken signed into law the Uniform Condemnation Act, which had already won the support of the Michigan Department of Commerce, the City of Detroit, the State Bar of Michigan, the County Road Association of Michigan, and Consumers Power Company. Two months later the mayor of Detroit announced his intention to use this law to condemn 1,400 homes, 144 businesses, sixteen churches, two schools, and a hospital to make room for a General Motors Cadillac plant. One of Detroit's most prestigious law firms worked closely with General Motors and the city to ensure that nothing delayed the project.

This use of the new law prompted Paul G. Citkowski, chairman of the General Government Committee of the Board of Commissioners, to write angrily to one of the bill's sponsors in the House:

> I suspect the legislation . . . was adopted to make things easier for General Motors in its current project. . . . I should emphasize that I am not necessarily opposed to, nor am I addressing myself to, any such past or current projects. I am, however, very much interested and alarmed over the undeserving power this legislature gives to private concerns. It appears to me that the law reads in such a fashion that it subjects our citizens to psychological pressure and actual influence from outside their city and neighborhoods which could move them out of their homes against their will rather quickly, under seemingly short notice—killing off a living, breathing neighborhood. That's a dark cloud to live with overhead."[11]

In the early months city officials generally played fast and loose with the figures, causing even the city council members to complain that they weren't being given adequate information to make a decision. The city planner primarily responsible for handling Poletown was Emmett Moten. Moten's main talent during the Poletown debate was obfuscation. When the council was preparing to vote on the merits of the project, councilwoman Maryann Mahaffey listened to Moten's rendition of the costs and benefits and then said, "What I'm hearing is a crock of shit."[12]

The *Detroit News* described Moten's interaction with the council this way:

> One tactic [Moten] employed when pressed for answers [by the council] was to deluge members with highly technical financial data or complicated explanations of the innovative schemes drafted by his staff. . . . Sometimes during the many discussions with the council, depending on the toughness of council questions, he'd simply say those answers "haven't been worked out yet" and no one could contest him. Once, when particularly pressed, he promised answers "tomorrow." But he didn't show the next day. . . . Another time, instead of addressing the council as a body with another set of answers as he had promised, he decided he and his staff would talk separately with each council member. This, said Larry Brown, one of Moten's aides, was because when it came to complicated issues, "There are different levels of understanding among the council members." Councilman [Ken] Cockrel told Moten that the development staff had supplied council with "a veritable mountain of paperwork, much of which is inconsistent, incomplete or downright lies." [13]

Finally, in mid-November lawyers representing Poletown residents were able to extract some concrete figures by taking depositions of the staff members at the Community and Economic Development Department. The costs breakdown, excluding the cost of interest on loans, appeared to be as follows:

Land acquisition	$62 million
Relocation	$26 million
Demolition	$35 million
Site improvement	$77 million
Total	$200 million

Officials indicated by September 30, 1980, the city had applied for the following grants:

UDAG (Urban Development Action Grant)	$30 million
EDA (Economic Development Administration)	$30 million
EPA (Environmental Protection Agency)	$6.8 million
State Road Funds	$38.7 million
State Rail Funds	$17.8 million
Urban Mass Transit Administration	$1.36 million
State Land Bank Loan	$1.5 million
Block grant money	$3.5 million
Total	$129.66 million[14]

The city anticipated a shortfall of $70.5 million. Thomas Cunningham at CEDD said this would be made up either from existing block grant monies or from section 108 HUD loans which would eventually have to be paid off through block grant funds. He added that, in any case, the city would draw on $10 million to $11 million of section 108 money a few years down the road.

Poletown's attorney then asked if all the figures combined would add up to a discrepancy of $10 million to $11 million. "I don't know if it would work out that way or not," Cunningham answered. "I know that the schedule we are on anticipates using $10 to $11 million of the 108 loans in about two to three years to complete site improvement. Now, whether you could add all of that up and come out with this difference, I don't know. I haven't done it." Even as late as February 1981 economic planners for the city were saying that they could not pin down hard figures for the project. Ernest Zachery, principal economic planner for CEDD, told *In These Times* that "there are a lot of unknowns. We don't know what federal programs will exist a few years from now. We can't have everything secure, but the city, state and federal government are generally interested in the same things."[15] Critics began to wonder if the Poletown project was going to be approved solely on the basis of the ungrounded but optimistic projections of the city's planners.

One thing was clear. If no money could be found, the city intended to use the HUD Community Development Block Grant (CDBG) monies to pay off HUD loans for the project. The irony of this was that block grants were created in order to give neighborhoods some control over how federal funds were used in their community. Block grants were created in an attempt to compensate for the damage done by urban renewal projects.

Although observers speculate that such a project in the private sector would have been rejected as unsound, the business people in the city's coalition groups felt comfortable endorsing the project because it was a public sector risk. GM could not lose. If the city failed to raise sufficient funds to clear Poletown, the corporation would go elsewhere. If the city came up with the money or pushed the project through solely on bravado, the corporation had a space for its profit-making plant. It would be of little matter to GM if the city spent the next thirty years cannibalizing its own monies to pay off the debt it incurred accommodating the corporation.

How GM would fare in Poletown appeared to be clear from the outset. The powers-that-be were prepared to welcome the plant and the neighborhood residents were largely lower-income and elderly. Many people assumed that these people would not have the resources or the know-how to fight back.

Chapter

4

"This Isn't Russia!"

This is America, not Russia. We're not going to let you do this. We're going to fight like hell.

— Josephine Jakubowski, Poletown resident

The first Poletown residents to become aware of General Motors' plan for the neighborhood were Tom Olechowski and Richard Hodas. They stumbled on the information inadvertently through a June 23, 1980, *Free Press* story outlining the area's potential for renewal.

Mention of the $100,000 grant they had obtained for renovating senior citizen housing in Poletown came as no surprise to them; nor did the comments about the feasibility study they were planning for the commercial strip. What stunned them was that an official at the Community and Economic Development Department (CEDD), an agency with which they had worked closely for a couple of years, completely disavowed their Poletown redevelopment plans. "This plan is too extravagant," Tom Cunningham was quoted as saying. "It's nothing we could possibly accomplish right now. We have no plans for new projects in this area."

Olechowski called Emmett Moten just before midnight. He later recalled he'd said, "God damn it, I am pissed. I'm standing here with a *Detroit Free Press* article quoting your guy Tom Cunningham saying you don't think Poletown is shit. If that's the case, you've been bullshitting me, jacking me round for a long time, and I don't appreciate it. Now either he's a bullshitter or you are. Which is it? If he's the bullshitter, you better get on the phone with the *Free Press* and tell them to pull that."

Moten did contact the *Free Press* and the quote was pulled from the later edition. The next morning Olechowski and Moten met outside the city council chambers. Olechowski had a letter in hand that he wanted Moten to sign and send to the Free Press. Instead, Moten looked at him and said, "Tom, I'm about to go into secret session to advise the council we're building a General Motors plant in Poletown."

Soon thereafter Hodas and Olechowski were invited to Moten's office. A sophisticated map of the GM plant and the land mass it would cover was tacked to the wall. "The project was already an accomplished fact," Hodas said. "There was just the question about how they [CEDD] were going to inform the community about it and that's where they were trying to get our support. Moten thought we were going to work with him. They asked us to get together a list of the quote unquote leaders in the neighborhood to discuss this with. Basically none of them knew anyone in the area except Tom and me."

Both Olechowski and Hodas took issue with the way the plant site was designed. They pointed to a rerouting of East Grand Boulevard and asked why it had to jut down into part of Poletown south of Interstate 94. In response, city officials modified the plan to stay north of Interstate 94. This gave Hodas, who lived north of I-94, the impression that the city might be flexible, so he said, "This is absurd, taking this amount of land for this plant, especially when you see how small the plant is in relationship to the size of the total parcel." Moten responded: "We had no choice. General Motors came to us." Hodas says that when he asked about the churches, Moten "kind of shrugged his shoulders and said, 'This is the site that fits the criteria. We have a crisis that has been engendered by General Motors coming to us and threatening to leave. We have to do something.'"

Hodas and Olechowski had a few days to consider how they wanted to respond to what they perceived as the city's betrayal. But most Poletown residents were caught completely off guard when headlines in early July heralded the new plant and announced that it would be built on top of their homes.

Word of GM's plans for the Poletown community spread from house to house like wildfire. During the first several weeks, residents clustered on the streets, reading and rereading the relocation information that had been hand delivered to them by the police. They received visits from appraisers. They were informed they could attend a public meeting on July 9.

The situation was utterly foreign to everyone in the neighborhood. Residents were unsure how to assess the scope and method of the project, much less how to organize to oppose it. Ken Fireman, a veteran city hall reporter for the *Detroit Free Press,* noted at the outset that GM and the city had designed their project with the intent of moving it along as quickly as possible in order to prevent strong opposition from developing. The formality of the documents presented and the speed with which things seemed to be being accomplished did serve to knock residents off balance.

Bernice and Harold Kaczynski were in North Carolina, visiting their daughter, son-in-law, and a new-born grandchild, when there sons called to tell them that they were soon to lose their home. They cut short their vacation and headed back.

"People couldn't believe it," Bernice Kaczynski explained.

> They thought it would be something that would pass by. They couldn't believe they were going to take this [Immaculate Conception] church. Everybody believed the project would take two, three, maybe five years. People said, "How can they take the property so quick? You know you have a chance to fight this and it will take years." And then we started to learn about the quick-take law at our own meetings at Immaculate Conception where people were looking into it. They came up and says, "Hey, Act 87—do you know what it's all about?" And that's where we learned about the quick-take law and about its being valid, that Governor Milliken passed it through in April and in June they told us this is how they're going to operate here.

Ann Giannini, who prior to the news of the project had never met Bernice but soon became a very close friend, said the reaction was much the same on her block. People just failed to acknowledge that everything that was familiar to them could be destroyed by a city edict. "My husband didn't believe it from the beginning anyway," she explained. "He was always kidding about it until they started tearing the houses down, and then he saw it was really going to happen. Most of the old folks—they are in their seventies—they just didn't want to get involved in it because they didn't believe it was going to happen. You couldn't get them to understand it.

"I've been married almost fifty years and our anniversary is going to be next July," Giannini added. "So on our golden wedding anniversary we're going to get kicked out of our house. I got up this morning and I was going through the house singing and my husband is looking at me. He says what the hell am I doing singing? I'm getting kicked out of my house, it's raining outside. . . . " She laughed. "I say I don't give up. We don't want to go because, although it's not much, it's all we have. I always said the only place I'd move to from here was Mount Olivet [Cemetery]."

Fr. Malcolm Maloney, pastor at St. John's Roman Catholic Church, did bury a Poletown resident soon after the project was announced. Maloney recalled that most of his parishioners were distressed. Some had never celebrated Christmas in any other church. But one incident in particular stood out in his mind. A woman in her forties, who carried scars from falls caused by epilepsy, came to his office with a blue HUD relocation booklet in her hands. Maloney was concerned about her because she seemed frightened and disoriented. He tried to reach her family and her doctor but finally sent her home with the phone number of a shelter where he suggested she stay for a while.

"She walked back to her building, leaving her little blue book on my desk," Maloney said. "Some guy tried to grab her purse when she got home. She went up the stairs and jumped out the window. She was killed." Maloney paused. "So how would you feel? You get a notice of displacement—none of it having anything to do with saving your house. . . . " He shook his head. Another of his parishioners had a heart attack and was hospitalized when she saw the first woman plunge from her apartment window next door.

Confusion permeated the neighborhood. While many people refused to believe that the neighborhood was truly in jeopardy, others insisted that the neighborhood was doomed and that there was no point in resisting General Motors. The news media, of course, reinforced the latter perception. Newspaper and TV coverage generally rejoiced about the Cadillac plant project; the mourning of residents only served as a minor dissonant counterpoint to the story.

Rumors flew wildly—one in particular, which warned that if you didn't sell your house quickly, the city would run out of money and you'd lose your home and neighborhood for next to nothing.

But when the first public meetings were called at Parke elementary and Kettering high schools, 1,000 people showed up and most of them were angry. They listened to presentations by city council members, representatives from CEDD, an appraiser, staff people from the state and national Historic Preservation councils, the Citizens District Council, and GM officials. They were shown slides of the Oklahoma prototype plant, of the new plant site design, and of alternate housing available in Detroit. Then a brief question-and-answer period followed, during which those who got to speak were limited to three minutes. Residents repeatedly asked why the citizens weren't allowed to vote on whether they should be displaced by General Motors. They asked whether GM had made any binding commitments about the number of jobs it would provide at the plant and whether the city council was really going to give the corporation a tax abatement on top of everything else. They also questioned the amounts of money people would be offered for their homes, when they would receive it, and whether the elderly would be able to get mortgages.[1]

Donald Ludwig, a Poletown resident and former GM engineer, gave the city council a written statement raising his objections, among them the concern that the plant would be highly automated and that the relocation would traumatize residents. Ludwig, a price-cost analyst for the Army, complimented Poletown residents for not allowing their homes to fall into tax delinquency and HUD-ownership, a process he called "being HUDized." And he regretted that the homes would be taken over by CEDD official Emmett Moten instead—a process he called being "Motenized." "It is a pathetic sight," he wrote, "to see aged couples hugging each other, sobbing on the sidewalks, looking at their homes perhaps for the last time before being Motenized. Such scenes are not pleasant and it is not imaginable that a great city like Detroit could be so cold-hearted and gluttonous for the almighty buck."

John Saber's complaints were equally passionate and brought down the house at the Parke School hearing. Saber, sixty-eight, railed at the city council members: "I been living in this neighborhood for over forty-six years, and I don't intend to move because you con artists are trying to pull a rip off. Nobody can tell me up to eighty percent of the value of that house, how much that house is worth. To me it is a million dollars. My house has a brand new bathtub and I don't intend to move to a clunker, God-damned, cockroach-infested house that you pick out. I want to live on Kanter and I love every rotten board in that house."[2]

To the surprise of Emmett Moten and other city officials who had expected their cooperation in selling the GM project to neighborhood residents, Olechowski and Hodas handed out leaflets urging people to fight the GM project. They invited residents to a Poletown Neighborhood Council meeting in the basement of the Immaculate Conception Church. According to Hodas, most of the people attending the public hearing were very hostile to the demolition of their neighborhood. But some were mollified when city officials invited people to sign up for jobs preparing the GM site. Plus, he said, people were told they could apply to be paid appointees on the Citizens District Council (CDC) that the mayor would soon create.

Nearly 400 people attended the first meeting of the Poletown Neighborhood Council. Some of the residents had already begun organizing on their own. Lists of the names and addresses of city council members, the mayor, and the chairman of General Motors were passed from hand to hand. People pooled envelopes and stamps. Second-generation Poletown residents, some of whom had studied at area colleges, helped their families and neighbors put their objections into writing.

It was at these early Poletown meetings that the Kaczynskis, the Crosbys, the Dockerys, and Karen Apollonio first met the Gianninis and the Jakubowskis. Bonds began to form in a number of directions as people recognized in each other the same resolve to stop the project or, at least, to make it as publicly costly as possible for the city and GM.

The prevailing sentiment in the neighborhood seemed to be that the neighborhood and the plant could co-exist. Residents resented being portrayed in the media as people whose selfish concerns posed an obstacle to the possibility of a new plant and jobs. "It's not the plant we're against," explained Hodas, who was elected vice president of the PNC. "It's the uprooting of history and human beings. We've seen the plans and we know that the site of the Immaculate Conception [Church] is supposed to be a flat, 50-car parking lot. We've tried to talk them into building vertical parking structures, which would be more efficient, but they won't even talk to us about it."[3]

Residents also resented the way city officials were implying that sacrificing the neighborhood was no great loss, since it was already blighted and deteriorating. "They say this is a slum area," complained Sally Harris, a Poletown resident who was laid off from GM's Chevrolet Gear and Axle plant. "They don't know how good it is. We probably get along better than people out in Grosse Pointe. We all have to scuffle to make it and everyone looks out for everybody else. You keep thinking you're making some moves in your life, some progress, and then something like this comes along and you have to start all over again. . . . The only way I would really be satisfied about moving is if they built that plant and gave me a job. But it's not going to happen. They're going to put robots in there and nobody's going to have a job."[4]

Many residents also expressed a strong sense of betrayal by an America they had believed in and fought for in the past. Harold Kaczynski, who fought in World War II and sent several of his children into the Service, complained, "I fought for this country for four years, and what do I get? They're trying to run me out of my home. I don't think that's justice. I'm not selling and I'm not moving. I'm not moving until the bulldozers come and knock me down in it. I got nothing to lose."[5]

Walter Jakubowski, retired from Chrysler, felt much the same way. "I've lived here for 60 years," he told the *Michigan Catholic*.

> My parents lived in this house. Two of my children were born upstairs

because we couldn't afford hospitals during the war. I went to that [Immaculate Conception] church as a boy. I was married there. My children were baptized there. And now they want to tear it all down. I'll fight that. It's just too hard to take. I want to live here. If I didn't I could have moved a long time ago.... We're not interested in how much they'll give us for our homes. A house can be replaced. But you can't replace memories. A neighborhood is your life and a church the hub of your social and religious life. If they destroy all that, what do you have left? The government talks about protecting human rights in Asia and Africa, but they're trampling human rights in their own backyard. There is no democracy. You have democracy as long as you don't tangle with the power structure.[6]

The PNC meetings themselves were bold stabs at challenging the project, but they were hampered somewhat by the de facto leadership of Tom Olechowski, who became the group's president partly because he had been involved in organizing the area prior to the announcement of the GM project but also because he claimed to have connections at city hall and in the state capitol. Many Poletown residents said in retrospect that Olechowski served a real purpose in pulling the organization together and in giving people confidence that they could dare to argue with the authorities. But his leadership was the cause of much doubt and dissension. People complained that he was from the southern part of Poletown, which would not be affected by the plant site demolition, and that he also had a tendency to play his cards too close to his chest. Olechowski insisted on meeting with political and corporate leaders himself and discouraged others from trying to make contact on their own.

Olechowski's first objective may well have been a wise one. He wanted to establish a clear name for the neighborhood, so that the media would refer to the area by a community name rather than as the "proposed Central Industrial Park" area. It proved effective to designate the area as "Poletown," a name popular at the turn of the century. Non-Polish residents complained that the name alienated them, but it did recall the area's history. Consequently, the neighborhood was perceived as having an essence prior to and distinct from the Cadillac plant project. Within a few weeks the media had adopted the name.

This so infuriated the mayor that he denounced Poletown as a myth and constantly referred to the area as "so-called Poletown." Young's constant attacks on the integrity of the neighborhood earned him the hostility of many Poletown residents. "When he first got into office he was doing good," explained Bernice Kaczynski. "But when he got re-elected he started going another way. I'm saying now 'a mayor is a mayor.' The black politician isn't going to do any more for me than the white politician because he never listened to me anyway. And now, he's calling us a myth."

Early on, a Citizens District Council (CDC) was set up by the mayor. This body was supposed to represent the public interest and oversee the project in compliance with Public Act 198. Hodas was asked to provide the names of ten community leaders for appointment to the CDC. Hodas did this, only to discover that business owners who were in favor of the GM project had also assembled a list of ten names. Officials at CEDD selected five names from each list.

The chairperson of the newly formed CDC, James Paczkowski, attended most of the early PNC meetings. According to residents who hoped to stop the GM project, he came intending to disrupt the meetings and to discredit the PNC leadership. "We couldn't stop him from coming, they were open meetings," Bernice Kaczynski explained, "but when he came in he caused a lot of chaos. That's how we found out about the Act 87, which is the eminent domain law, the quick-take law. We checked into that because he came to discredit Tom because he felt Tom didn't tell us about it. So Tom, I guess, wasn't aware of it at that point and that cost, because when the people finally found out what the Act 87 was, they were down on Tom for not telling us about it."

It was hard for residents to figure out the validity of these kinds of complaints, because the technicalities of the law under which they were being evicted were completely new to them. Most residents complained that when they tried to call city relocation offices or CEDD, the lines were busy or their calls were not returned. Deciphering the truth of the situation was nearly impossible and the pressure of time shortened most people's patience.

In addition, many Poletown residents were not used to having to challenge the government. Except for those with a labor union past, they had never been in a position to try to manipulate the political process. Some people tended to believe that if the Congress and the president learned about the situation they would intervene personally and put a stop to it. They believed that elected officials would put the rights of American citizens before the interests of General Motors. At one meeting an elderly woman expressed surprise when she reported, "I wrote a letter to President Carter, and I wrote about what's going on here. And I didn't get an answer from him, but somebody in his office answered me and told me that the president doesn't answer letters. He has a staff working for him, and he says they can't do anything but referred me to the HUD office downtown."

Clearly there was a need for someone to provide perspective. But Olechowski may have stepped beyond his limits when he promised at meetings to check out and pursue the multifarious suggestions that were raised. Eventually, residents became irritated with his lack of follow-through.

Fr. Malcolm Maloney, a newcomer to Poletown who was appointed pastor of St. John's church just a few weeks before the GM project was made public, complained later that "there was a lot of dissatisfaction over the way meetings were run. Practically everyone wanted to resist but it seemed like a couple of big egos got off on a head trip. They wanted everything to fall under their banner. Every week their goals changed. They had demands that they were going to make that were really good, but the next week they changed and they had added a whole new set." Maloney started to pursue independent plans to sue the city, which he finally abandoned when Fr. Joseph Karasiewicz, of the Immaculate Conception Church, gave his financial support to Olechowski's endeavors.

However, most agree that while Olechowski assumed the most visible power position in the Poletown resistance, another second string of leadership was forming. In fact, Olechowski's mobilization of the PNC did buy time for others who wanted to become active in Poletown. Karen Apollonio, who lived with her parents on Mitchell Street, teamed up with Bob Giannini, whose parents lived on the other side of East Grand Boulevard. Working with some other second-generation Poletown residents, like Connie Patrick, Pat Barszenki, and David Tylenda, they started planning more confrontational demonstrations by late September.

In four short months Poletown residents had banded together in a way that demonstrated a clear neighborhood identity. Their spokesman was articulate and passionate, even if his leadership was questioned. And the layer of leadership which was in the making promised more aggressive mailings, phone-calling efforts, and protests. The people who hung in behind the younger and less visible leaders, like Apollonio and Giannini, were primarily women, many of them elderly. These women may have taken the biggest risks of any when they decided to challenge the institutions they had depended on for so many years.

Rather than subside in disillusionment and bitterness, many of Poletown's women learned to fight back, carrying the American flag and the crucifix with them to protests. They drafted letters to their elected representatives, who rarely bothered to respond. They petitioned GM for a meeting to consider whether an alternative plant configuration could accommodate the plant and the neighborhood. And, finally, they overcame their hesitancy and were willing to march down city streets with signs and chants.

All of this took a toll. Many of the women had to leave husbands

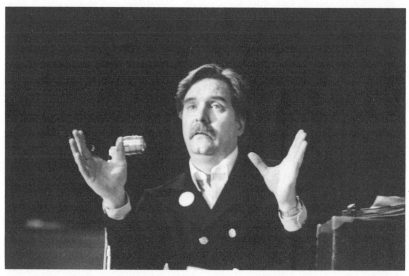

Tom Olechowski was president of the Poletown Neighborhood Council.

Poletown Neighborhood Council meetings were attended by spirited older women who had the courage to make demands.

and families to attend endless meetings. They had to expose themselves to the hostility of people who didn't share their views. They had to learn to speak out against critics who were often better-educated and more influential than they were.

Of course the city and GM were not standing still in the interim. While Poletown residents were aligning themselves and learning to grapple with the laws and executives that threatened their homes, the city and GM pushed ahead relentlessly toward clearing the land by May 1, 1981.

By fall Poletown residents were preparing to file suit and readying themselves for their first demonstration. But by then the city had already officially designated Poletown the Central Industrial Park Project. It had gotten a waiver from the Council on Environmental Quality to expedite preparation of the Environmental Impact Statement and contracted researchers to complete it. The city had held two public hearings to satisfy state and federal requirements and amended its application for federal monies to include an advance of $60.5 million in block grant monies to free up Section 108 loans. It had completed all its relocation surveys and 85 percent of its parcel appraisals.[7] In addition, the city's Economic Development Corporation (EDC) had passed a resolution stating that construction of the plant would serve a public purpose—a measure required to enable the city to use the new quick-take law to condemn people's homes.

Moreover, the city and GM had secured the support of the Roman Catholic archdiocese and the United Auto Workers. The union issued a brief statement commending GM for being socially responsible enough to build in Detroit. The church described itself as taking a neutral posture; however, it encouraged its Poletown parish priests to help their congregations move out by relying on Catholic Social Services. It also made the two priests cochairs of a church committee intended to defuse criticism and dissatisfaction with the project.

Both Poletown Catholic priests were new to their parishes. Fr. Malcolm Maloney, a Capuchin priest, arrived at St. John's one week after he had learned it was to be demolished. Fr. Joseph Karasiewicz, pastor of Immaculate Conception, had been at that church for only one year. However, Karasiewicz had a long history in the neighborhood. He had been raised in southern Poletown and had been carried into the Immaculate Conception Church (ICC) when he was only two years old.[8]

Predictably, the two priests responded differently to the pressures they received from the archdiocese concerning Poletown. Maloney was confused by the situation. "I called a meeting as soon as I got there," he later recalled, "just to find out what was going on and what [the parishioners] thought we should be doing. They were crying at that meeting. There were some that looked on this as an opportunity kind of thing, but the older ones had never moved. They were born in that neighborhood. . . . They'd retired and fixed up their homes to die in and had never been to another church. This one lady was crying and saying it would be the first time in her life that she would not have gone [to St. John's] for Christmas mass.

"Practically everybody wanted to resist, wanted to do something," Maloney said. "Nobody just wanted to hand this thing over. But you start playing both sides of the street. I'm a pastor and I'm responsible for a lot of old people. We started planning. If this thing in fact was going to happen, there's going to have to be some geriatric counseling, some kind of help so that people can move into parishes that are already prepared to take them."

In late September, twenty black and white Poletown residents picketed outside St. John's Church during a Sunday mass. They were angry that the priest was preparing his parishioners to leave rather than to fight. (Maloney felt the battle was to be fought in court, not in the streets by his parishioners.) The protestors resented the forums which Maloney held at his church for parishioners to learn about the relocation process from city officials. They saw his whole approach as a betrayal. Their signs read: "The church supports GM," "Fr. Maloney— Present Day Shogun Priest," and "GM Desecrates Churches for Profit."

Maloney responded to the demonstration in the *Detroit Free Press*: "These people outside, these neighbors, their approach is atrocious. That's why they get a 'no' from the start. They don't want to discuss. They back you into a corner. . . . I hope this relocation doesn't happen, but if it does, it will happen soon and we've got to be ready. . . . I'm afraid of how this is going to affect the little old lady in her kitchen, wondering what's happening as the wrecking boom hits her building. There are a lot of people who are going to die over this. We are trying to bring in the social workers to help."[9]

Maloney started receiving hate mail, some of it scrawled on toilet paper, from other Poletown residents. "I became the guy on the scene who was the bishop's boy," he said. "They needed a fall guy. I felt like the Old Testament prophets when Jerusalem was going to be destroyed. They got stoned and persecuted, because they were telling people to leave. But we started telling people, 'You'd better move out. We'll help you.'"

Olechowski denounced the picket at the next PNC meeting, but those involved were satisfied with the results and pleased by the press coverage it generated. "It worked," Bernice Kaczynski said later. "We started to be noticed. We, as residents of Poletown, were being heard for the first time and not in some basement of a church. It was a new venture for all of us. We mostly raised our kids. You stay home with the kids and you elect your politicians to work for you and here the politicians were taking over and we had no say-so. And so it was nice to see the reaction of everyone. My son, who came home from the Navy, helped make the billboards. It was nice. There was a little bit of everybody there. Everybody we could get on short notice."

Karasiewicz's early role in the Poletown struggle was much more low-profile. He had an innate sympathy with the residents that probably came from his background in the area. (His father had been a janitor at Ford Motor Company by day and a shoemaker by night. His mother had been a seamstress and had taken in boarders.) Like others in the area Karasiewicz doubted that the project would actually be put through.

"I think a number of people never thought it would be a reality," Karasiewicz said, "because the money wasn't available and nobody thought GM would go through with it. GM was threatening to go to the sun belt. I thought it wouldn't affect the church at all and I hoped it wouldn't affect the people either, at least the majority of them."

In time, Karasiewicz became extremely outspoken about the project, and his critics would suggest that this was a radical deviation from his early position. However, when asked by a reporter for the *Michigan Catholic* in October what he thought of the archdiocesan committee he cochaired, Karasiewicz said he was upset that it "does not have as its goal to forestall the plant from reaching into the residential areas. They want to recruit as much help as possible for this committee, which doesn't make that much sense to me. It's like saying, 'We won't help you live, but when you die, we'll dress you up real nice.'"[10]

City officials spent time in September lining up the support of the Advisory Council on Historic Preservation (ACHP). The ACHP, a national agency intended to help protect historic structures that are either on or eligible to be on the National Register, had the right to make suggestions about ways to minimize the destruction of historic structures during the completion of projects. The first representative sent from Washington, Patrick Steele, toured the area and concluded that "the ethnic background" of Poletown entitled it to protection. But his superior, Robert Garvey, arranged to take his own tour of Poletown with Emmett Moten. Steele says Moten described the neighborhood as a rundown residential area and pointed out that it stood in the way of a

$700 million development project. Garvey reportedly told Moten: "I don't see anything historic about this. I don't see that it would be a problem." Steele complained that at a policy briefing session "I was told, at two different times, that 'this is no time for integrity.' Shortly after that we had a policy committee session. Nobody came out and said anything direct, but it was pretty clear that we were going to give the needed papers to Detroit."[11]

On October 14, the city held its third public hearing. Like the previous ones it was top-heavy with presentations by GM and city officials. The question-and-answer period followed several hours of pro-plant talk by the panelists. Residents were allowed a few minutes to speak and were frequently angry that their questions were deflected, not answered.

Fr. Francis Skalski, rector of St. Hyacinth's Church in southern Poletown, attended. "I remember the meeting at Kettering High School very vividly," he said. "It was a mass meeting. There was about a thousand people there. It was hard to believe the amount of people there—blacks and whites and everyone. At that meeting I don't think they had more than six people speaking for the project. All the people there, young and old and middle-aged people, were against the project. Especially vocal were the people presently working for General Motors—they said they'd be losing jobs.

"My position throughout the whole thing was that you can't barter with a giant," Skalski added.

> I was probably the only one who said we don't need the project in this part of the city. I felt you couldn't win concessions from the city or GM. I brought up the fact that it was a shame that people like General Motors were coming in and taking over an area from poor people. It reminds me of a medieval king—there's a massive area, a nice big fence in front of their property, beautiful landscaping, and behind they have their castle—their plant. But nobody outside the neighborhood would listen to us. They thought we were antilabor, antijobs, just antiprogress when we started to fight. No one was giving too much attention to the fact of eminent domain, that this was a precedent-making affair.

At that meeting, residents were given a pamphlet titled *Acquisition Notice—When the City Acquires your Property*. This provided simplistic explanations for why the state could take your property against your will. There was no mention of the recent revisions in state law which were facilitating the GM project. Worse, there was a blatantly misleading paragraph stating that "in most states" residents who sued the condemning agency would have to pay their own attorneys' and appraisers' fees. The pamphlet failed to mention that in Michigan this was not the case. The Michigan Condemnation Act provided that the condemning agency would always pay appraisers and would also pay attorney fees if successfully sued. Emmett Donnelly, a representative of the Christian Service Department, pointed out the error and asked the city to amend the pamphlet. This was done within two weeks, but any Poletown residents who received only the first issue would presume that the state had no responsibility to help residents make their claims defensible in court.

Olechowski asked the city and GM officials at the meeting if residents could have forty days to consult with architects and industrial engineers to develop alternative site configurations which could accommodate the plant and the neighborhood. The request was denied.

Sandra Kotz, a Poletown mother at the meeting, accosted the city council and won rounds of applause. "My child is attending the same school that her grandfather attended," Kotz said. "I'm upset that I will never be able to afford to buy one of the cars that this plant will produce. Why don't they move it out to Grosse Pointe or Birmingham where the rich people live? You're taking away our freedom. You're not asking us—you're telling us. We're being ruled just like the gestapo."[12]

The next day, the draft Environmental Impact Statement was released, indicating that the city had adequately considered other possible sites and recommending approval of the project. The city's Economic Development Corporation, which was staffed by the Economic Growth Corporation, authorized a "letter of commitment" to GM. And on October 20, the city council's planning commission approved the project despite its concern about "real risks to the city in terms of financing and human impact." The report also said "the direct economic benefits to the city in terms of additional revenue have been somewhat overstated in the draft EIS."

In October Poletown residents began to express fear about living alone. The arson rate in the neighborhood had doubled since the project was announced, and even police arson investigators said that fires plaguing the neighborhood were a direct result of the GM project. But in the meantime residents worried that their neighbors would sell and move, leaving them next door to abandoned houses. The neighborhood began to feel transitional.

On October 31, the city council approved the project, declaring it "hereby determined to be for the use and benefit of the public." The only councilperson to vote against the project was Ken Cockrel, a Marxist known city-wide for his independence. On that same day, HUD authorized the city to draw on its $60.5 million in Section 108 loan guarantees.

The Poletown Neighborhood Council's efforts to challenge the constitutionality of Michigan's Uniform Condemnation Act were hampered by the group's difficulty in finding an attorney. This was partly attributable to Olechowski's preference for big-name Polish attorneys. But Poletown residents claimed it was also because most Detroit attorneys were unwilling to tackle General Motors and city hall. The PNC would eventually issue a press release to this effect.

Finally, labor attorney Ronald Reosti agreed to take the case, despite the fact that the PNC could not back the litigation financially nor coordinate a legal team to help with the case. Reosti decided to challenge the constitutionality of taking private homes for corporate profit. An expedited hearing was scheduled before Judge George Martin, a retired judge contracted by the city for the duration of the Poletown project. Reosti's motion for a temporary injunction to halt the taking and demolition of property until the legal issues were resolved was refused.

"This project violates the basic constitutionally guaranteed rights of the residents of Poletown," Reosti explained to the press. "If the court allows this takeover, it will set a precedent which can be used to undermine and erode the rights of citizens and neighborhoods in any part of our city or in any city in the country."[13]

In November and December Poletown residents picketed city hall and the Economic Development Corporation. At the EDC demonstration, protestors were denied access to the entire building which housed the Detroit Economic Growth Corporation, the EDC, and the Chamber of Commerce. When Jim Delcamp, a Poletown resident, and Nick Kubiak, whose aunt lived in Poletown, tried to insist that it was a public building, they were arrested. The charges were eventually dropped. At city hall, a group gathered to leaflet. One of those present was Teofilo Lucero, an American Indian in his seventies, who came to the demonstration in full Indian headdress. At PNC meetings Lucero was always the one who insisted that the government would be unrelenting in its relocation of the residents. He urged immediate action and was disappointed by people's confidence in letter-writing:

> People here are facing the same thing that the American Indian faced. We've been relocated ever since the white man came here. Our treaties meant nothing to them. And that's just about what our city fathers, GM, the mayor, the lawyers, the judges, and the governor are doing to us now.

I said we got to retaliate before they hire the planners, but the residents didn't believe things were going to go through.

The old people will never start over again. They'll be put in nursing homes. People here don't want that. They want to live here and die here. But what does GM and the city care? All they care about is the Almighty Dollar. We don't want that. We want to be humanly treated. Now you know what it's like to be relocated. It's a trail of tears.

One of Poletown's early demonstrations was a march through the neighborhood, which organizers hoped would draw the media into the neighborhood and force them to look closely at its character. Residents carried signs that read: "GM says get back—We say fight back." Members of the Revolutionary Socialists League who lived in the area helped organize the march, making some of their political skills available to Poletown residents. No other Left groups were willing to involve themselves, either because of the mayor's former reputation as a radical or because they saw battles for property as "petty bourgeois."

When he took the Poletown case, Reosti said he broke ranks with Detroit's Left lawyers, many of whom openly said that challenging the mayor was tantamount to facilitating racism. "I kept looking over my shoulder," he said.

But I don't think it's proper for a corporation to extort these conditions. The residents are as concerned about jobs as anyone else. But to hold this neighborhood hostage to the loss of jobs is to concede that the GM plan is the only way to save jobs, and that is simply not true.

Instead of using its vast energies and know-how to develop a plan for this urban area, GM has arbitrarily insisted on enough acreage to accommodate a plant designed for a flat, open area because that is what they did in Oklahoma. To force this design on this neighborhood and this city establishes the "government/business partnership" as a one-way deal. . . . GM could have its plant and at the same time save much of the Poletown neighborhood and millions in tax dollars with a more space-efficient design. There are several alternatives to allow for building the plant and saving both the neighborhood and taxpayer dollars. The neighborhood is still functioning; people still want to live in Poletown. Some have decided to leave, but the great majority will maintain this community.[14]

Reosti was given just under three weeks to present his case to Judge Martin. He presented several alternate design configurations which had been prepared by a local architect. Each one included the plant, its power plant, and raillines but also accommodated the neighborhood. A primary change from the GM site design was the creation of a vertical parking structure and rooftop parking.

Reosti argued that the city's use of eminent domain was unconsti-

Houses throughout Poletown sported signs saying their land was not for sale. Some added that arsonists, thieves, and GM "will be shot."

Teofilo Lucero, a Native American and a Poletown resident, holds the sign in front. Lucero told neighbors: "Now you know what it is like to be relocated. It is a trail of tears."

Walter Jakubowski, a Chrysler retiree, joins in one of the first Poletown protests.

Barbara Sokol (center) surprised herself by joining in one of the first demonstrations against the GM project.

tutional because it primarily benefitted General Motors and the exchange of private property for such a purpose was illegal. He argued that taking the entire 465-acre site was an abuse of discretion because the construction of parking structures would eliminate the need to take the whole neighborhood. The absence of any such changes in GM's original design indicated that GM had forced the city's hand. Reosti also argued that Poletown, because of its history and ethnicity, was an area resource warranting protection under the Michigan Environmental Protection Act (MEPA).

Mayor Young testified before the court that unemployment was at a crisis level of 18 percent as compared to a national rate of 8 percent. Unemployment for minorities was estimated at 30 percent. The mayor also said that Detroit's industrial facilities were largely obsolete, which resulted in decreasing employment and a decreasing population in the City of Detroit. Young testified to the relentless efforts of the city to lure new industries into Detroit.

Judge Martin stated at the outset that his purview was relatively narrow, because he was bound by the quick-take statute to presume that an agency's finding of necessity to take the property was legitimate, unless there was evidence of "fraud, error of law, or abuse of discretion." The broader questions—such as whether it would be wise to take hundreds of parcels of property to build a Cadillac plant—were outside his jurisdiction.

Martin ruled that Poletown's presentation fell "far short" of proving the city abused its discretion because the city examined the residences and the people affected by the proposed plant, offered relocation help, and provided financial assistance for relocation. "General Motors held no gun to the head of the City of Detroit," Martin wrote, adding, "General Motors could go elsewhere." No doubt, the judge's intent was to show GM had not insisted on this particular site for the Cadillac plant, but he unintentionally acknowledged the argument of Poletown residents, which was that by threatening to leave Detroit GM *was* putting a gun to the head of the city.

Martin also ruled that the city's refusal to insist on the construction of parking structures was not an abuse of discretion but simply "having regard for all the features involved, including how workers rush to parking spaces on entering and exiting." The judge dismissed the MEPA argument, saying that the protection of cultural resources was outside the scope of the act.

Most importantly, Martin wrote that construction of the plant would serve primarily a public purpose, because "unemployment deeply affects the lives of citizens and of the city and state in which they are resident. Governor Milliken has approved this project, and it comes most definitely within the goal of federal programs. In large part how a city and state can avoid more decline depends upon the employment of its citizens. *The emphasis on this project is not upon GM but upon the employment and attendant revitalization of the city.* The use of the power of eminent domain for the Central Industrial Park Project serves a public purpose because the use of such power is indispensable in order for the city and EDC to take action to 'alleviate and prevent conditions of unemployment.'" (Emphasis added.)[15]

The Poletown Neighborhood Council immediately appealed the decision to the state court of appeals, as well as applying to the State supreme court for an appeals court bypass.[16] But by the third week of December, the city began demolishing Dodge Main and some of the very first residents began to leave. Many people held their breath through the Christmas season. Their faith was lodged in court appeals for the duration, but they were painfully aware of neighbors who were already searching for new homes.

"The court decision was a rotten deal," Mary Mitchell, a Poletown resident, complained. "When Judge Martin ruled in favor of GM, it was telling me you might as well give in. It was like saying, 'I work for the city, I get my paycheck from the city and I'm not supposed to go against them.' They say judges are supposed to be impartial. They're working hand in hand—the city, Reagan, big business. I wish the poor people and private citizens had control over the city, as much power as GM has. I feel anger and helplessness because of the whole situation. Why me? Why this area? I don't know what to do, who to turn to. I felt I didn't have the power to overcome big business."[17]

During this same time, residents began to receive notices giving them 20 days to "object to the necessity" of the city's condemnation. The city began to remove water meters from some homes. And the arson in the area began to escalate. Residents complained that they were being subjected to psychological warfare. While all the wheels were being greased with public agencies in Washington and with the UAW and the archdiocese in Detroit, the comfort and the safety of their neighborhood were being disrupted in an effort to deliberately undermine their ability to resist.

"I think the city is behind it to scare people out," Carol Dockery, a mother of five, explained. "I blame General Motors and the city and these damn businesses that wouldn't stand behind us. If all the people

Moving day was hard on many Poletown residents who began to flee the community as early as the fall.

DAVID C. TURNLEY

Carol Dockery worked hard to stop the GM project, often attending meetings right through meal times, leaving her husband, Randy, son Brian, and the other children to fend for themselves. Carol's mother, Louise, and step-father, George Crosby (right), lived just down the block.

would stand together, it would make a difference. It's something I've never seen before. I've got an education out of all this, I'll tell you."

Early on, most Poletown business owners were put in touch with condemnation attorneys who assured them that selling their properties to the city could be immensely profitable. They would be able to sue the city for monies above and beyond the assessed value, partly because the law required that the condemning agency help prevent the relocated business from going bankrupt. So few of them did more than make a token financial contribution to the community's resistance. In fact, the attorneys did eventually succeed in forcing the city to spend at least $100 million more than it had originally estimated for property acquisition and relocation.

One business owner who attempted to fight the project was Eddie Niedbala, owner of the Chene Trombly Market. Niedbala bought his market, renowned both for its homemade kielbasa and for its record sales of state lottery tickets, for $50,000 in 1947. Niedbala was popular in many circles and claimed the mayor as a "personal friend." An autographed picture of Coleman Young hung on a wall in the store.

When Niedbala first heard about the project, he telephoned Young. He was told, "'Don't fight it, you're going to lose.' And I says, 'You're full of it. I am going to fight it.'"

> I called [Senator Carl] Levin. I called [Senator Don] Riegle. I went right down the chain of command. I found out there's nobody to stop this. Nobody wanted to stop it. They wanted the plant. Young wants this plant bad and I can't blame him. Detroit needs that plant. But they could have made it smaller. GM is getting it for nothing so they take what they can get.
>
> I think the whole shot was illegal. The quick-take law, Public Act 87, that is wrong. I told that to the mayor. I told that to anybody that would listen. They just confiscated my property. It's just as bad as Russia. It's confiscation. I'm not being funny. They gave me half of what I paid for this place in 1947. I remodelled my whole upstairs living quarters. They're taking my home and my business for $34,000."[18]

Twenty-six months after the project was announced, after the Chene Trombly Market was destroyed, Niedbala died of a heart attack.

It was never precisely determined how many of Poletown's residents were willing to leave the area. The Citizens District Council claimed 70 percent of the people it interviewed wanted to leave, but researchers from the Social Research Application of Montana called the CDC study unscientific and published their own results which showed that two-thirds of the residents wanted to remain in the neighborhood.

Recent residents and renters were the group most likely to take the city's offer of money and go. Each renter was offered $4,000 to relocate. It doubtless did not escape the city's attention that most renters were young black families living below the poverty line. These people could have been formidable adversaries to the mayor if they had chosen to fight the project, particularly since the mayor often charged that people resisting the GM project were racists. Young claimed that no one had protested the destruction of Black Bottom for freeway construction, because the neighborhood was black. He insisted Poletown generated interest only because it was white. This argument could fly only if the majority of Poletown's black residents, who constituted half the community's population, did not fight the project.

But for the many who wanted to stay in Poletown, the primary question was not how much money they would be offered for their homes. Again and again residents explained that they were fighting for principle.

"If we allow this to happen, our ethnic backgrounds, our religious backgrounds, our America has no way to stand because we're laughing at the laws men gave their lives for," Fisher complained from his Famous Bar-B-Q Restaurant. "Some of these people are affected mentally. They walk around like they're drunk, some of them saying 'What am I going to do?' Invariably we get a phone call or two every day. 'Did you hear anything, Carl? Do you know anything?' Who's to stop the same thing that happened in Germany? It may sound ridiculous to a lot of people, but then a lot of things sounded ridiculous to me until I seen with my own eyes what went on in Germany.

"I spent a whole year with the third armored division and I seen it all," Fisher said. "We spearheaded all the first army's moves. We were the first ones to overrun and release a German concentration camp. What we seen is deeply embedded in my mind. And I say it can happen any place. This is what we're allowing to happen here."

Chapter 5

The Powers-that-be
Play Pilate

GM says "you give us what we want—land and services—or we'll put our plant somewhere else." Then the courts, our elected officials, even our union leaders, fall all over themselves, kowtowing. Well, I call that blackmail.

—Bernice Kaczynski, Poletown resident

Not a single institution in the city of Detroit rallied on behalf of the Poletown residents. Residents attempted to contact the chief executives at General Motors, the mayor and his staff at CEDD, the cardinal and his adjuncts at the archdiocese, the local and high court judges, news editors and station managers, officials at the United Auto Workers, Detroit area clergy, community groups, and members of the Left.[1] None took the time to respond in a genuine manner. None even advocated a meeting of all parties to discuss possible compromises. For a variety of reasons, all of which could be reduced to a collusion of class, the power brokers in Detroit embraced GM's Cadillac project.

At every possible juncture these institutions—some of which Poletown residents had been prepared to fight and die for—rejected the community's appeals. Some people confided to Poletown residents that they did believe something needed to be done, but they would add that publicly they would endorse the plant since GM might move out of state. Detroit, they said, should do everything possible to accommodate the automaker.

The workers who struck the auto companies in Flint and Detroit in the 1930s had a vision of a different way of living. They placed themselves in opposition to unrestrained capitalism, which they saw quantifying workers and deliberately creating surplus labor pools in order to make workers insecure about job availability. They opposed wages that kept workers in debt and protested working conditions that were inhumane. They adopted a far-sighted, visionary attitude toward community, the environment, and the resolution of international conflict. The UAW's first president, Walter Reuther, argued: "What good is a dollar an hour more in wages if your neighborhood is burning down? What good is another week's vacation if the lake you used to go to . . . is polluted and you can't swim in it?"[2]

Fifty years later the UAW maintained the same reputation. Nationally, it was recognized as one of the most progressive unions. But Pulitzer-prize-winning reporter William Serrin noted that the UAW was actually a right-of-center union with a left-of-center reputation. "What the companies desire—and receive—from the union is predictability in labor relations," he observed:

> Forced to deal with unions, they want to deal with one union, one set of leaders, and thus they have great interest in stability within the UAW and in a continuation of union leadership. They also want to have the limits of the bargaining clearly understood and subscribed to. "GM's position has always been, give the union the money, the least amount possible, but give them whatever it takes," says a former negotiator. "But don't let them take the business away from us." The union has come to accept this philosophy as the basis of its relationship with the companies. It will get money, some changes in work procedures, usually nothing more. . . . Both the union and the companies, a mediator says, have one major goal—"They want to make cars at a profit."[3]

In her book *Corporate Power and Urban Crisis*, Lynda Ann Ewen notes that "the entrenched labor union leadership has accepted the basic premise that there are no irreconcilable contradictions between labor and management and that what is good for management is inherently good for workers as well."[4] And GM vice president George B. Morris agrees. "I guess it was understandable when the unions were beginning to organize that they had to be militant and aggressive. And they adopted a vernacular vocabulary that was militaristic, aggressive, and inculcated into the minds of their constituents this idea of conflict, of war between the classes, between the worker and the employer. Hell, that day is gone. That's nickel beer and button shoes. It's gone."[5]

And so it would seem. Routinely in the 1970s and 1980s, union leaders entered into corporatist arrangements smiling. All wore suits and some boasted that they had never walked a picket line. Unions tended to increase their reliance on management experts and to run white-collar organizations. In 1978, then UAW president Doug Fraser was applauded by the *Detroit News* for understanding that "the yelling and the violence advocated by many union stalwarts was the style of a bygone era." The article commended Fraser for knowing how to "make lots of noise," so that "members 'know' their president is giving them his best because they see and hear him," while actually cutting deals in corporate suites. "Business leaders don't think less of Fraser for the bravado," the article continued. "They have come to expect reasonable compromise in the end."[6]

The recessions of the late 1970s and early 1980s only underscored the cooperation between the UAW and the automakers. Nationwide, there seemed to be a consensus that labor had outgrown its britches and was due for a tumble, and the UAW did little to combat this image. It was actually among the first unions to cave in to the demands by employers for concessions. Afterwards, Ford's Willow Run plant, just outside Detroit, hoisted two huge signs that advertised "FORD-UAW / Team up for Quality."[7]

"The process which brought the American labor movement to its current weakened state began years ago," labor analyst Jane Slaughter writes in her book *Concessions and How to Beat Them*. "Throughout the boom years of the 1950s and 1960s, the labor movement avoided major confrontation over the size of labor's slice of the economic pie. As long as the pie itself was growing, members' standards of living could improve without a basic challenge to corporate practices and philosophy. . . . Now the pie is shrinking, and corporate leaders want workers to donate more of their slice. The labor movement, its militant traditions rusty from lack of use, is left with no way to protect members' income. . . . The irony is that concessions will shrink not only the absolute size of the workers' slice but its proportionate size as well."[8]

The situation in 1980 appeared to be as bleak for the UAW as it was for its members. Employment levels in the auto industry had always been cyclical, but the crisis which struck Detroit at the end of the 1970s paralyzed an unprecedented number of workers. Chrysler Corporation's federal bailout in 1979 was dependent on UAW concessions. So, under national scrutiny the UAW agreed to forfeit $1.068 billion in members' wages and benefits.[9] The agreement broke the parity among the Big Three and invited similar concession demands from Ford and GM.[10]

Between 1979 and 1980 the UAW lost 29 percent of its 1.53 million members.[11] The union's hastily devised survival plans disappointed many because they failed to call for organizing the unemployed. There were no mass meetings or rallies pushing for plant closing restrictions, local content laws, forty-hour pay for thirty-hour weeks, or industrial conversion. Instead, the UAW granted concessions, including forced overtime, and put its hopes in organizing workers in other industries like secretaries, nurses, and government workers.

Stanley Aronowitz observed in The Nation in 1980 that most big unions were cannibalizing other smaller unions to compensate for membership drops. "The weak response of the union leadership to manufacturing decline reflects their greater concern with organizational self-preservation than with saving workers' jobs," he wrote.

> As their dues rolls decline, the response of the big manufacturing unions has been to organize or swallow up existing unions in unrelated industries. The rise of conglomerate capitalism is being paralleled by the rise of conglomerate unionism. Today, the number of members of the United Auto Workers who do not work in the auto industry is greater than the number of those who do. . . . Unions representing aircraft, agricultural implements and nonferrous metal workers, as well as retail employees, university clerical workers and professionals, now dominate the U.A.W. If the auto industry continues its projected decline in the United States, car workers will probably constitute no more than a third of the U.A.W.'s entire membership by 1990.[12]

The desperation of unemployed auto workers and UAW staff people at Solidarity House was channeled, with the union's blessing, into vicious anti-Japanese propaganda. Solidarity House banned the parking of foreign-made vehicles in its parking lot. The guard booth at the driveway sported red, white, and blue bumper stickers that invited drivers to park Japanese cars in Tokyo and to remember Pearl Harbor. The news media gave nationwide play to pictures of unemployed auto workers destroying Japanese cars and motorcycles.[13]

The union mounted a massive "Buy American" campaign in early 1981. During March, when Poletown residents were pleading with union officials to persuade GM to modify its Cadillac plant, the UAW spent $200,000 to encourage Americans to feel unpatriotic if they bought a fuel-efficient compact car made overseas. Local and state agencies in Michigan passed resolutions prohibiting the use of foreign-made vehicles for government business.

The irony of the Buy American campaign was that it was abandoned by the automakers almost immediately. By the mid-1980s GM had joint venture plants with Isuzu, Suzuki, Toyota, and Daewoo in South Korea. GM also built plants in Mexico and Brazil. Ford gained 25 percent ownership of Mazda. And Chrysler was continuing its relationship with Mitsubishi, building a joint venture plant in Illinois.

This was the state of affairs when Poletown residents approached

Solidarity House and asked for UAW support. On March 2, 1981, Tom
Olechowski presented a letter to the rank and file, care of Doug Fraser,
which read in part:

> The people who make up our Poletown Neighborhood Council and
> our area are workers. Almost none of us have huge holdings or live off
> the dividends, interest, labor or sweat of other people. We, like you, are
> rich in every way except materially. Most of us, if not all of us, have been
> members of a union or are members of a union family. Like you, we
> suffer from low, inadequate or declining incomes. We struggle to make
> ends meet while fighting off the ravages of high taxes and high inflation.
> Many of us also suffer the cruel indignity of enforced perpetual jobless-
> ness. In addition, inasmuch as we are creatures of an inner-city long
> abused, neglected, and manipulated by government, corporate and bank-
> ing policies, we suffer more than some of our brothers and sisters in sub-
> urban America.
>
> Many of us are retired, living in homes we have long ago paid for and
> once or twice rebuilt at great personal expense. We have neighbors, not
> all of the same ethnic group, whom over the years we have learned to
> love and come to depend on for our daily comfort, needs and sometimes
> for our very lives. We have lived in and made our history in Poletown
> with churches and institutions older than most of us. Now we are told
> that we must forfeit all these friends and neighbors, forfeit networks of
> mutual help, aid, and trust which took years to build and which allowed
> us to live in dignity conferred by personal caring free of bureaucrats,
> forfeit our historic churches, our clubs and gathering spots, our institu-
> tions, forfeit our neighborhood. All this we must forfeit to the General
> Motors Corporation, the most rich and powerful multinational industrial
> corporation.
>
> Brothers and sisters, we don't believe we must forfeit our neighbor-
> hood and we know we can prove it to you. We want our brothers and
> sisters to have jobs—more than GM will let us have. From the very first
> days of the Poletown Neighborhood Council when we learned about the
> plant, we were not against the plant. Nor were we indifferent to jobs. We
> can prove to you that the GM plant can be built in Detroit's Poletown and
> in Hamtramck and provide taxes and jobs—while keeping the neighbor-
> hood intact and indeed improving it.
>
> You should know that many of our brothers and sisters in Poletown
> are being cheated, manipulated and lied to with regard to benefits, serv-
> ices, and costs, both economic and social. Promises were made as early as
> September which have yet to be implemented in March. We need your
> help to insure and guarantee the interests of our people. We need your
> help in a number of ways.
>
> In a recent letter from GM to the Poletown Neighborhood Council,
> chairman Roger B. Smith smugly states, "We have the whole-hearted
> support of the United Automobile Workers."[14] Only a decision made in

the absence of known facts would justify such support. Once we have examined these facts and documentation together, we know that you, our unionized brothers and sisters, will speak loudly, clearly, and effectively for yourselves."

Olechowski's letter went on to enumerate four points. First, the plant could be built without destroying homes south of East Grand Boulevard. Second, it would cost less money to revitalize the neighborhood than to destroy it. Third, job prospects would be improved by strong community and plant relations. Fourth, that otherwise "working class neighborhoods will be endangered and treated like landed plantations where retired sharecroppers will be evicted from land they are told never really was theirs but belongs to Master GM, Master Bendix, or Master Ford, and that the city will act as sheriff to evict them."

Predictably, this appeal was rejected by the union leadership. In the spring of 1981 Walter Duda went with several Poletown Neighborhood Council members to Solidarity House. They made their appeal to Brad Brasfield, administrative assistant to Doug Fraser. Brasfield told them the union Duda had helped organize couldn't offer any help. "That didn't set well with me," Duda recalled later, "because I thought that the UAW certainly should have taken an active part in helping the Poletown residents. The union was stupid not to support the people in this area. Of course, there was a lot of bullshit at the beginning about 'creating' 6,000 new jobs. We know better than that now."

In the locals there were more union members willing to express sympathy for Poletown residents. But they, like the others, were not willing to risk the promise of 6,000 jobs by speaking out. M. L. Douglas, vice president of UAW Local 22, which represented 9,000 Cadillac workers, summed it up: "It is a matter of balancing the pain. We have feelings about uprooting a lot of older people, but the way things are going, we can't afford to lose those jobs. . . . I can't in good conscience, speak out against the plant when there are so many families around here out of work."[15]

Only a handful of UAW members made their support for Poletown residents visible; these were dissidents within the union who published a rank-and-file paper called *Fighting Chance.* In the spring of 1981 Glen Janken, who worked at Chrysler's Lynch Road assembly plant, came to a Poletown Neighborhood Council meeting. He complained to Poletown residents about the concessions the Big Three were demanding of labor, the new popularity of profit-sharing during a time when there were no profits, the decline of health and safety standards.

"It's real similar to what's happening here in Poletown," Janken said. "It's being done with no consideration of alternatives. The way it's being presented you're against jobs, the plant and progress. But it's not progress; it's who is going to pay for progress? We have the same interests as you people here. If we can get more people together, they won't be able to pick us off one at a time."

Janken was very well received by the Poletown residents, who called a joint demonstration for April 4, 1981, when GM president F. James McDonald was to speak at the University of Detroit on "Detroit—Managing the Uncertain '80s." The staff of *Fighting Chance* distributed a flier that read "No Wage-Benefit Cuts/Save Poletown & Jobs." But only a handful of auto workers showed up for the demonstration.

Most of Michigan's state and federal elected officials embraced the GM project. U.S. Congressman George Crockett, who had a good reputation as a civil rights advocate, served as the acting corporation counsel for the city during the planning phases of the project. Crockett's friendship with the mayor dated back to when Crockett represented Coleman Young before the House Un-American Activities Committee. In a letter to Bernice Kaczynski, Crockett said: "I believe it is vital to the future economic condition of our city that projects such as the GM plant be encouraged. The shrinking tax base, increasing unemployment, and reduction of federal support for Detroit have jeopardized our economy. We must act for the economic survival of the entire Detroit community."[16]

U.S. Senator Donald Riegle criticized Poletown residents for resisting the project, saying that there are no alternatives. Staff aides in Detroit said Riegle believed "the project must go as is." Riegle declined repeated invitations to meet with Poletown residents, but he did appear at the University of Detroit conference on the economy with McDonald. At that conference Riegle said that he hoped more projects like the GM Poletown plant would be pursued. Eventually, Riegle pronounced that the resistance in Poletown "borders on the irresponsible."

U.S. Senator Carl Levin complained that Ralph Nader's request that he conduct congressional hearings on the Poletown project was "audacious" and said that he would take no active role in Poletown, since the issues were already being litigated. His posture did not change after the litigation was complete.

Michigan's Republican governor, William Milliken, embraced the project and freed up state rail and road funds to help pay for Detroit's site preparations for GM. Milliken, who held the governor's office for twelve years, had a good working relationship with the mayor and had helped insulate Detroit from the budget-cutting proposals of state officials who favored suburban or rural areas.

The only Michigan politician to break ranks with GM's corporatist alliance was U.S. Representative John Conyers. Conyers met with Poletown residents in June of 1981 and discussed the possibility of setting up congressional hearings on the project. Although the hearings never took place, Conyers did send the mayor a letter questioning the ethics of proceeding with the project when the federal funds were not in hand, or even necessarily forthcoming. Conyers said: "The community rancor that has grown out of the project is very disturbing. I am told that the level of tension in Poletown is dangerously high. The impression has been spreading—rightly or wrongly—that the city has shown too little flexibility in addressing the neighborhood's concerns and in considering alternative designs and site development plans whereby the neighborhood could be saved."[17]

The Detroit City Council enjoyed a far-Left reputation in 1980. Council members were constantly passing resolutions that supported popular struggles in Central America and South Africa as well as in the United States. But when it came to legislating local affairs, the city council toed the mayor's line almost without fail. Rebellious rhetoric often divided the mayor and his council, but on the first vote, or the second, the council conformed to his intentions.

Prior to the October 1980 council vote approving the Poletown project, several council members went on record opposing it. Councilwoman Maryann Mahaffey told a labor conference that GM's offer to the City of Detroit was an insult and that she would refuse it. "The only alternative that General Motors ever gave us was that they were going to move out," she said. "The tragedy is the fact that we have a world economy, and the corporations are transnational corporations that operate in a world economy. We're colonies attempting to survive in this world economy. We're trapped between the long-range in trying to pull the corporations into line and the short-range of survival. It's just a tragedy all the way around."[18]

City Councilman Ken Cockrel criticized CEDD officials, saying, "You talk about saving jobs, but what you're really doing is paying for their [GM's] automation."[19] He gave his own position to Michigan Avenue Community Organization members:

> Year in and year out, they have been moving poor and working people, but this kind of struck people's conscience over in Poletown,

because it was such a dramatic example of the power, the raw naked power, of government in coalition with a multinational corporation.

General Motors, knowing that there are other states in this country that are prepared to do the same or worse for them, knew that it had us over a barrel because they could go anywhere. People are falling over themselves in states now to build plants and lease them to the corporations, to write down land costs, to give them tax abatements, to come up with grants whereby they can train the workers. They can get this all over this country and, for that matter, in many other places in the world. And they know they have units of government in a bind when they come and talk with them.[20]

Ten days before the city council was to vote on the Poletown project, the city council's planning commission issued a report which cautiously endorsed the GM project but recommended major modifications in the arrangements between the city and GM. The report said, in part: "The CPC staff believes that the Central Industrial Park Project presents some real risks to the city in terms of financing and the human impact. The direct economic benefits to the city in terms of additional revenue have been somewhat overstated in the draft EIS [Environmental Impact Statement], and the resources to fully pay for the project are not in place. The relocation of such a large number of persons in such a short period of time will require a monumental effort by the city and the EDC [Economic Development Corporation] in order to ensure that relocatees' needs are addressed with sensitivity to minimize the human trauma involved."[21]

During the council hearings on the project members made repeated efforts to get hard facts from officials at CEDD and from General Motors but were usually stonewalled. Helen Cunningham, a council staff person who did post mortem research on Poletown, reported four years later: "As far as I can see, council made its decision in a vacuum. CEDD submitted a financial plan indicating projected sources for the funds. Unfortunately, the actual sources of income were 50 percent short of the projections. There are no factual indications as to whether or not CEDD's projections were based on solid financial commitments, but I think not. Having reviewed the source documents and the Journal of the city council, my opinion is that the figures in the financial plan were grossly exaggerated in order to complete the balance sheets." Council approved the project with only one dissenting vote, that of Ken Cockrel.

Most media organizations in Detroit expressed sympathy for the elderly being required to leave their neighborhood. But enmeshed in these same reports was an assumption that although we all feel sympathy for these people we also know that their claims must not hinder GM's project. It's natural to feel pity, but it would be unforgivable to act on that pity in any way that might obstruct the project.

Television news reports from Poletown nearly always included a sequence with a weeping Polish woman, sometimes in a babushka. But the image of grief was followed by a corporate or city official, or even the TV anchorperson, saying that progress has a cost, sometimes a bitter one, but in times like these Detroit can't afford to say no.

The ingredient missing from most of the Poletown coverage was a serious consideration of the constitutional issues raised by the people of Poletown and their claim that the plant and the neighborhood could co-exist. It became the prevailing wisdom of the media that events in Poletown were tragic (and good color and copy) but necessary, even acceptable.

The *Detroit Free Press*, a Knight-Ridder newspaper which is reputed to be liberal, did an interesting flip-flop early on. The paper published a sympathetic piece about Poletown just days before GM's plans for the neighborhood were made public. The article accurately depicted the deterioration of Poletown but rejoiced in its ethnic flavor, its history, its churches and markets, and indeed its future as a neighborhood.[22]

But after GM and the City of Detroit announced their plan to level the neighborhood and build a Cadillac plant, the *Free Press* editorialized in favor of the plan and did very little, if any, truly investigative reporting on the behind-the-scenes negotiations or the steps that might be required to build the plant and preserve the neighborhood. Veteran city hall reporter Ken Fireman told his editor at the *Free Press* that it seemed clear to him that the groundwork for the project had been laid well in advance and suggested that a team of reporters be assigned to investigate. Instead, the story was given to a general-assignment reporter, Luther Jackson.

Many of the *Free Press* headlines about the Poletown story focused on GM's demands or perspective. For instance, a story in September was headlined, "GM's Commitment on New City Plant Expected This Week." The story outlined the corporation's expectations in terms of when its letter of commitment would be released. It mentioned the sorts of items that might be listed in the letter and stated that the new plant would replace two older west-side plants. The only allusion to the people who were going to be thrown out of their homes was made two-thirds of the way through the story on the jump page: "If the council approves the plan Oct. 15, the city is expected to begin making acquisition and relocation offers to some 1,362 residents and 143 commercial, industrial, and non-profit organizations shortly thereafter."[23]

On October 6, Patricia Chargot, who three months earlier had written the *Free Press* piece on the potential comeback of the neighborhood, coauthored a piece headlined "GM Site: A Doomed World: Detroit-Hamtramck Residents Anxiously Await Bulldozers." The article indicated the forced relocation would be a hardship to many but added that at first glance "the site looks like an area begging to be bulldozed." The reporters added that, given the city's economic straits, "No one, including condemnation attorneys hired by some of the area's residents and businesses to deal with the city, believes the project can be stopped."[24]

Five days later a *Free Press* editorial read: "The attempt to assemble for industrial development so huge a block of land within a city is perhaps the most audacious effort at industrial renewal ever undertaken in the country. . . . Yet, it seems to us so abundantly clear that the city simply must renew its industrial base—must find ways to provide space for putting up new plants while tearing down the old—that it would be wrong not to try to bring it off. The only way we are going to preserve and restore jobs in the central city is by undertaking some very difficult steps."[25]

With the exception of Ken Fireman's exposés of the mayor's behind-the-scenes lobbying the *Free Press* reporting on Poletown was generally competent and unimaginative. It espoused the inevitability of the project and offered no new angles on the story and no voice of advocacy for compromise. By the summer of 1981, when the story was nearly over and the opportunity for resistance past, reporter Marianne Rzepka was allowed to write a few lengthy pieces about residents' opposition to the project. Likewise, the *Free Press* published a special magazine section that displayed exquisite photographs of Poletown, its residents and multiple cultures. The display was terribly poignant, composed largely of photographs by David Turnley and Taro Yamasaki, both of whom had gotten to know the residents and the area. However, the spread wasn't published until fall of 1981. At the time of its publication all the residents pictured at family dinners and tending their shops had long since been moved out, their homes and businesses destroyed.[26]

The *Detroit News* coverage of the project was better, perhaps because the *Detroit News* is an afternoon paper which, to remain competitive, must offer more thorough local reporting. Perhaps it also helped that Robert Roach, who was assigned to the Poletown story, was a native Detroiter with a sense of the city's history.

On October 22 Roach wrote an article which the News headlined: "New GM Factory Won't Add Any Jobs." Roach reported that during a city council meeting a city aide admitted that no "permanent new jobs" would be created by the GM project. Ernest Zachary, under aggressive questioning by Ken Cockrel, even admitted that the promise of new jobs was added to the city's federal grant application to make the appeal sound better. Zachary called it a "psychological grantsmanship statement. We say they are 'new' jobs because that carries more weight with the people in Washington."[27]

Three days later, after the city released some optimistic figures about the project's financing, Roach double checked the figures and revealed that the State of Michigan had no intention of turning over $28 million for the repayment of Detroit's federal loans. Roach had also called HUD to see how officials there felt about Detroit's misrepresentation of the jobs offered at the plant as "new." Interestingly, Jack Flynn, the HUD spokesman, said grant reviewers expect "overstated" benefits and that "we take none of these figures at face value." Roach constantly raised the question of actual funding in his stories, citing the reservations of some of the city council's advisors who asked the council to get written commitments.[28]

Likewise, it was the *News* that ran a profile of Emmett Moten that exposed his propensity to gloss over facts and to obscure issues. Roach and Steve Konicki wrote a front-page piece headlined, "Quick Talker Sells GM Plant—But He Buys Criticism, Too." The article ran through a litany of lies and confusions offered by CEDD to the city council.[29]

But the reporting notwithstanding, the *News* editorialized constantly in favor of the GM project. In October the *News* ran two pro-plant editorials in one week. The first acknowledged that the Department of Housing and Urban Development semed to be moving awfully quickly in its approval of grants for the GM Poletown project but commented that this was appropriate since "the new GM facility is a must for Detroit."[30]

The second editorial followed an announcement that GM would invest $10 billion in the state of Michigan during the following five years. The *News* editorialized its glee about the announcement which had been made by Roger Smith, who was to succeed GM chairman Thomas Murphy on January 1. The paper admonished state and local politicians to do everything in their power to cooperate with GM to improve the business climate in the state. "General Motors, as vast as its enterprises are, is our friend and neighbor. Its birthplace and headquarters are here. Its resources are enormous and its alternatives are many. Thus, the company's dramatic reaffirmation of faith in our state and our people is, especially in these times, a cause for pride and confidence."[31]

The only mainstream paper to challenge GM's estimates on the numbers to be employed at the new plant was the *Macomb Daily*, a small suburban paper. In March of 1981 that paper published an article by Robert Selwa which indicated that GM was actually only promising 3,000 jobs. It quoted a letter from GM's director of real estate, Stuart R. Hock, to David S. Cordish, director of the UDAG program, which said that the Poletown plant had "the capacity to employ about 6,000 people at full employment. GMC will, however, commit to employ no less than 3,000 people within the next four years." Despite this public memo, most media continued to report, well into the next year, that the plant would put 6,000 auto workers on line.

The *Macomb Daily* was also one of the few, perhaps the only, metropolitan paper to editorialize against the city's use of eminent domain. Its editors wrote: "We can understand condemnation of properties to build roads or parks or municipal facilities, which in theory are beneficial to all residents, but we can't accept the reasoning that allows the city to clear out 3,438 residents for a profit-making corporation."[32]

Television reporting was poor. The stations preferred personality conflicts—between old women and mammoth GM, between the mayor and Ralph Nader—to anything substantive. All three commercial news stations inundated viewers with Poletown stories—poignant church services in a condemned church, prayer vigils, a balloon release, community picnics—but the reports lacked content. They were generally slanted toward the necessity of the project.

WDIV-TV 4's Beth Konrad explained to TV viewers in February that "Detroit has the highest unemployment in the country. It has an eroding tax base. Numerous plants have either moved to the suburbs or sunbelt states. GM's Cadillac plant will provide 6,000 jobs. Ground has already been broken. Two-thirds of the Poletown residents have already accepted bids for their homes. Moving families out of their homes is disruptive, but it is necessary and they have been fairly compensated."[33]

WJBK-TV 2's editorial by station manager Bob McBride was perhaps the most offensive to Poletown residents because he attacked the integrity of the neighborhood itself. "There's a big myth about Poletown," McBride said. "A hoax. It's been foisted on the public by a few well-intentioned Detroit citizens pulled along by some publicity-grabbing manipulators and out-of-towners. . . . These people would have you believe that General Motors is guilty of bulldozing its way over thousands of innocent Poletown victims and cheating them out of their homes in order to build a gold mine of a factory. Well, there is no grab of Poletown. The fact is, the true Polish community is Hamtramck, and that city is delighted to have part of the new GM plant. . . . The over-whelming number of residents are ready, willing and eager to move. This is a racially integrated area, equally black and white, but it has suffered from urban blight. . . . The way we see it, it's about time the Poletown myth was exploded. What do you think?"[34]

The editorial policy of WXYZ-TV 7 was akin to the others. Jeanne Findlater said in a March editorial: "The issue revolves around which is the lesser evil: relocating an entire neighborhood to accommodate a giant job-producing industry, or leaving the neighborhood unscathed while the giant industry moves its plant and its jobs somewhere else. While General Motors and the City of Detroit are seen as the villains in this struggle, nearly 1,200 of the 1,500 families who live there have accepted the city's fair buy-out offer. The remaining 300 families vehe-mently protest having the fabric of their lives ripped apart and that's why we have a lawsuit. We wish it were an easier choice—that it was a case of creating jobs rather than just saving existing jobs. In this case, we reluctantly say that building the plant and saving jobs is the best way."[35]

Toward the spring, when GM's deadline for the land was fast approaching, reporter after reporter visited the area and concluded the story with the quip "and this is the day Poletown died." This verdict punctuated every court decision and every major fire in the neighbor-hood. Each Poletown demonstration was depicted as a final flourish.

What about other local media?

The *Michigan Chronicle,* a weekly paper targeted at middle-in-come, black city residents, didn't choose to focus on the Poletown struggle. But when it did address the issue, it followed the mayor's lead and referred to the neighborhood as "so-called Poletown." It reported the city's figures on those residents who had moved willingly as fact, even though that number was impossible to calculate. No one could estimate the number of homeowners who would have preferred to stay if given the option. *The Chronicle* also highlighted a pro-plant demon-stration which was advertised as being indigenous but which was actually attended by people bussed into Poletown.[36]

Monthly Detroit, a slick city magazine tailored for upscale subur-ban readers, condemned the Poletown struggle as well. Kirk Cheyfitz, a former *Free Press* reporter who edited the magazine for its owners in Cleveland, Ohio, wrote a full-page, smugly condescending article titled "Why It's a Good Idea to Bulldoze 'Poletown.'" Cheyfitz, who soon thereafter founded a competing magazine heavily subsidized by financier Max Fisher, imputed a racist motive to the people who originally chose to live in Poletown: "Let me try to get this straight: The Detroit neighborhood where General Motors wants to put the southern end of its Cadillac plant (the north end is going in Hamtramck) is not Poletown. Old Poletown actually lies well south of this much publicized neighborhood, on the other side of the Ford Expressway. . . . The place the newspapers call Poletown is the neighborhood to which many Poles and other ethnic whites fled after blacks began moving into old Poletown. The only historic value of this misnamed neighborhood is that it memorializes a small part of the history of white flight in Detroit. Since there are now a substantial number of blacks living there as well, it also documents the ultimate futility of white flight."[37]

Cheyfitz didn't say where he got his information about Poletown's boundaries, but it conflicts with Jim Anderson's University of Michigan study and with *Free Press* reports from the turn of the century. More importantly, it casts a slur on the people living in Poletown by suggesting that they moved there to avoid having black neighbors. White flight was a central urban issue after the 1967 riots, but the northern end of Poletown was established well before then and was, as noted in the city planning commission's report, a well-integrated and stable neighborhood early on. (It seems obvious that if Poletown's residents were primarily motivated by racism, they would not be fighting to preserve their half-white, half-black neighborhood.)

When Cheyfitz attempted to turn a critical eye on the City of Detroit and General Motors, he faulted them for not planning ahead and for not allowing more time to complete the project. What Cheyfitz failed to appreciate was that the accelerated time line of the GM project was not the result of poor planning. It was GM's experience that if it imposed an immediate deadline and threatened to build out of state, government leaders would bend over backwards to accommodate the corporation. Meanwhile, community groups and opposing interests would barely have time to form opposing arguments.

The *Hamtramck Citizen* followed events in Poletown faithfully, but its editorial board was opposed to the residents' struggle to keep their homes. In a letter to the *Detroit Free Press*, the *Citizen's* editor, Greg Kowalski, wrote that "Poletown—and it is disputable whether it should be called Poletown considering the black, Arab, Albanian and Yugoslav makeup of the area—has been deteriorating for years. Fifteen years ago my mother stood on a sidewalk in the Chene-Milwaukee area at 6 A.M. waiting for a Dearborn-bound bus. Today, standing there at that hour would be dangerous. But a few blocks north of Poletown is Hamtramck. It is not paradise; but it is a stable community, one that has a viable future thanks to GM. . . . Poletown was dying long before the

GM plant was proposed. But now Hamtramck has a chance to survive. I think it's a fair trade."[38]

The *Detroit Metro Times*, a news and entertainment paper run by socialists but aimed at young, trend-setting, upwardly mobile people, published very early on a two-part series which laid out the issues in Poletown clearly. In an article titled "Push Comes to Shove," Michael Betzold wrote of the community: "They broke their backs making cars for Packard on the Boulevard, Chrysler at Dodge Main, for the old Hupp Motor Company on Mount Elliott. With pennies saved from their scrawny paychecks they barely met mortgage payments on their frame houses, but they kept their yards clean and their homes painted. They watched in horror as their community was torn in two by the Ford Freeway so that fatter fellow Detroiters could drive the cars they had built away from the city, leaving it barren and desolate. Still they fought for survival, kept alive their neighborhood and its traditions, and dreamed of revitalization. Now they are simply in the way. Their valued homes and small businesses will be leveled by edict of the world's largest corporation—so that it can build a new plant and manufacture more cars."

Betzold gave an accurate sense of the time pressure the community was exposed to. He gave space to the residents' claim that the plant could be built without destroying the neighborhood and outlined the redevelopment plans Hodas and Olechowski had put in place prior to GM's plant announcement. He rebelled against the news media's depiction of Poletown as blighted, saying it was a neighborhood of "neat houses, small green lawns, and well-swept sidewalks where children of all races play together."[39]

Radical Left newspapers like the *Torch* and the *Revolutionary Worker* sometimes saw the Poletown story as an opportunity to examine the weaknesses of capitalism. But the paper that gave the best continuing coverage was the *Bulletin*, a paper produced by the Workers' League. Poletown residents spoke warmly of the paper, often saying it was the most accurate of all. The *Bulletin* covered Poletown's suits, its negotiations with the church, its appeals to the UAW, and its proposed alternatives. The paper also ran photographs of residents with full pages of uninterrupted comments. This may have been the only forum in which residents were allowed unedited versions of their opinions. The *Bulletin* was faithful in presenting the views of black residents, many of whom were very bitter about the project and who were often overlooked by the mainstream media.

The national press paid little attention to Poletown until Ralph Nader intervened in early 1981 on the residents' behalf. Generally, the national media did a better job of reporting the issues than local media, but the quality was mixed.

Time magazine published a piece titled "The Last Days of Pole-town—A Neighborhood Faces Doom and a New Plant May Rise," which outlined GM's plans and the city's cooperation. The article stated as fact, despite clear indications to the contrary, that 6,000 people would be employed there and that the plant would generate $8.1 million in tax revenues. *Time* claimed the city examined twelve alternative sites for the GM plant and finally picked Poletown. It stated that 90 percent of the homeowners "voluntarily sold" their property and quoted Emmett Moten of CEDD claiming there was no opposition. "How many mass meetings have been held? Where do you see evidence of mass support?"

As for the other 10 percent, the article continued, "That feisty minority vows to save the neighborhood from the wrecker's ball. Yet even if Poletown were saved, the community would never flourish as it did a generation ago. Concedes Henry Michalski, a Poletown Neighborhood Council supporter: 'Over the long term, the place would continue to deteriorate because the old people will die off and the young people have moved off.'"[40] The slant of the piece enabled General Motors executives to cite it in justification of the project.[41]

Several nationally syndicated columnists wrote articles critical of GM and the City of Detroit. Colman McCarthy wrote one titled "GM, the Gentle Goliath, Is Winning," which argued that the scope of GM's project and the public subsidies required provided "greater cause for alarm" for citizens already "fearful of excessive corporate power." He noted with irony that the Poletown residents were not being presented as victims by the media. Instead, General Motors was presented as a well-intentioned but terribly harassed Goliath.[42]

Jack Anderson wrote a similar column which opened with Bernice and Harold Kaczynski's opposition to moving and then turned to irregularities in the Environmental Impact Statement, the neglect of the alternate site designs, and the fact that GM was not legally bound to ever employ anyone at the plant. "So WHY is the city doing this to Poletown?" Anderson asked. "The answer seems to be that Detroit, which has been the big automaker's private fiefdom for more than half a century, will do anything to please General Motors."[43]

It is revealing that the *Free Press*, which regularly carries Anderson's column in Detroit, chose not to run this one. When Poletown supporters complained, they were told that too much had already been written on Poletown and that Anderson's column didn't contribute anything new. Only when Poletown supporters threatened to picket the paper did the *Free Press* run the column.

William Safire wrote a column condemning GM's Poletown project from a private property vantage point. "At a time when we are encouraging the Poles in Poland to turn toward capitalism," he wrote, "it is ironic to have Americans in Poletown facing expropriation of their property. Why are we so reluctant, in these rights-minded times, to defend property rights? Possession of land or valuables is nothing to be ashamed of or to feel guilty about; we should lustily own up to ownership."[44]

Both *In These Times,* a socialist weekly out of Chicago, and New York's *Village Voice* ran lengthy articles on the issues involved in Poletown. David Moberg's piece ran in *In These Times* in early February 1981 and explored Detroit's past use of tax abatements and federal funds, the projected financing in this case, and the rationale of GM and the city. Moberg's reporting was unparalleled, cutting through corporate and political rhetoric to reveal the real power dynamic at work.[45] The *Village Voice* cover article ran in July 1981. It examined much of the same material as Moberg's piece, adding details about the political and court struggles which continued through the May ground-breaking ceremony, the incidence and cause of arson and vandalism in Poletown, and the dismal history of GM's plant construction in Oklahoma, Kansas, and Orion Township, Michigan.[46] [See Appendix B.]

CBS produced a one-hour special which aired in August, 1981 called "What's Good for GM." The documentary included exclusive interviews with Mayor Young, GM officials, and union leaders and analysts. The intent was to examine the cost of reindustrialization. The mayor set out the desperate circumstances. The corporation explained its needs and demands. A variety of economists and analysts gave their opinion on whether the circumstances warranted the demolition of a neighborhood. Visuals of Polish dancers, interviews with residents, and magnificent footage of homes being vandalized and demolished were used as a backdrop. The documentary was not intended to, nor did it, examine the appropriate role of the community in that situation.

WDIV-TV in Detroit produced a documentary in late 1980. Called *Land Grab: The Taking of Poletown,* this one-hour piece produced by Detroiter Harvey Ovshinsky hit on many of the key issues in the Poletown struggle: the question of the site design, the fairness of the quick-take law, and the question of automation. The documentary's flaw is that it presents the GM plant as inevitable.

Three Detroit filmmakers and activists produced a film called *Poletown Lives!* which subsequently won five national awards, including a blue ribbon from the 1983 American Film Festival. This documentary is a colorful and dramatic film that approaches the story through the voices of the residents. They are not the emotional backdrop; they are the ones framing the debate and keeping the film focused on questions about who does and who should run the country.[47]

Overall, Poletown residents grew very disillusioned with the media and equally astute in their criticisms of it. Early on, residents felt excited and nervous about being singled out for an interview, but by 1981 many had learned how to handle reporters and even felt free to chastise them for their errors.

Bernice Kaczynski expressed concern when she explained that on trips around the country she and her husband had stumbled on all kinds of local struggles: strip mining, water pollution, land foreclosures. At first she was surprised these stories weren't making big news but then concluded that the omissions were deliberate. "The less anybody hears of any tragedy going on the better," she said, "then they don't get nobody involved in it." The protests that did get aired on television used to look foolish to Kaczynski, partly because of the way they were presented by the media. "But now I respect the people that go out there and picket. When I see a demo on television now, I says, 'Wow, I was doing that just a short time ago.' And I have deep respect for it now, because I understand it better too."

Carol Dockery found that the media had biased her view of Ralph Nader just as it had biased Kaczynski against demonstrations. "He comes across bad on the media too," Dockery said, "because a lot of people say, 'Oh no, not that troublemaker.' And then you meet him and find out his views for real. I was telling my husband last night, 'He's not what he appears to be. He's really a nice guy and he's smart.'"

One might assume that the Left turned out to support the people of Poletown in their battle against GM. Certainly, the situation pitted one of the most powerful capitalist multinationals against a small and aging working-class constituency, both black and white. But even though Detroit is home to many radical parties, only one—the Revolutionary Socialist League—built relationships with Poletown residents and helped them organize an early march through the neighborhood. Every other group kept its hands off entirely, unless it was merely to publish an opinion paper, most of which came out long after the Poletown struggle was over.

People speculated that this was partly because the old Communist party maintained a deep respect for Coleman Young, grounded in his radical past. During the Poletown crisis, the American CP published a statement saying that the mayor should not be blamed for the dislocation in Poletown. These leaders also let it be known that they personally supported the mayor and saw the principal issue as one of jobs versus homes. Anyone on the Left who criticized the mayor was likely to be accused of wounding the movement, because he was historically a part of the Left and a black politician always exposed to flack from the Right.

Dan Luria, a UAW researcher and a socialist, had this to say about Poletown: "I don't believe in community. Community struggles always have the same feel as strikes, but they always lose. The only lesson of Poletown is that GM is powerful. We don't need another populist lesson. The public is already populist. We don't need to know that business calls the shots. We need to know why they call the shots." Luria added that community struggles are always petit bourgeois struggles revolving around private property. Life and even where you live, he said, shouldn't be organized around your neighborhood but around where you work.[48]

Ron Reosti, with deep roots in Detroit's Left, had to soul-search for answers to the progressive attorneys who condemned him for taking on the Poletown law suit. "A lot of lawyers had very sincere reservations about the case," he said. "They just didn't agree with the politics of the case. They thought that given the economic condition in the city that jobs took precedent over homes and the neighborhood, that on balance it was a progressive thing to do." It took months, he said, to persuade other lawyers that "contrary to press accounts—this was not a good deal for the City of Detroit, that it was economic blackmail. They were concerned with confronting the mayor's popularity and they were scared off by the racial aspects of this issue. . . . I had to keep looking over my shoulder to see if I was doing the right thing."[49]

The National Organization for an American Revolution (NOAR) was one of the few Left groups which issued a statement condemning proceedings in Poletown. In August 1980 the group criticized corporations for their lack of loyalty, adding "GM will bulldoze our communities. Then it will turn around and spend millions in advertising to make us believe that it is doing this for our own good. GM comes like a knight in shining armor to revitalize our communities when, in fact, it is destroying the few communities that still remain."[50]

ACORN (A Community Organization for Reform Now) focused largely on legalizing homesteading. ACORN members were lobbying to get the city to free up abandoned, government-owned houses for low-income people. This was a proposal that Mayor Young had first endorsed after his election.[51] But by 1980 the mayor was absolute in his opposition to ACORN's homesteading plan. In the spring of 1981 Poletown organizers asked ACORN organizers if they would consider moving people into the newly vacant homes in Poletown. PNC members hoped this might preserve a sense of hope in Poletown and protect the vacant houses from arson and vandalism. ACORN organizers refused. They had just succeeded in persuading the city council to set aside $1.2 million for homesteading and now needed to maintain relations with the city to get a homesteading ordinance passed over the mayor's objections.

Similarly, the Michigan Avenue Community Organization, which was trying to stop GM from closing the Cadillac plants in southwest Detroit, was deterred from joining the Poletown struggle because it had grant requests pending with the Roman Catholic church. MACO received a great deal of support from the church and informally told Poletown organizers that they were unwilling to join forces because it would antagonize the church.

The Roman Catholic archdiocese, under Cardinal John Dearden, had tremendous power in determining how the GM Cadillac project would proceed. Nearly half the residents in Poletown were Catholic. The cardinal was in a legitimate position to demand negotiations and corporate compromises. He could speak from a powerful and highly visible position. He could mobilize area clergy and congregations and he could make use of the archdiocesan public relations staff and resources.

Dearden did none of these things. He assumed a position which he described as "neutral." He neither campaigned for the plant nor supported preservation of the neighborhood. But to fail to speak out in the interests of Poletown residents was to embrace the GM project, given its momentum. Dearden's voice was conspicuous in its absence, and this was not lost on Poletown residents, many of whom had believed that the cardinal would intervene to make sure they were given a fair hearing.

Instead, Dearden said the most compassionate thing he could do was to help facilitate the relocation process. This posture, of course, undermined the stamina of some who were challenging GM's right to take the neighborhood and actually expedited the exodus.[52]

Unfortunately for the residents, Dearden's understanding of denying "positive support" to either side did not include reserving judgment about whether the residents should be relocated until all the issues had been discussed, protested, taken to court, and resolved. From the outset, the archdiocesan position was that the plant was a blessing for the city and that Poletown residents should be treated as humanely as possible during the relocation process.

On July 2, just days after the GM project was announced, Bishop Arthur Krawczak, who served as the cardinal's liaison with Poletown, was already telling the *Detroit Free Press:* "We are concerned, of course, for the people involved—and I mean all people, Catholic and non-Catholic alike. We're concerned that they get proper compensation for their homes and adequate moving expenses. . . . I have no problems with the way the city has operated so far. The important thing is for all parties involved to address ourselves to the needs of the people." [53] And Auxiliary Bishop Thomas Gumbleton added: "The overall good of the city is achieved by cutting away a certain part. When you're trying to make something grow, you prune."[54]

When the Poletown Neighborhood Council approached the archdiocese for a grant to help underwrite a lawsuit challenging the city's use of the quick-take act for GM, they were refused. In October, just after some PNC members had picketed a mass at St. John's because they felt Fr. Maloney was discouraging his parishioners from fighting the project, the archdiocese created what it called a joint committee. The committee included Maloney and Karasiewicz, from Immaculate Conception, and some others. Maloney, who had attended meetings with city officials and with Bishop Krawczak before the GM plan was made public, told the *Michigan Catholic* that the committee had "nothing to do with fighting this project."[55]

Karasiewicz took a low profile at the beginning. Karasiewicz welcomed the Poletown Neighborhood Council into the basement of his church; he didn't take his views to the media or to the streets. However, Karasiewicz told the *Michigan Catholic* that he would appeal to the archdiocese to allow him to use $50,000 of the Immaculate Conception's reserves to fund a legal battle over the GM project. If the archdiocese refused permission, Karasiewicz said, "We would be forced to broadcast that fact to the media."[56] In time Karasiewicz became more and more bold until he stood out as one of the community's principal spokespeople. As that occurred, rumors began to spread through the network of urban clergy that Karasiewicz was taking on the Poletown fight because he was angry at the cardinal for failing to make him a bishop.

There was truth mixed in with the allegations that Karasiewicz had a history of dissension with Cardinal Dearden.[57] But it was disturbing to some that Detroit's inner-city clergy were so willing to believe the disparaging things that were said about Karasiewicz's motivations in Poletown. Vicar James Robinson even went so far as to say that Karasiewicz's concern about events in Poletown was evidence that he had been "brainwashed" by Ralph Nader.[58] Both Robinson and Norm Thomas, an influential pastor of a parish neighboring Poletown, were said to be unwilling to take a critical stance in Poletown because "they didn't want to undermine Coleman Young," according to a staff member at the archdiocesan peace and justice office.

Karasiewicz himself summarized his convictions this way: "I'm not one to be disobedient. But every priest will see this: if you're with the people, you are always right. Not as a follower of the people, but with the people to the extent that you appreciate their feeling. If you know that they are giving their life to the parish and they love it here, they are dedicated to the parish, their whole life centers around it—then you have to be with the people. No matter who you go against. No matter what may happen."[59]

Maloney, on the other hand, felt deeply conflicted but concluded that if his parishioners ended up being caught unaware by the project and suffering because they had been ill-prepared, he would feel he had failed them. "If one group wants to fight the project, if they feel that's necessary, then maybe they can slow things down," Maloney said. "That's okay, but if we don't back that, I don't want it to look like we're not for the people. It's more complicated than that. What I hate to see is old people at the end of their lives. . . . they shouldn't have to go through all this."[60]

At PNC meetings and at demonstrations through the fall and spring Poletown residents debated the reasoning behind the archdiocese's decision to endorse their relocation. Over and over again they complained that Dearden "doesn't like Polish people." Signs carried outside the chancery asked, "Why do you dislike Polish people?" Residents recalled that Dearden had been nicknamed Polakozerca, or "devourer of Poles."[61]

These accusations were taken seriously enough that the *Michigan Catholic* ran a guest column by Fr. Wladyslaw Gowin, who wrote that the accusations were "a great injustice to Cardinal Dearden." He added that they were "not very well censured expressions, which are not to the credit of those who expressed them." Gowin pointed out that Dearden had appointed a Polish bishop, Arthur Krawczak, and had appointed forty-four priests from Poland, more than any other diocese in the U.S.[62]

Critics said that Dearden and GM's chairman Thomas Murphy were friends who attended the same exclusive suburban country club, jetted together in private planes, and had the same interests—interests of class. Murphy was a devout Catholic who received communion daily. Both he and Dearden frequented the elite Bloomfield Hills Country Club, and Dearden did meet with an association called the Cardinal's Club, a group of prestigious Catholic businessmen convened to honor and meet with the archbishop.

Still others said the archdiocese had probably arranged a lucrative price for the two churches, based on the archdiocese's cooperation during the taking of the property. Poletown residents pointed out that whatever price the archdiocese accepted it would be profitable since the cost of constructing and staffing the churches had been borne by the parishioners.

But it was also true that the trend in the archdiocese was toward closing ethnically identified churches with dwindling congregations. In fact, in 1988 Dearden's successor, Edmund Szoka, would announce that forty-three inner-city Detroit churches would be closed or merged, causing a furor among parishoners.[63] There was, partly as a result of Vatican II, an effort to universalize the church by breaking down ethnic ties and replacing them with what was forecast to be a vibrant new Catholicism. Dearden was also reluctant to create shrines, arguing that the church is not confined to its buildings.

Mayor Coleman Young was unwilling to accept an interview for this book. When his press secretary was approached, she said, "There are lots of applicable quotes from the mayor such as that there never was a Poletown before this conflict erupted." Joyce Garrett added, "I don't see how the mayor can be the bad guy if he's getting 6,000 jobs for this city." Asked why the mayor wouldn't be interviewed about his position on Poletown, Garrett explained that "he's disgusted with it."[64]

The city's public relations campaign concerning Poletown took two paths. The first was a positive one, which suggested that GM's proposed plant would be a lifesaver for the city, attracting revenue and new investors. This approach usually implied that the city had acted ingeniously to persuade GM to locate in Detroit. "I have no doubt this will go down in modern history as one of the most significant projects in urban history," the mayor said expansively. "There's nothing wrong with our city that two or three of these plants couldn't solve. This could mean the difference between a greater Detroit and a deteriorating Detroit. If the flak goes with it, it's a cheap price for progress."[65] At such times the mayor was also likely to poke insults at his detractors, labelling them "saboteurs."

The second approach, which was often employed in court or when the GM project was being criticized, involved protestations that the city's back was to the wall. GM was inflexible and the city had no choice but to conform or lose the plant. Most often, this defensive line was run by city officials other than the mayor, presumably because it would be bad politics to make the mayor look powerless.[66]

Of course the principal issue, in the city's view, was jobs. The city clung to GM's initial estimate that the plant would provide 6,000 jobs. It then applied a multiplier to achieve an estimate of 24,000 spinoff jobs that would result from the original employment. The spinoff estimate was calculated to include temporary workers who would work on neighborhood demolition and plant construction. It included employees at supplier plants that would presumably service the new GM plant. And it included people who would offer services to the auto workers, like grocers, bartenders, shoe salespeople, and sandwich vendors.

However, Michael Patin, former research chief of the Michigan Office of Economic Development, says the figures were inflated. It was his computer model that came up with the estimate, but Patin says that the new GM plant running at maximum capacity wouldn't provide any more than a maximum of 20,000 jobs.[67] Nonetheless, the city estimate carried weight, and it generally went unchallenged in the media even after GM admitted to HUD officials that it would promise no more than 3,000 jobs at its new Cadillac plant. City planning department head Corinne Gilb was persuasive when she argued: "One after another industries have been leaving the city. We have more than 130,000 unemployed. If we didn't move to keep General Motors in Detroit, we'd have lost the anchor and magnet for all major job providers. It would have been the height of irresponsibility to cater to a tiny handful of people when you realize what is at stake—the life blood of the city."[68]

Several things generally went unmentioned in these types of city protestations. The first was that the estimated jobs were not new jobs for the city but were actually retained jobs for auto workers at the two closing Detroit Cadillac plants and for service people already selling parts or sandwiches or shoes. The second detail generally passed over was that HUD regulations required that priority be given to employing low- and moderate-income people for HUD-funded projects. Residents of Poletown and some of the neighborhoods to the south heard through semi-official channels that they would be likely to get jobs at the new plant. Alice Lyte, head of a powerful community group called Semi-Quois and a member of the Poletown Citizens District Council, threw her support to the GM project partly for that reason. The catch, of course, was that GM's contract with the UAW guaranteed jobs to auto workers with seniority at the Fleetwood and Clark Avenue plants. The media never pursued this discrepancy. The third, and perhaps most important, point was that the Poletown residents *wanted* the plant built in their neighborhood but modified in order to save their homes.

As with the promise of jobs the projected tax revenue from the GM plant was grossly exaggerated. Early estimates were that the plant would generate $20 million a year in property taxes. City officials suggested that Detroit would net more than $12 million, with Hamtramck receiving the remaining third. City officials were quick to say that the older Cadillac plants only generated a little over $3 million a year, so it would be a gain of $9 million.

However, if GM demanded a tax abatement, the amount would be diminished. GM could either ask for a 50 percent, twelve-year abatement for a new facility, reducing the city's share of the annual tax revenue to $6 million, or it could argue that the Poletown plant would be a replacement facility for the older plants and require that only the old $3-million-plus tax be imposed on the new plant for twelve years.

When the city council's planning commission examined the city's calculations, it warned that even with no tax abatement it would take the city fifteen years to recoup its investment in the GM plant. If a 50 percent abatement were granted and the payback period at least doubled, the commission asked whether the city could count on the plant still being in operation in the year when the city's investment would be paid back.

An additional possibility escaped scrutiny. If GM prevailed upon the city to create a Tax Increment Financing Authority, as some considered likely, then whatever revenue was generated by the plant would be recycled into improving the plant area. That revenue would never be channeled into the city school system or city services.

6

Enter Ralph Nader

My principal concern is that General Motors Corporation, the second richest corporation in the world, makes the decisions in the city of Detroit, not the city government.

—Ralph Nader
Detroit News, 12 March 1981

The new year began on a mixed note. In early January headlines indicated that more of the federal funding necessary for the project had been approved and that full-scale demolition of Dodge Main would begin in earnest. But during the same week residents learned that the Polish-American Congress, the Michigan Environmental Review Board, and consumer advocate Ralph Nader were willing to lend the community their support.

The first two offers of support were without lasting consequence, but people were encouraged to hear that Kazimierz Olejarczyk, president of the Polish-American Congress in Michigan, was urging GM to revise its plant design in order to save the neighborhood. Since Olejarczyk worked for GM as an engineer in the suburban Tech Center, he appeared to be taking an additional risk.

The Michigan Environmental Review Board issued a similar appeal, saying that revision of a proposed boundary road could save "a large number of substantial homes that are slated to be taken." The board said the social effects of the project were not adequately documented or mitigated and that GM's need for a ring road around the plant should be reconsidered since its construction would destroy most of the homes.[1]

After Nader read an article about the proposed GM plant that appeared in a back section of the *Washington Post,* he sent an attorney to

Detroit. Gene Stilp, who arrived in Poletown on January 5, chuckled that the article was buried among the real estate ads and would have been overlooked by anyone less persevering than Ralph Nader. During his first days in Poletown Stilp toured the neighborhood, met with residents, attended a Poletown Neighborhood Council meeting, and told residents that Nader was concerned about the course of events in Poletown. He was welcomed with open arms, partly because he was the first representative of a national group to take an interest in the community.

"At the time when I arrived, there was deep snow, very deep snow," Stilp recalled. "It was ten degrees. Like any community that's snowed in, it looked quiet, not too many people on the streets. But I started going into people's homes. One by one they'd invite you, and you might as well have been at your grandmother's house for Christmas. It was my impression that the people wanted to stay."

At the end of his visit Stilp recommended that Nader throw his support and resources behind the Poletown residents who wanted to save their homes. "I have to commend you people," he told the residents. "You have a lot of guts for sticking it out under all this pressure from the governor, from the mayor, from General Motors. A lot of pressure. There is no reason anybody in this country, or any country in the world, should be allowed to take your church, your homes . . . to build Cadillacs. It's just silly."[2]

Nonetheless, two weeks later mass condemnation hearings were held by Judge Martin in Cobo Hall, one of the city's largest auditoriums. Harry Kaczynski went to that hearing believing that his property was protected because he had filed an objection. What he didn't learn until later was that the judge was rejecting more than sixty such objections because they hadn't been filed as legal motions.[3]

"We filed this, which we were told was legal," Kaczynski explained. "We were told to sign the first one of these with the lot number. This would take care of what we were after. And then we appeared at Cobo Hall on the 21st of January. And he [the judge] never said one word. All the city did was read off all the lists of parcels they wanted. He granted them the parcels [1,366 of them], and that was the end of it. Plus, they searched us coming in like we were a bunch of criminals."

"Yeah," Bernice Kaczynski interjected, "they had guards there. When it came time for some questions from the people, they had two doggone Wayne County sheriff's deputies there in the middle of the aisle with their hands on their guns, ready as if we were going to pounce up there and kill somebody. We're good people. If we do something, it's a demonstration, but nothing in violence. Maybe that's where we made our mistake—we should have been a little more violent."

The media concluded that, Ralph Nader's interest notwithstanding, the gradual approval of federal funding and the abrupt taking of title signaled a virtual end to the neighborhood's chances of survival. And this took its toll on the residents. "With the negative publicity of Judge Martin's ruling, a lot of people lost hope and gave up because he said the government was in the right," Bob Giannini, an employee at Chrysler's personnel department, told the *Bulletin*.

> They resigned themselves that this is a lost battle. If this project manages to succeed, I think that this city is bound to see a revolution in the streets. The city is planting the seeds of revolution by destroying this multi-ethnic neighborhood. It's not all white or black or Arab—it's a multi-ethnic neighborhood that doesn't exist anywhere else in the city. This whole thing has really rekindled my thoughts about the efforts in the 1960s when people took to the streets demanding power. This country has to give more power back to the people. We don't control our own destiny. It's controlled by the power structures. No matter how much they tell you they want your input, no matter how much you protest, their minds are made up behind closed doors."[4]

Behind those closed doors the principals were largely in agreement with each other, but there were some disputes. The Council for Environmental Quality (CEQ) believed that officials at HUD were proceeding prematurely and should have been gathering and considering environmental information, including the social impact of the proposed plant. But HUD Secretary Moon Landrieu, Emmett Moten's former employer, rejected this, saying that HUD would go ahead and publish regulations for the GM project in the Federal Register. Three days later Gus Speth of the CEQ sent an angry letter to Landrieu complaining that "no other federal agency disputes the authority of the Council's regulations on this issue, nor supports HUD's view of NEPA's application to the UDAG program. We repeat our statement of October 31, 1980, that any further processing of UDAG applications or release of federal funds without consideration by HUD of environmental documents and information would violate the procedural provisions of NEPA."[5]

However, these disputes were not aired publicly, and HUD continued approving the funding for the project.

At the end of January a flurry of activity sent restless and hopeful sentiments through the neighborhood. Residents learned that the state supreme court had agreed to hear their suit. And Ralph Nader announced that he would be sending a team of organizers to Poletown. Nader announced that he would launch an investigation of possible corruption of federal and local government officials. And he sent a letter to GM's chairman requesting a meeting during which they could discuss alternatives to destroying the neighborhood. However, its tone was sarcastic.

"Once upon a time in American economic history," Nader began, "companies established production facilities by purchasing a parcel of land and building a factory with their own money. Times have changed for corporations who used to believe in free enterprise. Now, even the wealthiest multinational corporations such as General Motors prepare a prospectus for building a plant and then dangle it before various municipalities and states to ascertain how large a subsidy the taxpayers will be compelled to provide if they want the plant in their area. Of course, General Motors is keeping a low profile on this sensitive public relations problem, preferring to have the City of Detroit be its bulldozing agency . . ."[6]

The Detroit newspapers editorialized against Nader. They regarded his intervention in Poletown an outrage which would have the direst of consequences. And while the editors could hardly argue that the Poletown residents didn't have a right to their day in court, their editorials begged the question of the verdict by recommending that the supreme court act quickly lest delay kill the GM project.

The Motor City media were quick to remember that Ralph Nader first became nationally known when he wrote *Unsafe at Any Speed*, a book which revealed flaws in the GM Corvair that jeopardized people's lives. Nader's continuing interest in auto safety was often interpreted as a personal assault on the city's livelihood. When Nader committed himself to advocating the resistance of Poletown residents, the newspapers saw it as more of the same.

"Mr. Nader has long demonstrated an antipathy toward Detroit that goes beyond his early interest in safe cars," the *Detroit News* wrote. "Well, the Motor City today stands bruised and bleeding, at least in part because of his and his disciples' continuing assaults." The editors applauded the mayor for calling Nader "a carpetbagger" and reveled in the fact that Smith had refused to meet with him. They applauded GM for "bucking ferocious headwinds to press for the Detroit site to help its hurting hometown." The editorial continued: "Now the nation's best-known vigilante is filing requests under the Freedom of Information Act as part of his investigation into the relationship between Detroit, General Motors and two federal funding agencies, the U.S. Commerce Department and the U.S. Department of Housing and Urban

Development. It's our guess that he's crawling up a blind alley, and that the new GM plant will be built on schedule, with fair recompense to the families displaced. But Mr. Nader isn't making things easier. Detroit is battered and barely breathing. Under such grim circumstances, we don't welcome a visitor who comes with dagger in hand." [7]

The *Detroit Free Press* editors took a less exaggerated stance but came to the same conclusion. They seemed to fastidiously avoid name calling and attempted to give everyone the benefit of the doubt. As is so often true, this liberal position ended up being more damning for the Poletown resistance than the conservative outcry of the *Detroit News*. At least with the latter it was always eminently clear whose interests they were serving.

The *Free Press* editors disavowed the mayor's use of the word *carpetbagger*, saying that everyone has a right to express an opinion and that the truth from any quarter would be enlightening. But they added, "We believe that he [Nader] is wrong on the facts, that the plant will serve the greater good of the people of Detroit and that the city can and must deal fairly with the people. It is a difficult call, but it is an essential step in rebuilding the city's economic base." The editors applauded the community for its persistence and determination to make its case in court but added, "It would be a mistake to let the dimensions of the plant site get bogged down in a prolonged dispute. . . . There seems to us to be a clear-eyed case that the building of that plant, with enough land to provide suitable buffering from those neighborhoods adjacent to it, will contribute more to community survival and to neighborhood stability than Mr. Nader's approach." The alternative would be to "condemn much of the city to a slow, degrading death."[8]

Nader's team of five, including three lawyers, set up an office in the basement of Immaculate Conception Church. They put in three phone lines and a couple of typewriters and began generating press statements and releases to increase the public pressure on GM by attracting national news coverage. Fr. Karasiewicz was impressed by Nader's volunteers' courtesy and diligence, often pointing out that they worked twelve- and fourteen-hour days. Sandy Livingston, a student volunteer with Nader's office, recalled later that Karasiewicz "was incredibly warm and hospitable with us. Besides giving us space in the basement, he made his office supplies available to us, gave us use of his washer and dryer, and ping pong table. FJ [Father Joe] was a mean pingpong player and we sometimes had matches with him at night. He supplied us with large blocks of cheese, cookies, etc. Father Joe came downstairs a couple times everyday—to bring in the mail, to see how we were doing and give us news. He was a refreshing change from others who would call and tell us to do things that they were unwilling to do themselves. FJ would initiate his own projects and ask us what we thought of them."

The five Nader staffers, most of them in their late twenties and early thirties, stayed in a Poletown house provided by Louise Crosby on Mitchell Street. The Crosbys, the Kaczynskis, the Dockerys, the Watsons, Mary Mitchell, the Bargos, Karen Apollonio, and Mr. Martin were all their neighbors.

The atmosphere at Poletown Neighborhood Council meetings changed. While the Nader support team took a low profile, there was more sense of follow-through. Likewise, the status of court proceedings or of city maneuvers was more clearly explained. And residents were more prone to believe that they had a legitimate constitutional complaint because Nader said so too. The Nader team generally attempted to develop residents' leadership and self-reliance without rocking the ego of Tom Olechowski.

A major contribution of the Nader team was that they were available in the church basement twelve hours a day, seven days a week. Residents who had the inclination to stuff envelopes or write letters could come to the church to do that. When news broke about a funding allocation, an eviction date, or a comment from city hall or GM, people had a place to congregate and brainstorm. And community relations were built between residents and the team each time Josephine Jakubowski, who had hosted parish dinners most of her life, decided to bring fresh perrogies down to the basement.

When the Nader team arrived, the Workers League, which publishes The *Bulletin*, decided to withdraw its support from the Poletown struggle. They believed that Nader's team would divert residents' faith into the courts and the media, instead of helping them to become more militant.[9]

So the Nader team operated in a tentative framework. They were condemned as carpetbaggers by the power structure, written off as counter-productive liberals by one of the only Left groups that supported Poletown, and eyed warily by Tom Olechowski, who worried that they'd usurp his position. Of course, the momentum GM and the city had established did not slow down to allow the team time to find its bearings.

In early February residents began to receive ninety-day eviction notices. Realtors eager to sell residents their new homes plastered the neighborhood with flyers. The city hired gerontologist Leon Pastalone to oversee the relocation of the elderly. Hamtramck was awarded $30 million from UDAG, the largest grant in the program's history, only after Hamtramck resolved a race dispute.[10] And Governor Milliken met with newly inaugurated President Reagan to learn that Detroit would most likely receive its own $30 million from UDAG.

The Nader team decided to challenge the mayor at a press conference. "It was my intention to question him about Poletown," Gene Stilp explained. "I was going to go on the attack. Olechowski went crazy. He wanted to show deference to the mayor in the press statement. He was always deferring to these higher authorities—it seemed as if he were trying to fight the project and protect himself at the same time." As a result the Poletown Neighborhood Council issued a press statement that praised the mayor for a variety of things but ended with a paragraph calling on him to save the neighborhood. (The run-in with Olechowski was less than amicable, but both sides kept the conflict quiet. Although the run-ins continued frequently, some even peaking with Olechowski's threats to denounce the team to the press, most people in Poletown were unaware of them.)

Despite the internal and external tensions, the Neighborhood Council went toe-to-toe with the city and the federal government. Ron Reosti went to the state supreme court and requested a temporary injunction which would prevent the demolition of property in Poletown pending the court's eventual decision on the legality of Detroit's use of the new quick-take act. Three days later the residents filed a motion to prevent the city from sending out more notices to vacate pending the supreme court decision. On February 14, residents held a demonstration at a National Bank of Detroit branch which had announced that it was closing on March 27. Residents carried heart-shaped signs and chanted: "Hey, hey, NBD / Take our money and then you flee."[11]

"The main reason for the demonstration," Carol Dockery explained, "was that the bank doesn't have to move. It's psychological warfare to close it so early because people are still here. The people with accounts are getting notices that they must tell the bank by February 23 where they want their accounts transferred to. If you don't tell them, it's automatically transferred to the branch at Mt. Elliott and Gratiot." The bank's policy posed an obvious problem for residents who didn't drive. In addition the land the NBD branch stood on was located in an area that did not need to be cleared for the GM project before September.

Bernice Kaczynski and her neighbor Ann Giannini agreed that the time they were taking to demonstrate and to sue and to speak out to the media was worthwhile. Bernice summarized their activity for the press one afternoon, saying, "We're standing ten feet tall right now. We're fighting something so big. But I think we have to win, to show that the people have a voice in America once again. . . . We didn't know that we could fight either. We're used to staying home and cleaning house and taking care of the home front. This is a different kind of involvement. We're learning that politicians are just cold to the human needs of the people. But you have power over politicians, power as a human being for a voice in the community and the country without being locked up as a traitor because you're speaking out as you feel."

On February 20, residents learned that the state supreme court had issued an injunction preventing any demolition in Poletown prior to its ruling on the constitutionality of the GM project. It was the first institutional response to the neighborhood's crisis that seemed to indicate a community victory. People stopped into the basement of the Immaculate Conception Church all weekend to congratulate each other. Residents speculated about whether the court would preserve the neighborhood and whether neighbors who had moved out would return. If they didn't, would their houses remain the property of the city or would they be for sale? What creative things could be done to restore and even improve the neighborhood?

That Sunday, residents read in their church bulletins that the cardinal had signed a purchase agreement with the city, selling St. John's for $1.09 million and the Immaculate Conception Church for $1.3 million. Both churches would be deconsecrated on April 30.

Feelings ran extremely high that Sunday. Ann Locklear, who lived downstairs from her aunt and uncle, the Jakubowskis, said: "They're traitors. They've sold us out to the city and General Motors for thirty pieces of silver. What I have to say about him [Cardinal Dearden] is unprintable. He knows how much our parish church means to us. And also, just for the record, I don't care who knows that I'm not moving out of my house either. Home and church, that's what's important."[12]

"How can they sell the churches that the people built?" Ann Giannini asked. "That wasn't right that they should sell the churches. They are just taking them over like they are nothing, and the people support them, doing everything that they can to keep them churches up." Harold Kaczynski agreed. "The people are the ones that built them in the first place. It ain't built by the archdiocese."

Katherine Patrick, seventy-five, told the press: "I don't want to be a Catholic anymore after they knock my church down." Patrick had been a parishioner at St. John's since 1929. Her six children were baptized and confirmed there. "I'm going to stay until they bulldoze me," she said.[13]

At the next Poletown Neighborhood Council meeting Bob Giannini complained that "the cardinal and his immediate circle of incompetents, including Bishop Krawczak, sold the entire archdiocese down the river. They purposely chose to sell the churches at this point in time, prior to the supreme court decision. And the reason is to wear us down, to demoralize us. We're going to demonstrate, either in his office or downtown at the chancery, to show them that we're angry, we're upset, and we're not going to take this any longer."

Fr. Karasiewicz sent Roger Smith a letter saying: "While I am aware that His Eminence, Cardinal Dearden, made it known that he would not oppose your project, I dare to presume a more 'on the spot' appreciation of the situation here in our parish. If our church should be demolished, the resulting harm inflicted on our people would be absolutely devastating, causing, as I can envision it, irreparable personal harm." He offered Smith a "cook's tour" of the neighborhood and the church, as well as a ride in his 1972 Oldsmobile stationwagon.[14]

On February 26, forty Poletown residents, both black and white, circled in front of the chancery with enormous, round signs that read: "Sold, for Thirty Pieces of Silver," "In GM We Trust," "Dear Lord Forgive Them, They Know Not What They Do." And the perennial, "Cardinal Dearden, Why Do You Hate Polish People?" The group handed out a leaflet which called for the cardinal to rescind his church sale agreement, to disclose all archdiocesan dealings with the city in regard to Poletown, and to remove Bishop Krawczak from office.

Local newspaper photos the next day pictured Barbara Sokol, who worked at the main branch of the Detroit Public Library, carrying a huge round silver sign that read "In GM We Trust?" and showed a wrecking ball striking a church. At two the following morning, she stood on her front porch, confused and in shock. The fire department had just brought her flaming garage under control. The streets were flooded with water and the air was damp and smoky. As friends learned that Sokol's house roof had sustained fire damage and called to make sure Sokol's sister and brother-in-law were on their way over, Sokol kept repeating that she was sorry she had allowed herself to fall asleep. She said that ordinarily, these days, she tried to stay awake at night to protect her house. No one could say whether or not the fire in her garage was set in retribution for her participation in the demonstration at the archdiocese.

An increasing number of Poletown homes were being vandalized. Residents complained that the looting and arson escalated when

DAVID C. TURNLEY

Ann Giannini protests the archdiocese's decision to sell Poletown's two Roman Catholic churches for $2.8 million. The sale was announced just days after Poletown had won its first victory: the Michigan Supreme Court stopped demolition in the neighborhood pending a decision on the project's constitutionality.

DAVID C. TURNLEY

Barbara Sokol takes advantage of a moment of quiet in the Immaculate Conception Church. Shortly after this photograph was taken, Sokol would stand on her street in tears at 2 A.M. because her garage was in flames and the roof of her house had caught fire.

As vandalism and demolition increased, parents began to fear for their children's safety.

DAVID C. TURNLEY

the temporary restraining order was issued by the court. Residents saw it as an extra-legal way to drive them out. Part of the problem was that the city marked newly vacant homes with a big blue spray-painted *X* to signal that the water meter could be removed. The Xs served as invitations to anyone who wanted to steal leaded glass windows, wood molding, flooring, or bathroom fixtures. As vandals became more bold, they even stripped the aluminum siding off houses. Residents complained that the people stripping the neighborhood were helping to sign its death certificate, since it would be hard to restore the community—even with a court victory—if the area was butchered.

The police, they said, seemed to be looking the other way. Windows in vacant homes were smashed. And house after house went up in flames. Some residents gave up then and packed up their grandparents or their children and left. By June arson and vandalism were epidemic. Some homes were painted with warnings: "Death to Arsonists, Thieves and GM," "Kill GM," "Anyone breaking in will be shot," "Warning: This place is guarded 24 hours a day. All thieves and looters will be shot dead. This is no joke."

During this time the Mitchell Street residents began what they titled the "Poletown Patrol." Often in the evening Bernice and Harry Kaczynski or Carol Dockery could be spotted bicycling around the neighborhood. Police revealed in May that most of the looters were suburbanites who admired Poletown's old, crafted, stained-glass windows and woodwork. None of the news agencies ever reported what Police Captain Robert McClary (an arson investigator) told residents during a spring Poletown Neighborhood Council meeting. "It's not unusual for a fire to occur in an abandoned building and sometimes help expedite the demolition process," McClary said. "The city hires a contractor; they hire subcontractors. Sometimes subcontractors, knowing full well that juveniles will be blamed, hire agents and send them in. With enough money you can do anything." McClary added that the last time he had seen arson on this scale was when GM had gentrified the New Center Area.

During the last week of February the Poletown Neighborhood Council sent a letter appealing to all Detroit area clergy for help. The council also released letters to state and local bar associations accusing lawyers of failing to aid Poletown residents because they were afraid to take an unpopular position. Tom Olechowski wrote to the pope, the bishop of Chicago, Senator Levin, the Polish National Alliance, and Governor Milliken. In his letter to the pope, Olechowski asked the pontiff to address the demolition of Poletown, saying, "This destruction is unnecessary and contrary to the desires, deepest feelings and

Children learned to regard fires in the neighborhood as commonplace. Within six months of the announcement of the GM project, fires were up 300 percent.

DAVID C. TURNLEY

needs of the parishioners and the people of Poletown. We will document and demonstrate our assertion that the destruction serves economic, bureaucratic, political, and wholly secular considerations which
stand in deepest contradiction to our spiritual, cultural and historic
values."[15] Olechowski added that the archdiocese had a history of
Polish dissension and would benefit from the appointment of a Polish
archbishop.

One week before Poletown hearings were to begin before the state
supreme court, residents complained to the media of declining city
services. Garbage pickups were becoming irregular. Bernice Kaczynski
complained that a Detroit Edison worker had removed one of two
electric meters from her home. While the meter was not in use, Kaczynski
said she was upset when the worker said, "The meter is Detroit Edison
property and besides, you live in Poletown." She protested that "as
long as we are intact, I don't think any meters should be taken out. It's
pure harassment. It's very upsetting to the older persons who don't
need to be constantly scared that the neighborhood is lost." Both the
city and Detroit Edison denied that they were altering their services.[16]

Just two days before the supreme court hearings, the *Michigan
Catholic* published an article titled, "Is Supreme Court Too Late for
Poletown?" Fr. Maloney was quoted as saying, "There's lots of empty
houses now and there's going to be more. The neighborhood is destroyed now as far as I can see. What can save it? A court ruling? I really
doubt that's the answer. It seems so late now. We needed that supreme
court decision back in December. If the project is defeated in court all
the contracts that have been signed already will be invalid. You think
those people who have gone through the pain of being uprooted will
want to move back?" Maloney added that the final mass at St. John's
was set for May 24.[17]

The doomsaying notwithstanding, a school bus and several cars
full of Poletown residents traveled to the state capitol to hear the
arguments in the supreme court on March 3. Fr. Karasiewicz was out of
town, but Fr. Skalski went in support of the residents. Pat Barszenski, a
second-generation resident, provided rosaries for anyone wishing to
pray. For many of the seventy residents, this trip marked their first visit
to the state house.

Four members of a Polish dance troupe, which had always practiced in the basement of the Immaculate Conception Church, sat in the
front row of the court room. Fr. Skalski sat toward the back. Other
residents, both black and white, filled the benches in between. Some
spilled over into the hallway. When the city's attorney, Jason Honig-

man, entered the court room, residents noted that he was clearly well known to the justices and greeted warmly. Their own attorney, Ron Reosti, did not receive the same signs of recognition. The *Detroit News* described Honigman as "the patriarch of the prestigious law firm Honigman, Miller, Schwartz and Cohn."[18]

During the oral arguments Reosti stated that the Poletown case would set precedent. "There is no place in the country in which a condemnation for the express purpose of conveying land to private users has been approved. The issue in this case is whether the city can, through eminent domain, condemn a viable neighborhood for the use of a private corporation." Reosti cited a Kentucky Supreme Court ruling which warned that "the opportunity for tyranny exists to a much greater degree in condemnation than in taxation." That court added that if a government body is allowed to be "a land broker for private interests . . . the property of citizens would never be safe from invasion."

The Fifth Amendment, Reosti argued, was designed to protect Americans from sovereigns who would seize land and turn it over to their political allies. This application of eminent domain law promised to undermine the amendment's intent. "There are no restrictions on GM or its use of the land—it's clearly for private use." If Detroit's use of eminent domain were upheld by the court, Reosti said, then it would serve as a tool for "any corporation which is powerful enough or politically influential enough" to demand it.

Reosti argued that the Michigan Economic Development Corporation Act, to which the quick-take clause was an amendment, violated the state constitution as well. The act authorized the taking of private property for industrial development, while the constitution only authorized it for public use. The direct benefit of the Central Industrial Park Project would be GM's, Reosti said. The promised 6,000 jobs would only be an "incidental benefit" to the public.[19]

Reosti dismissed arguments that the GM plant was "essential to economic survival," saying the argument was a "smokescreen" designed to obscure the fact that the city was "functioning as a public realtor for a private corporation." The city had many other ways to "aggregate land for industrial expansion without using the power of eminent domain." In addition, the neighborhood itself was a valuable community asset that warranted legal protection as a "natural resource," Reosti said. "Poletown is a unique, historic, viable integrated neighborhood with many important cultural and social institutions which would not survive the physical destruction of the neighborhood and the dispersion of its residents."[20]

Honigman argued that as "Mayor Young told us: 'Jobs are vital for our survival.' That's what this is all about." The GM plant would be more important to Detroit's future than the $337 million Renaissance Center, according to the mayor, and would support between 500 and 600 sandwich vendors alone. Honigman said GM's plant promised to be primarily a public gain. He stated that the Detroit Economic Development Corporation was established to create industrial parks and that its application of the power of eminent domain was consistent with the state's 1974 eminent domain act. "It is a *condemnation* law," he added.[21] Honigman questioned Poletown's value as a cultural resource and urged the court to act quickly, saying "we are not in control of our destinies at this time."

"'If General Motors was able to dictate the amount of land, isn't the public purpose incidental to GM's private use?' Moody asked. Honigman responded that the city, with 15.3 percent unemployment, is in dire need of jobs. Asked by Justice Thomas Kavanaugh whether 'government should' play the role of realtor for industry, Honigman said, 'What is necessary changes with the times.' Honigman added that he is uncomfortable with the expansion of state power during the last fifty years but said one must act within the context of the time."[22]

The attorney for the Detroit Economic Development Corporation, David Lewis, argued: "At issue here before this court is the power of a municipality to perform major surgery to stop the hemorrhaging of jobs, a procedure that no doubt is painful but is necessary for the survival of the patient." Lewis told the court that the framers of the constitution did allow for land acquisition for public use and that public purpose was the equivalent. He said the Economic Development Act authorized their conduct in this case and that the economic situation in Detroit was extreme enough to warrant use of the power of eminent domain. He added that the Economic Development Corporation, the Citizens District Council, the city council, and the trial court all had jurisdiction in this matter and all had approved the project.

In the afternoon twelve of the Poletown residents who had come to listen to the oral arguments were permitted to meet with the governor. They were delighted when Milliken offered to relay their suggestions on how to build the plant and save the neighborhood back to the mayor and GM. "I will try to reconcile the desperate need for jobs with the desires of people who have lived in the community for years," Milliken told them. "It is essential that the plant be built and here in the state if possible. A lot of lives depend on that too. There is no easy solution to the problem."[23]

Mayor Young was livid when he learned that Milliken had given

Poletown's residents a hearing. "With all due respect to the governor, that is not his purview at all," he told the press. "We have reviewed alternative sites. All that is past. I believe the governor ought to let the Supreme Court handle it. I object to the fact that anyone would attempt to delay at this time, since delay is tantamount to defeat. Any delay will jeopardize the project. [That] would be one of the greatest economic setbacks Detroit and Michigan have ever received. It'll be a disgrace. It'll be a shame."[24]

When the Poletown group returned home, they gathered in the basement of the Immaculate Conception Church, where Reosti made a statement to the press. They also learned that Charlie Garlow from Nader's office, who had worked in Poletown for two months before returning to D.C., had organized a picket outside GM's Washington offices. Later that night several Poletown residents saw themselves on CBS national news. Spirits were high. Demolition had been halted at least temporarily, the supreme court was well aware of their arguments, and resistance activities abounded.

On March 8 Poletown was in the news again. Maggie Kuhn, the founder of the Grey Panthers, came to Poletown to support the residents and to call attention to the danger forced relocation poses to the elderly. "People here are not receiving the kind of consideration from General Motors and government officials that civic responsibility in a democracy requires," said Kuhn, 75, to a gathering of 200 people in the basement of the Immaculate Conception Church. Gentle and dignified, Kuhn urged GM and the city to enter into dialogue with neighborhood residents and concluded: "We all have a stake in Poletown—to allow local governments to abdicate their responsibilities to corporations and to allow the rights of citizens anywhere to take a back seat to the demands of corporations can set the stage for a dangerous erosion of important constitutionally protected rights.

"Relocation trauma has been documented in the movement of people out of their neighborhoods and into nursing homes," Kuhn added. "The rate of decline—mental and physical—has been very, very high. This is a kind of pioneering social research that would be very, very important to do here."

After Kuhn's talk, two white-haired women rose to object that Kuhn was too genteel in her remarks. The first dissenter complained that GM was taking advantage of socialism for the rich, while she would prefer to see real socialism with companies owned by the people making socially useful goods. The second, Doris Siefert, a secretary at Wayne State, objected: "I'm speaking as someone who during the thirties had some experience with eviction. I have sat on the sidewalk with furnishings around me. And I think we are being entirely too kind. I personally want to express my disgust with the way that the mayor of the City of Detroit and some of its well-meaning council persons have sold out to corporate blackmail, to promises of that corporation that this will produce 6,500 jobs. That is not true. I hope that half of that comes to be. The rest of the jobs will be automated and people must be aware that we are not going to sit still anymore while our government sells out to corporate power. I personally refuse to do that!"

These remarks were greeted with vigorous applause from elderly Poletown women who might at one time have considered such remarks un-American.

On March 9 the Nader staff initiated a nation-wide postcard campaign asking sympathetic friends and others to send a card to GM chairman Roger Smith. The same night Nader spoke to college students at Eastern Michigan University then came to Detroit to meet Poletown residents. Although Nader had invested a lot of his resources in the Poletown struggle, he was a stranger to the community. Nader's straightforward style and clear appreciation of their struggle won their hearts.

The next day Nader announced to the press that a federal suit would be filed on behalf of Poletown residents under the National Environmental Protection Act. Nader said that the city's "steamroller tactics" to advance the project violated federal laws by not considering alternate site designs that would preserve the neighborhood and by approving the project before the Environmental Impact Statement had even been filed. Nader faulted Moon Landrieu for delegating all NEPA responsibilities to the city and for failing to oversee the project. Nader called Detroit "merely an instrument of GM blackmail" and said: "This is not capitalism in action. GM is demanding that it be given a welfare payment of some $320 million by the federal, state, and local taxpayers, and a 465-acre site for the privilege of making a profit. That's not capitalism. That's corporate socialism in its most pristine form and it's a radical departure from free enterprise." The press briefing was followed by a Polish dinner which Fr. Karasiewicz had hurriedly asked Josephine Jakubowski to pull together, as she had so many times in the past.

Mayor Young was angry. He told the *Detroit News*: "Ralph Nader is psychotic in his hatred of GM. It's obvious that they just want to kill the project. The real residents of Poletown are voting with their feet. They've left." The next day Young called a press conference to say: "What's happening now—it's very, very clear—is an obvious attempt

DAVID C. TURNLEY

Ralph Nader sent five staff people to Detroit to fight the GM project. He also visited the Immaculate Conception Church and ate a meal with Poletown residents.

Ralph Nader and Fr. Joseph Karasiewicz stand silhouetted in the Immaculate
Conception Church.

to sabotage. It's very, very possible that one month's delay could kill the whole project and those who belatedly make this challenge are very well aware of that." Of Nader, the mayor said: "This man has a phobia. Whenever General Motors is mentioned he froths at the mouth, but I don't know why the City of Detroit should be punished for his phobia."[25]

Victoria Roberts, an economic development attorney, told the *News* that "all but 190 of the 1,700 parcels" had been acquired, so that if the suits did stop the GM project the city would "end up owning a lot of property." At that time, however, more than 1,500 of the parcels were still occupied by the owners.[26] During the same week Poletown residents went to the GM world headquarters and leafleted GM employees. The flier read in bold print: "People of Poletown Welcome General Motors."

"Dear General Motors Employee," it read: "We believe that in your hearts, you support the people of Poletown. No human being wants to be displaced from his or her home, church, business, or neighborhood of a lifetime—especially when the displacement is unnecessary. We wish to show you that the displacement of Poletown residents is totally unnecessary."

The flier invited GM employees to visit Poletown, meet with residents, and to discuss alternatives. It asked them to consider speaking with those responsible for the plant's design and inviting them to visit Poletown too.

On March 12 television actor Max Gail came to visit Poletown. Gail, who starred on the "Barney Miller" show as a Polish police officer, was coming home to visit family and look into events in Poletown. Gail's involvement in Native American issues made him quick to see parallels between that concern and affairs in Poletown. He hired a video crew and did interviews which he hoped to edit into a docudrama. Residents were charmed by Gail. They were surprised that he was balding in real life. They were put at ease by his casual clothes and his relaxed, even slow, train of thought. They were surprised by his support, since they knew that his sister, Emily, had made a career out of Detroit boosterism.[27]

Gail shot interviews one afternoon on Mitchell Street. Bernice Kaczynski ran door to door collecting all her neighbors. The crowd soon exceeded twenty-five people, both black and white, who ranged in age from little Brian Dockery to Mr. Martin, who was in his eighties. The sky was blue and the sun was out for one of the first days since Michigan's winter had begun. For the moment, demolition was halted and both the supreme court and the federal court were having a crack at saving the neighborhood. People felt good. They were angry and under threat—but finally getting a hearing.

Television and print media people were present to cover Max Gail's visit to Poletown. But roles became confused when reporters began to enter arguments and residents started interrupting interviews. For a rare moment Poletown residents had a chance to air their views before an outsider and the press while on their own turf. They were not limited by the constraints of a press conference or a court room. They were at home.

Therefore, when Carol Dockery saw *Detroit News* reporter Michael Tucker jotting down that Gail was in Poletown to "learn about" the situation, she interjected,"I just want to see how that's going to come out in the paper." She complained that the *News* would report that Gail wasn't there in support but just there to learn. Gail's soundman, George Corsetti, asked Dockery, "You feel like the media is on the side of big business?" She snapped, "Yes I do." When Gail responded with a little lecture on how editors often change a reporter's copy, Dockery interrupted: "Then what the hell is the point of reading the paper? What's the point of reading the paper?" Gail laughed and responded, "A lot of people don't." Tucker seemed uncomfortable throughout the exchange and then asked Gail for a precise and representative quote.

Shortly thereafter, Harold Kaczynski and Ann Giannini were complaining to Gail about the archdiocese's sale of their churches. Television news reporter Jim Harrington entered the discussion as an explicator. In a modulated tone he explained the obvious. "It belongs to the archdiocese and the archdiocese says 'We will sell it.'" When that failed to disarm Kaczynski, Harrington repeated, "Legally it belongs to the archdiocese. It belongs to the archdiocese, right?" He shrugged as if to say that's the way the law works. Faced with the increasingly articulate and radical anger of these Poletown residents, the reporters began to look like apologists for the status quo. They were the only people on the block in suits. They were the only people on the block persuaded of the absolute legitimacy of "the Law."

The only time the residents took issue with Gail was when he suggested that the media was being sensationalist in reporting that Poletown residents might resort to guns. "Anytime you say something about guns," he said, "you might be just joking. . . . " Gail was interrupted by Kaczynski: "Under pressure I don't know what I'll do. Since June we been going through this. They don't stop and think the effect it's got on my life, my wife's." Bill Larkins, one of Louise Crosby's sons, said, "Mr. Gail, all we're trying to do is protect our homes. I sleep with my shotgun laying on my bed, and it's loaded. They have been burning houses all over this neighborhood. I think Coleman Young's behind it. They're destroying the neighborhood so they can condemn it."

March 13 brought dire news. The Michigan Supreme Court, in a five-to-two decision, ruled that the city acted legally when it employed the power of eminent domain to take land for the General Motors Cadillac plant. The *Detroit News* sported banner headlines and a front-page feature, running through page three, which included a photo of the mayor, excerpts of the court's ruling, and a mood piece titled "Ruling Cheers Many: They're Ready to Move." The latter article opened: "A lot of people in Poletown seemed relieved yesterday after the Michigan Supreme Court ruled that the city of Detroit can proceed with acquiring their neighborhood for a General Motors Corp. plant. Contrary to the message of Poletown supporters (that the residents want to stay where they are), people were getting ready to spend the checks they get from Detroit for their old homes on newer homes and other items."[28]

The article shows the problem that beset every report about Poletown. No one could ascertain the numbers of people who wanted to stay versus those who wanted to leave. However, to report the court loss as a cheerful event was certainly insensitive and misleading. In addition, the second paragraph was peculiar in that it didn't identify the "message of Poletown supporters" as coming from Poletown residents, nor did it identify the "people" who were champing at the bit to spend their city checks beyond the three people quoted in the article.

The court's ruling indicated that five of the justices felt "the city presented substantial evidence of the severe economic conditions facing the residents of the city and state. . . . and the lack of other adequate sites." The justices added the city had in mind "the essential public purposes of alleviating unemployment and revitalizing the economic base of the community. If the public benefit was not so clear and significant, we would hesitate to sanction approval of such a project. In [this] case the benefit to be received by the municipality. . . . is sufficient to satisfy this court. *The benefit to a private interest is merely incidental*" (emphasis added). [29]

The two dissenting justices disagreed violently, saying the decision was "unprecedented" and could lead to "the most outrageous confiscation of private property for the benefit of other private interests without redress. . . . The potential abuse in the use of eminent domain power is clear. Condemnation places the burden of aiding industry on the few, who are likely to have limited power to protect themselves from the excesses of legislative enthusiasm for the promotion of industry."

Justice Ryan added:

> There may never be a clearer case than this of condemning land for a private corporation. The reverberating clang to its economic, sociological, political and jurisprudential impact is likely to be heard for generations.... Behind the frenzy of political activity was the unmistakable guiding and sustaining, indeed controlling, hand of General Motors Corp. The evidence then is that what General Motors wanted, General Motors got. The corporation conceived the project, determined the cost, allocated the financial burdens, selected the site, established the mode of financing, imposed specific deadlines for clearance of the property and taking title, and even demanded 12 years of tax concessions.... The location of the CIP is, to say the least, solely a result of conditions laid down by General Motors, which were designed to further its private, pecuniary interests. Those are facts of private significance. The level of employment at the new GM plant will be determined by private corporate managers primarily with reference, not to the rate of regional employment, but to profit.
>
> When the private corporation to be aided by eminent domain is as large and influential as General Motors, the power of eminent domain, for all practical purposes, is in the hands of the private corporation. The municipality is merely the conduit. Eminent domain is an attribute of sovereignty. When the individual citizens are forced to suffer greater social dislocation to permit private corporations to construct plants where they deem it most profitable, one is left to wonder who the sovereign is.
>
> What has been done in this case can be explained by the overwhelming sense of inevitability that has attended the litigation from the beginning; attributable to the combination and coincidence of the interests of a desperate city administration and a giant corporation willing and able to take advantage of the opportunity that presented itself. The justification for it, like the inevitability of it, has been made to seem more acceptable by the "team spirit" chorus of approval of the project which has been supplied by the voices of labor, business, industry, government, finance, and even the news media. Virtually the only discordant sounds of dissent have come from the miniscule minority of citizens most profoundly affected by this case, the Poletown residents whose neighborhood has been destroyed.
>
> With this case the Court has subordinated a constitutional right to private corporate interests. By its decision, the Court has altered the law of eminent domain in this state in a most significant way, and, in my view, seriously jeopardizes the security of all private property ownership.[30]

The mayor rejected Nader's allegations that the ruling came from a "GM court" and said it was a "far-reaching" vindication. "Detroit is undergoing an economic crisis," he said. "We have to be able to find some way of rearranging our people in order to be able to attract and accommodate new plants." Any further attempts to halt the project would amount to "conscious sabotage" and "shooting dice with Detroit's economic future. Nader doesn't live here. He doesn't know a damn thing about plant design. He comes in. He sues. He leaves."[31]

Fr. Karasiewicz, of course, saw it from a different perspective. He told the *Detroit Free Press*: "We're fighting for a principle—the principle that 'eminent domain' does not apply for private business. This is not a public necessity. This is a diabolic precedent that makes no one safe. Any mayor, any corporation will be able to destroy anything they please."[32]

But insult was added to injury. The *Free Press* reported that the mayor's press secretary jubilantly carried a hand-made poster through city hall after the court decision. It showed a hand making an obscene gesture; the name "Nader" was emblazoned across it. The next day that same poster was hoisted high in a pro-plant demonstration that was designed to appear as if it was an indigenous Poletown demonstration.

Jim Paczkowski, chairman of the Central Industrial Park Project Citizen District Council—the same agency that Olechowski warned early on would have no real power except to rubber stamp the project, told the *Free Press* that the supreme court decision was great, adding, "I think it's giving the majority of the people the justice they want."

The pro-plant rally was greeted with loud headlines in both dailies' Sunday papers. The *Free Press* story, titled "Rally in Poletown Celebrates Court Approval of GM Plant," was accompanied by a photograph of a largely black crowd carrying a huge drum and signs that read: "Job Creation, not Job Elimination," "Jobs will keep Detroit ALIVE," "March 13, 1981: Smile Detroit." "It was more than just a show of support for GM's plan to build a new assembly plant in Poletown on the Detroit-Hamtramck border," the story began. "The rally Saturday morning in Poletown felt more like a celebration. About 150 Poletown residents and business people turned out for a boisterous march that began . . . in front of the old Dodge Main, a landmark in the neighborhood for 71 years. In the background, a wrecking ball could be seen smashing away at the plant."[33]

The *News'* front-page story was titled: "Poletown: Its Spirit Fades as Neighborhood Dies." On the jump page the *News* carried a full page of maps and photos sandwiched between copy that indicated Poletown's struggle was over. Arthur Parker, a Poletown businessman, was quoted as saying, "The neighborhood is like a mouth with one tooth." What had just been authorized by the court had apparently already been accomplished by the vandals, scavengers, and arsonists. "Demolition, the unofficial kind, had been going on for weeks," the story observed. "Some blocks of homes look like ghost blocks, most of the houses already vacated and only an occasional light in a kitchen where someone hangs on. Housestrippers have descended as fast as the Poletowners have left. Aluminum siding is stripped from some houses, metal fencing has been skinned off at other homes and the fence poles. Bannisters, doors, wood molding—all have been carried off."[34]

The *News'* story made repeated reference to people's fear. The elderly were quoted as saying that they had trouble sleeping and were very eager to get out. Paczkowski indicated again that the silent majority wanted to leave. The pro-plant rally seemed to indicate this was true.

A month went by—an excruciatingly significant one for Poletown's future—before residents and Detroit newspaper readers learned that the $500 tab for bussing 175 people into the supposedly indigenous pro-plant rally had been picked up by New Detroit. In an irate April 15 letter, Richard Hodas chastised the board of New Detroit for involving itself in the Poletown struggle. "When New Detroit funds a demonstration," he said, "that advances the financial interest of its officers and board of trustees—which includes Roger B. Smith, chairman of General Motors, the heads of both other major domestic auto companies, two other GM officials including recently retired chairman Thomas Murphy, and Ben Maibach, chairman of Barton-Malow, which will build the plant—it raises serious questions about the organization's 'charitable' and 'civic' nature."[35]

New Detroit president Walter Douglas told the *Free Press* that Richard Hodas "is full of ——. Quote me on that. There's nothing secret about us. We're not the CIA. He's trying to imply that New Detroit is a front organization for business and that's bull ——." Douglas added that there was nothing wrong with providing the buses. "We bus welfare mothers to Lansing, too, when they ask us.[36]

The Poletown Neighborhood Council stayed busy during the rest of the month. Members wrote letters to Congress and other groups they hoped would decide to help. They held a balloon release with church-shaped tags asking people to write to Roger Smith. They appealed to the Detroit Economic Club, asking for a forum on Poletown. They wrote to Edmund Szoka, the new archbishop designate and the first Pole named for the position. And they heard Andrew Miller, of Laborers Local 334, explain that he'd been fired from the Dodge Main demolition crew after complaining about the community's exposure to asbestos. Miller also said that only 100 of the 3,000 promised demolition jobs at the site had materialized.

In return the PNC won the support of the Polish National Alliance, which wrote to Governor Milliken that the destruction of the neighborhood was indefensible. But they also received a ninety-day eviction notice for the Immaculate Conception Church and learned that title to the last remaining 190 parcels had been taken by the city.

One Saturday in March a cluster of women stood on the street. A house on Milwaukee was in flames, the third in a line of charred homes. A woman sobbed over and over again that two men had broken into her basement a half hour earlier. Knowing that the elderly woman who owned the house was napping and deaf, she had stood at the top of her stairs and yelled, "I'm getting my gun and I've called the police." The men fled, even though she had neither a gun nor a phone on the second floor. Even as the women talked, a garage caught fire behind them.

At PNC meetings, safety became a primary topic. The Nader team offered to put frightened neighbors in phone connection with each other. "The police department has the same attitude about Poletown as Mayor Young does," Olechowski remarked. "In fact, I wouldn't be surprised if they were instructed not to spend much time in the area." Gene Stilp noted that "gasoline smells are rampant in the neighborhood. Eight houses were lost in one weekend."

Soon rumors were circulating that the Economic Development Corporation had recommended that Poletown's problems be escalated in order to drive people out. As the pressure escalated, some residents made it clear that while they were still hoping to preserve their homes and churches, they were fighting above all for a principle. The political maneuvers and victories of the city, in combination with the destruction in the neighborhood, made a Poletown triumph seem unlikely. But for the sixty to 100 residents who continued to attend the PNC meetings (as well as others who did not make themselves publicly visible), the struggle was worth something in and of itself.

On March 20, Fr. Karasiewicz mailed a letter to Roger Smith inviting him to recant:

> General Motors is hurting and may well continue hurting even more in the foreseeable future. I cannot, I dare not gloat over this, because General Motors is people, and as people, it is an essential part of our beloved country. I may well be too simple-minded, but please bear with me just the same as I share with you the following thought:

General Motors could well call a brief press conference and announce something to this effect: "In studying the present Cadillac plant controversy, we have come to the simple, humble conclusion that the alternatives presented by the opposition do have merit. With this in mind, we will build accordingly—right here in the Detroit Hamtramck area. We will not be the cause of any community disruption; rather, we will help repair what disruption has already occurred in the process, and help renovate. We will build, and work, and live in harmony with all in the community." Can you imagine what a sensation this would cause, and what a feeling of mutual love and respect this would generate throughout our beloved country? And all of us would be victors, particularly General Motors. Really and sincerely, I wish you well. God Bless you![37]

On March 31 Poletown resisters gained an unlikely ally. The president of the Council for a Competitive Economy, a Washington-based lobbying group representing medium-range businesses including Getty Oil, came to blast GM for its conduct. Richard Wilcke told Poletown residents and the Detroit media that GM's role in Detroit's land grab was a "shameful . . . violation of property rights and repudiation of free enterprise. Eminent domain, government subsidies and loan guarantees do not constitute voluntary exchange, but its very opposite. Our organization is unalterably opposed to their use in the procurement of plant sites, or for any other purpose, 'public' or private. . . . The right to own homes or a business should not be subordinated to the political or economic gain of others. This is not an issue of business versus the people, but rather of liberty versus political power. We condemn anyone who aspires to use that power for any purpose. . . . As this case clearly and dramatically demonstrates, if property rights are not respected, there can be no rights at all."[38]

The Detroit media were perplexed that an advocate of business could criticize GM and asked how he felt about being on the same side of the fence with Nader. "Ralph Nader is on our side here," Wilcke replied. "I'm glad he's defending property rights in this case."

April 1 was a red-letter day in Poletown. Major discussions about the GM project's future began both in federal court and in the city council chambers. At the council hearing members were asked to designate the affected part of Poletown as a special tax district. It was understood that a 50 percent, twelve-year tax abatement valued at $120 million would follow. Walter Jakubowski, an officer of the PNC and member of the Citizens District Council, came with prepared testimony but was allowed only one minute to speak. He made a stab at summarizing the PNC's questions about the city's use of eminent domain, its unwillingness to consider alternatives, and the foolishness of granting GM a tax abatement valued at $120 million over twelve years.

The council heard city planner Maurice Loper echo some of Jakubowski's reservations when he said, "The city has already made extraordinary efforts to get this site prepared for GM. Any extra incentive, such as a tax abatement, is not needed." Loper added that "in St. Louis, a generous abatement was offered and they [GM] decided not to build there anyway. Meanwhile, GM built in Baltimore without a tax abatement. Tax abatements are not the overriding factor in a GM decision to build or not to build." The city planning commission also advised the council to reject the abatement.[39]

However, GM and CEDD officials insisted the abatement would be necessary. "We have no alternative plans [to build somewhere else] at this time," GM vice president David Potter told the council. "But without the tax abatement, we will have to go back and rethink the project to see if it still makes economic sense. Our position is that a tax abatement makes it more economically attractive to stay in Detroit. Without a tax abatement, it is not as economically attractive and we will have to go back and rethink it. With the abatement we will still be paying more taxes here than in other areas."[40]

Had the council questioned Potter as carefully as David Moberg questioned Donald Postma for *In These Times*, they might have learned why, corporate rhetoric about good citizenship notwithstanding, GM was insisting on a tax abatement. "We would be remiss to stockholders if we said we decided not to ask for a tax abatement," Postma said. "This is the system that exists, and now we are building the plant, and we would be derelict if we didn't take advantage of what is available. . . . This is similar to deductions available to us in filing tax returns. If they are available under the law, why shouldn't we take advantage of it?"[41]

City officials told the council that even with the abatement they would experience a net gain. Bob Holland of CEDD said the affected area in Poletown used to generate $732,000 a year in property taxes. Even with the abatement, Holland said, GM would pay the city $2.4 million a year.

The council was divided on the wisdom of the abatement. It had just been informed by the mayor that the city was in a state of economic crisis and that taxes would have to be raised. Council chairperson Erma Henderson complained that the mayor "talked of reducing services, freezing employees' wages, cutting back on police and fire services and other drastic measures. I think it's time for GM to really understand what this city is going through. We're carrying quite a load. . . . How can we in good faith give GM a tax break?"[42] Councilperson Ken Cockrel, of course, agreed with her, saying: "I don't see how we can justify giving a multibillion-dollar corporation tax relief when we are asking our citizens to dig down into their own pockets."[43]

On the other hand, councilperson Nicholas Hood argued, "The tax abatement must be approved. The city's budget deficit will be here no matter what happens. But by granting GM a tax abatement, we would be saving some 6,000 jobs and increasing the amount of taxes GM would eventually pay to the city."[44]

Councilperson Clyde Cleveland predicted a four-to-four deadlock. At the end of the day, Henderson scheduled continued hearings on the topic for April 13, the soonest she felt they could address it. However, when Emmett Moten interjected that in order to accommodate GM the issue had to be resolved earlier and when Potter reiterated that any delay might prevent GM from opening in time to produce 1984-model-year cars, Henderson moved the hearing up to April 3.

On April 3 when some Poletown residents were expecting to drive down to city hall for the tax district vote, the morning *Free Press* carried headlines that the matter had been decided April 2. In a surprise move Henderson had called for a vote on the tax abatement one day early. In an astounding reversal, all but one of the four council members who had vowed to oppose the tax abatement voted for it. Clyde Cleveland explained his shift by saying that "Emmett Moten said they had other offers. He said they had three real strong offers. He said they were backing off, and that if we did not approve it, they would pick another site."[45]

Ken Fireman reported the council's approval of the abatement this way:

> Last week's turnabout was startling, even for veteran city hall observers who have grown accustomed to the council's irresolution in the face of strong pressure from the mayor's office. . . . What caused this abrupt switch, according to sources familiar with the situation, was an intensive telephone lobbying campaign the night of April 1 by Mayor Young and his major domo for development projects, Emmett Moten. Young and Moten told council members that GM would pull out of the project if the abatement were not granted, sources said. And Young bluntly threatened political retaliation against those who opposed him. "They [council members] came in Thursday looking like they had been whipped," said one council staffer.
>
> Two things seem clear in the wake of this episode. The first is that council members, for all their complaints about how Young abuses them, have absolutely no stomach for standing up to the mayor on an issue of

importance to him. The second is that neither Young nor the council has any stomach for standing up to a large corporation such as General Motors when tax breaks are at stake. Opponents of the GM abatement argue the automaker would have backed down if the city had called its bluff. Perhaps they are wrong—but no one will ever know until someone tries.[46]

Fireman's article drew the ire of Mayor Young who lashed out: "This particular story . . . is a damn lie. It's a shame for any responsible person to tell a lie like that because it sets elected public servants at each other's throats."[47]

In the meantime, Poletown residents were attending the three-week federal trial before U.S. District Court Judge John Feikens. Hugh Davis, the Detroit attorney filing the federal suit, complained that Detroit was given an emergency waiver on the EIS because of GM's May 1 deadline for land acquisition. The waiver enabled Detroit to receive federal funds immediately and to compile an abbreviated EIS.

"If all it takes to get an emergency waiver is for a corporation to set an arbitrary date, there will never be a regular application of the law," Davis said. "That's an issue which many more people than the people in Poletown care about."[48] Davis also objected that the city knew when it put the EIS together that it was planning to confirm the GM plant's construction in Poletown. "The purpose of the EIS is to determine what the harms are going to be and to see if there are any ways to avoid the harms," and this was never done, Davis said. He told the press that one reason GM would refuse to have a parking deck built south of its administration building was that the corporation was afraid that someday urban guerrillas might shoot from the parking deck into the offices. The company wanted the plant and its offices totally insulated, he said.

Judge Feikens had gained a liberal reputation by ruling in favor of women who claimed sex discrimination at Triple-A and by leaving control of the metropolitan water supply in the hands of Mayor Young, despite suburban complaints.[49] In the Poletown case Feikens was brusque and impatient with John Sims and Bruce Terris, Ralph Nader's Washington attorneys who were flown in to try the case. When one objected that he did not understand why the judge was willing to presume the parties were bound by GM's timetable, Feikens said, "Well, I did, so let's knock it off."

Sims summarized his objection to the city's preparation of the EIS, saying, "If you limit yourself to these options, you might as well not do an environmental impact statement. They were doing an EIS where the conclusion was foregone. They sleepwalked their way through considering the alternatives."

The designs which would allow the neighborhood and plant to co-exist were presented to the court by Richard Ridley, a Washington architect who modified alternatives proposed earlier by Detroit architect Michael J. McCleer. Ridley's first proposed alternative cut 165 acres out of the plant's area by including two parking decks, reducing the amount of greenspace, and eliminating the ring road. In the second option some greenspace was eliminated and the whole plant was shifted north. This design required the demolition of some forty homes in Hamtramck. The third option involved turning the assembly plant to face east onto Joseph Campeau.[50] The fourth proposal, similar to the first, moved the plant north of East Grand Boulevard and relied on two-story parking structures, but it proposed putting the administrative offices above one of the parking decks.

Ridley testified that each of his designs allowed GM room for 20 to 30 percent expansion. Feikens asked if he had consulted GM about how much expansion room it required and Ridley said he had not. Under cross examination Ridley was criticized by city attorneys for the lack of detail in his drawings. Ridley responded that they were drawn to the scale ordinarily required in Environmental Impact Statements.

Feikens's questions often reversed roles and put Poletown and its lawyers on trial. On April 7 Feikens asked, "How can I be concerned about the Immaculate Conception Church if the cardinal has already sold it? What are you trying to do, preserve some kind of a blighted area?" He also demanded that Sims state whether he was trying to kill the GM project. Feikens showed little appreciation for the community's right to have the constitutional issues addressed without having to prove its own worth first. Residents pointed out that since Poletown was not condemned under the slum clearance provisions, consideration of its blight or beauty was irrelevant. They added, of course, that much of the area's blight was the direct result of the announcement of the GM project.

Bernice Kaczynski explained to the court that her last home had been bulldozed to make room for a GM parking lot in Hamtramck. Kaczynski testified that she and her neighbors were as committed to rebuilding the neighborhood as they were to saving it. When city attorney Eric Clay questioned her expertise, she tried to respond but was cut off by Clay, the judge, and her own attorney. Kaczynski, trapped by legal procedure and unable to express herself fully, murmured over and over again: "It's not fair. It's just not fair." The rest of her testimony was spiritless.

DAVID C. TURNLEY

Richard Ridley, a Washington, D.C. architect, testified in court and made presentations in the neighborhood about several ways GM could build its new plant without destroying the neighborhood. One partial solution was to build a parking structure rather than flat parking lots.

When Richard Hodas took the stand, he told the court that his parents had owned a store on Chene street for thirty-five years, that he lived in a home on East Grand Boulevard, and that he owned several others. He recounted the history of his efforts to organize the merchants on Chene Street, explaining that just three months before the announcement of GM's project the merchants had raised $10,000 for an architectural and planning study of the area. He recounted Moten's early visit and his enthusiasm about Poletown. He added that Mayor Young had approved a $325,000 grant for senior-citizen home improvements with $100,000 already released by the council for the first year. He told the court about the day that Olechowski called saying the GM project was about to be announced, and he testified that Emmett Moten said to him and to Olechowski that the city doesn't "seem to have much choice, because General Motors handed us this footprint and told us that if we don't give them this plant they would move somewhere out of state."

Asked about Poletown's viability, Hodas said that he had conducted an unofficial survey of the neighborhood. According to his survey, 500 of the area's homes were still occupied, 171 homes might be occupied, 29 houses were vacant but boarded up and in good shape, 100 were vacant and damaged, 139 were significantly vandalized, and 22 were charred. Feikens asked what would happen if GM's project were turned around, and Hodas said that they would organize to get people into the vacant homes and continue to improve the neighborhood. William Christopher, an attorney hired to represent the city, told the court that only one merchant (of 144) and one Catholic church (of two) were still operating in the affected area.

Leonard Hotstetter, who helped design the GM proposed plan, testified that GM had considered alternate designs but had rejected them because parking structures would cause traffic delays for workers coming into and from work. He also said that the Detroit design was already smaller than the Oklahoma prototype. "It is the smallest of our new plants. It does not provide as much flexibility and as much expansion possibilities."[51]

Wayne Conn, a regional director for Conrail Railroad, insisted that Ridley's alternate designs were unusable because they didn't allow adequate rail curvature. Later Conn revealed that his company would lose a contract to a neighboring plant if the design were changed.[52]

Mayor Young testified to Detroit's desperate future and its dependence on the Poletown plant. Under cross-examination, he was asked about the discrepancy between GM's promised 6,000 jobs as compared to the probable 3,000. Young responded that he would have pursued this project for 2,000 jobs.

*   *   *

Poletown residents stayed busy throughout the hearings. On April 3 Barbara Andrews took Fr. Karasiewicz's place at a forum of religious leaders invited by Rep. Crockett. Andrews, a Poletown resident, criticized Crockett for supporting the Poletown project and for selling out black people in the process. Andrews repeated her complaint at a May 7 press conference:

> It's my peoples that wanted to grab up the money [involved in the Poletown project] because the white man telling them to. They got to wake up before it's too late, because the white man is going to trample them and they ain't going to have nothing to lose there. Put that in the news and tell my people to wake up and quit letting the white man tell them what to do. Give us our homes back. If I leave here, I'm still going to fight for this church. I'm not Catholic. I'm Baptist. But I serve God. I don't think it's right for General Motors or the city or nobody to come and take this church. What kind of God do they serve? Is the God they serve the God we serve? No, it's not, because they serve the devil—that's with money. And this church is to serve the people. This is the people's lives."

Andrews was also the first of six black residents to a sign a letter to Coleman Young, which read: "We are shocked at the way you, an elected official, are catering to the desires of General Motors at the expense of black people and other Detroit residents. . . . There is still time for you to demonstrate some courage and work to bring GM to the negotiation table—we mean the kind of courage that has been demonstrated by blacks fighting for basic civil liberties, for a seat on the bus, a place in the classroom, and a voice in the political arena."

Andrews's protest required particular courage. Her mother feared for her safety, saying that you don't just take on the mayor that way. Prior to Andrews's complaints, the mayor was inclined to characterize anyone who opposed the GM project as a racist. Andrews was the first black person in Poletown to throw the charge back at him publicly.

"A lot of people are afraid," Andrews explained. "Blacks are afraid. My family says, 'Why are you fighting for them?' My mother's afraid of me speaking. She thinks I'm going to get killed. But this community has a lot of mixture—it's a good neighborhood. As long as we hate one another, we'll never make a world and we poor will always be stepped on. We going to have to speak up. The rich peoples know that we can be heard."

On April 7 the *Free Press* carried a two-paragraph story which quoted a laid-off policeman who was opening his own private security agency as saying that he would be available to contain "terrorists" like anti-nuclear and Poletown activists.

Two days later, on the Detroit Tigers' opening day, Patrick Steele of the Advisory Council on Historic Preservation (ACHP) protested to city officials that they were violating their October agreement with ACHP. In that agreement Emmett Moten had promised to preserve historic structures in Poletown, in exchange for that agency's approval of federal funds. Steele was assured that the city would provide ACHP with data about the historic structures, along with information about steps that could be taken to preserve the structures or the ornamentation.[53] The mayor, meanwhile, was at the ballpark throwing the Tigers' first pitch. Poletown supporters in the bleachers held up a huge banner reading "Poletown Lives!"

On April 10, residents appealed to the governor for protection from arson and vandalism. A letter, signed by six residents and Frs. Skalski and Karasiewicz, reported to Milliken that "the City of Detroit, in conjunction with GM, is engaged in a program to destroy a significant portion of the neighborhood. These abuses constitute a pattern of violence and intimidation that has been, and continues to be, condoned by elected officials of the City of Detroit. By failing to act swiftly to reverse this pattern, the city has declared open season on all residents of the Poletown Project Area—a declaration that constitutes nothing less than blatant official terrorism. This systematically inflicts lawlessness on a law abiding community, by terrorizing our elderly, victimizing the property owners, and undermining the businesses. As a result, city officials have inflicted fear, sickness, and despair upon these law-abiding citizens of Detroit." The signers asked Milliken to send the state police into the area.[54]

The city council voted to rezone Poletown for industrial use on April 13, but city officials were slapped the next day with a formal complaint from the Advisory Council for Historic Preservation. The ACHP indicated, in a telegram to the mayor, that the city was in violation of its October agreement and that demolition should stop. Steele said that he had finally received the promised data about Poletown's historic structures but that it was insufficient.[55] He also complained that the city had just recently torn down an 1890 Victorian home in Poletown, in violation of the assurances he had received just the previous week. Moten told the press that Steele's objection was based on "erroneous information," but before the end of the month these abuses would be raised in federal court and Hodas would report thirty-five similar abuses to the inspector general of HUD.[56]

On the same day that Steele sent the telegram to Young, Poletown residents received a visit from the leader of a community group opposing a GM project in Kansas City, Kansas. Richard Rosenthal told residents about the state of Kansas's maneuvers to float bonds to pay for GM's plant construction, the bond attorney's conflict of interest, the intimidation tactics used by the railroad, and the charges of racism that were aimed at those opposing the GM plant. Rosenthal surmised that if his community were successful in fighting off GM while Poletown was not, this would be partly due to class, since Piper Area residents were upper-middle class and had easy recourse to attorneys and the press. (See Appendix B.)

On income tax day, the city council approved the second step required in order to grant GM a tax abatement. Cockrel, the lone dissenter, complained that Moten's unwillingness to provide a copy of the development agreement between GM and the city "does not allow the council to know what it was voting on. The whole argument used all these years to support tax abatements—that it either creates new jobs or retains old ones—is something that has never been documented."[57]

On April 16 GM slipped from second to third on the Fortune 500 list and Poletown residents returned to Judge Feikens's court with a suit claiming violations of the Clean Air Act, the National Historic Preservation Act, and the Environmental Protection Act during demolition. Residents complained to the court that buildings "with possible historic significance" had already been destroyed. The following evening twenty Poletown residents and supporters took candles out to Roger Smith's neighborhood in Bloomfield Hills and held a vigil close to his house.

A week later Judge Feikens ruled that the city had acted responsibly in choosing to clear the Poletown site for General Motors and that the federal government did nothing wrong in releasing funds prior to completion of the EIS. He reached this conclusion despite the fact that he had the opportunity to review the newly released dissenting supreme court decision which slammed the project.[58] "It is now clear to me," Feikens said, "that all the acreage in the proposed area is needed for the new plant." Feikens said that the economic benefits of the plant construction outweighed the environmental cost to Poletown.[59]

In late April the Nader support team spoke with two black Poletown pastors who were upset because the city's money offer for their churches was inadequate for them to move to someplace comparable. Rev. Arkless Brooks, pastor of the Gospel Chapel Church on East Grand Boulevard, told Sandy Livingston that city officials "don't consider anything. They just want you to take what they offer you. And that's nothing." Brooks said he was offered $65,000 for his church, seven-room parsonage, and parking lot. "I'm so disappointed, I'll never

DAVID C. TURNLEY

Fr. Malcolm Maloney, rector of St. John's Roman Catholic Church in Poletown, said he had deep sympathy for the black pastors in Poletown, who received nothing like the $2.8 million the archdiocese received for its churches. Many of the storefront churches received only $60,000 and had the added problem of rebuilding a congregation after moving.

trust city hall again." Brooks said he was less frustrated with the mayor than with officials at CEDD who, he said, "won't tell you what they know." Rev. James Smith, of the Greater Triumph Missionary Baptist Church on the Edsel Ford Freeway, wrote to city officials that he'd been offered $39,000 for his church. "With what they are offering for our church we can't afford to move," he lamented. "All we ask is a little consideration. We don't want to go back to where we came from, but with $30,000 we can't even buy a storefront."[60]

On the last day of April, just one day before GM's planned ground breaking, six archdiocesan officials and two city officials came unexpectedly to the Immaculate Conception Church to evict Fr. Joseph Karasiewicz. The eight men requested all records of births, deaths, and weddings as well as the keys to the church. Karasiewicz explained that he had a letter from the city allowing him to remain until June 17 and that Bishop Krawczak had told him that the April 30 moving date was negotiable. When the eight persisted, Karasiewicz went down to the basement to ask the Nader team for support.

Karasiewicz later explained that Gerald Chuhran, from the archdiocesan real estate office, had called earlier in the week to say that he would come by with a man from Turner Construction but that he hadn't specified the purpose of the visit. "When he finally came, he said, 'This is the day.' Of course, I was very much upset about it. He had that smirky look on his face and he said, 'This is it. We want the keys and the books.' They had their van from the chancery to haul everything away. They had the men to do the hauling. And I have to say, I lost my cool. I probably never lost it in all my life." Karasiewicz laughed and dropped his voice, "I was calling all of them *barbarians*."

Members of the Nader team immediately alerted the press and Poletown residents, many of whom were in court for the federal hearings on their second suit. John Richard, of the support team, took Karasiewicz aside and jotted down the morning's events. Gradually the basement filled. Reporters from all three TV stations, both dailies, and both wire services gathered in one group, while residents greeted each other. Josephine Jakubowski, one of the first to arrive, walked around in a daze repeating, "That's terrible. God almighty, that's terrible. What are they trying to do to people?" Her niece, Ann Locklear, arrived angry. As she watched the scene, her body began to tremble and then tears slid silently down her cheeks. When Karasiewicz moved to comfort her, both dailies caught photographs of him holding her beneath the "GM Mark of Destruction" sign that was pasted high on the basement wall.

The Nader team distributed Richard's notes from his conversation with Karasiewicz to the reporters. Some of the media followed Vicar Robinson back into the rectory, but the group there withdrew into one room and refused interviews. Karasiewicz told the press: "I'm not bucking any one person, I'm bucking evil, so to speak. If there's evil in the chancery, then I'm bucking evil there."

A meeting was arranged between Karasiewicz and Dearden for 3:15 that afternoon. Fr. Skalski, of St. Hyacinth's, accompanied Karasiewicz, but Dearden refused to allow Richard or Gene Stilp to sit in on the meeting. Residents picketed outside, chanting,

> Cardinal Dearden, man of God,
> you have joined the GM squad;
> Cardinal Dearden, with his cross,
> sold us out to the GM boss;
> Cardinal Dearden, we all know,
> sold us out for a stack of dough;
> Cardinal Dearden, won't you say,
> save the church for people to pray.

After an hour, Karasiewicz emerged, saying he'd been given an extension until May 13. He said Dearden told him that he had gone "to great lengths to speak with the city and to get this concession from them." Dearden drafted an April 30 letter which said, "I personally intervened to delay this action until Monday, May 11, in order that you would have time to announce this matter to your parishioners at the Sunday masses this weekend and prepare to celebrate a final liturgy on May 10." He enclosed a decree of suppression dated May 11. Karasiewicz was to vacate May 13.

In the aftermath the Nader team learned that Karasiewicz had previously received a letter from the archdiocese indicating that he would have to be out by April 30. But he also had a letter from the city saying he had until June 17, and another letter from the archdiocese saying that he could observe the city's timeline. Russell Chambers, a city official, claimed the city and archdiocese had agreed to waive the June 17 date and exchange the property on April 30.

Karasiewicz said one of the things that hurt him most was that Chuhran and the others had come to evict him prior to any communication from the cardinal about where he was to go next. "In spite of the things that have happened here," he said later, "in spite of that notorious day when a group of people came in to boot me out. . . . I would say that I don't think it was intended as such. I think personally that God had blinded them . . . in their hurry to do what they wanted to do to boot me out. And God had blinded them to the fact that they didn't think about the most primary thing, what to do with me. . . . Not that I care about myself, but normally you would say, 'Well, we'll provide for you' or 'We'll keep in touch with you.' Anything like that."

One of Dearden's demands on April 30 was that the Nader team be evicted from the church basement. But nonetheless, Karasiewicz renewed the Nader team's lease for use of the church basement. The team had paid $10 for its use every month. The renewed contract promised to give Nader's staffers the status of renters in court when it came time for eviction.

On May 1, "May Day" to many but "Law Day" to others, headlines announced that the state supreme court had agreed to consider whether Hodas's rights were denied him by unclear city instructions about the process to be used in filing an objection to the taking of property.

Meanwhile, over at the Old Dodge Main GM held a groundbreaking ceremony. The mayors of Detroit and Hamtramck were on hand. Young told the press: "This could mean the difference between a greater Detroit and a deteriorated Detroit. If the flak goes with it, it's a cheap price to pay for progress."[61] David Turnley, a photographer for the *Free Press*, said he thought the time for the ground breaking was kept secret to avoid confrontations with protestors. He received a call to go to the GM headquarters and was told there to proceed to Poletown.

On May 4 Cardinal Dearden called Karasiewicz down to the chancery and told him that the Immaculate Conception Church would be suppressed as of May 10, regardless of any changes in the city's timetable or any appeals by the Nader team. He also recommended that Karasiewicz stay with Skalski at St. Hyacinth's after May 13. "For the most part, he was calm," Karasiewicz told Gene Stilp later. "I think he was perhaps disappointed that I was adamant about my thoughts, and I am sure he realized that, the way I was speaking, I would continue doing what I felt I should be doing."

That afternoon Dearden made a special trek out to one of the most elite suburban malls to bless a Gucci shoe store. Dearden stood near the women's accessories and prayed that customers see "the beauty that is captured and expressed by the human artist in his handiwork." He went on to say, "All about us here we see evidence of human artistry—may it lead us to You, the source of all that is beautiful. In that spirit we beg your blessing, Almighty Father, upon this enterprise, those who labor here, those whose craftsmanship is displayed here, those who will possess and enjoy these artistic creations. May we all be moved by

Mayor Coleman Young of Detroit (left) joined hands with the mayor of Hamtramck, Robert Kozaren (center), and Roger Smith, chairman of GM (right), at the groundbreaking for the new Cadillac plant. In the background stand the remains of Chrysler's old Dodge Main plant, which was also destroyed to provide a 465-acre site for GM.

a spirit of reverence and humility in our lives. We ask this in the name of the risen Christ, our savior, Amen."[62] In response, Poletown residents hung large banners on the outside walls of the Immaculate Conception Church reading "DEARDEN blessed GUCCI while destroying Polish shrine" and simply "GUCCI."

Karasiewicz's feelings about the archdiocese were increasingly mixed but always expressed in a quiet, respectful tone. Clearly, the priest believed the archdiocese's cooperation with the GM project was a sin and felt personally hurt by some of his dealings with the church. On the other hand, he genuinely did not want to judge people or breed hostility. Consequently, his comments were full of denials and innuendos. "Is this an evil thing, the destruction of the church?" Karasiewicz asked. "Yes, absolutely, absolutely. This is the only reason I am fighting it." But asked whether evil people were responsible for the destruction, Karasiewicz responded, "Now you're going into judges and I can't judge. I don't want to judge people. I would say that the actions are evil, no doubt about that. We have every right to judge actions, but to go further and say this or that person is guilty before God of a sin, deserving of punishment. . . . No, I can't go into that, never will." And after Cardinal Dearden stated publicly that both parishes had been consulted before the parishes were sold, Karasiewicz responded, "If you would ask me now the nitty gritty question, 'Is he lying?' In itself, yes. I would say the statements are lies. To what extent should we accuse him of lying? No, I wouldn't revert to that." Karasiewicz's congregation knew what he meant, as did the media which often quoted him. But Karasiewicz artfully avoided strong, damning statements. Too much of Karasiewicz's heart was quite seriously entwined with his vocation as priest for him to want to harm the church.

SWAT Team Seizes the Church

> These people responsible for this are worse than the Communists in Poland. That's the message I gave them before. They might as well get it straight now. It's a criminal act. To go down to a very basic definition of stealing, it is simply taking somebody else's property against their will.
>
> —Father Joseph Karasiewicz

On May 5 Karasiewicz was quoted in the *New York Times* as saying that "the neighborhood is gone already. The mayor has seen to that. There's only a handful of people left. My hope now is to save the church."[1] Karasiewicz expressed the sentiments of a lot of people, although most of those continuing to resist the project were reluctant to say so. Increasingly it seemed that the only shred of victory Poletown residents might get to celebrate would be the saving of the church.

Judge Feikens handed down his ruling on Poletown's second suit on May 5, saying that he dismissed the Historic Preservation Act complaint because the city and the Advisory Council for Historic Preservation had come to a mutual agreement and had amended the memo regarding the alleged violations. He did not consider the project in violation of the Clean Air Act.

On May 6, the state supreme court considered Hodas's request for a hearing regarding his objections to the necessity of taking Poletown for the Cadillac plant. This was the hearing Judge Martin denied to him and to many others because their objections had not been filed as legal motions. The acting corporation counsel, Sylvester Delaney, was extremely confident. He told the *Detroit News* that word that the court might rule in Hodas's favor was "a damned lie. We are absolutely, unequivocally, dead right. So was the trial court, and the Supreme

Court will bear us out."[2]   Nonetheless, the court ruled that Hodas's rights had been violated and remanded the case back for a hearing to be set by Judge David Vokes.

The following day Vicar Robinson paid his third visit of the week to Fr. Karasiewicz. Afterwards, he stopped down into the basement and argued with Russell Mokhiber, of the Nader team, about their activities. When Mokhiber said they were fighting for people's rights, Robinson responded: "When this guy (Fr. Karasiewicz), when he ends up in the nuthouse and this building is down, you think about him. You catalyzed him. You motivated him." As Robinson spoke, Sandy Livingston, who was seated at a nearby desk, started typing notes of the conversation. Robinson declared that both Karasiewicz's job and health were in jeopardy and that the Nader team was to blame. He added that the team was overzealous and probably wouldn't leave until the last person in Poletown had died. Mokhiber tried to talk about the church's betrayal of the parishioners, mentioning Josephine Jakubowski, who had spent her life's blood supporting the parish, but Robinson said: "This is no human rights issue. Mrs. Jakubowski understood the system . . . otherwise she has been duped." Robinson said that the church would be emptied after the last mass on Sunday. "You won't have any more April 30ths around here. I believe there are going to be cops, there are going to be arrests." When the Nader team suggested that the mayor seemed reluctant to face the publicity which would come with arresting people, Robinson responded: "That's bullshit. The city's playing games. It's going to be a little more than that."[3]

That evening officials in the City-County Building noticed that "Poletown Lives!" stickers were plastered on the walls near the mayor's office. Poletown supporters were also flooding the city, the archdiocese, and GM with letters asking them to at least save the church. They asked that the church be allowed to remain in the midst of what would eventually be a parking lot. People knew of other instances where this had been done, even one in Detroit, where a Catholic church had been moved when a freeway ripped through its old location.

GM's Donald Postma answered one such letter sent to him by Sigrid Dale. Dale, a German immigrant who lived in the suburbs, visited Poletown after reading about it in the paper. She was motivated to help intervene in Poletown and in other situations where she perceived injustice partly because her father had been executed under Hitler. In his May 7 letter Postma said: "From our position . . . the problem is not so easily solved. First, we do not own the church—the archdiocese sold it to the city which cannot afford to keep it. If we were to obtain it from the city we would have to maintain it, and candidly, we don't think it is right for a private company to own and run a Christian church. There seem to be no other sources of funds available to maintain it either. . . . So you can see the quandary in which we all find ourselves."[4]

On May 8 Vicar Robinson returned to the Immaculate Conception Church and told Karasiewicz he was going down to ask the Nader team to leave. Karasiewicz said, "You're free to do that." Later he confided, "I felt the aides would be able to take care of themselves quite well. They did, you know." Robinson told John Richard: "I am here now as the official parishional representative of Cardinal Dearden to ask you to vacate this building immediately. In spite of any other welcome you might have had from minor delegations [meaning Karasiewicz]." Richard told Robinson that their tenancy was in litigation and that it would be resolved by the courts May 11. He sent a memo to Dearden via Robinson to that same effect. Robinson returned that night with a letter from the cardinal indicating that Karasiewicz should take a three-month sabbatical at St. Hyacinth's. Karasiewicz said he did not consider that a disciplinary move because it did attach him to an active church and allowed him to remain in the same area.

On May 9, the day before Mother's Day, residents took a bulldozer to Roger Smith's house. The Nader team called all over town before finding someone who was not worried about losing a possible GM demolition contract by making a bulldozer available for the demonstration. But once they found one, residents decorated it with flowers from their own gardens. They taped on signs which read: "Happy Mother's Day, Mrs. Smith, talk to Roger," "GM, Don't Bulldoze our Church," and, in the scoop, "Flowers for Mrs. Smith/A Bulldozer for Roger/Save Our Church." A caravan of twenty cars drove the fifteen miles to Roger Smith's house, following the bulldozer, which was loaded on a flatbed truck that belonged to George Smiley, a former school teacher.

Just outside the street leading into Smith's Bloomfield Hills neighborhood, three police cars stopped the caravan and said that without a parade permit they couldn't proceed to the house. So, while some people gathered outside a nearby school, twenty others approached the house with the bulldozer. Mrs. Giannini and Mrs. Jakubowski presented flowers to the security guard stationed at Smith's driveway. Bob Giannini said, "This is a gift from the mothers of Poletown to Mrs. Smith. They're hoping that her Mother's Day will be as happy as it is for them, seeing their homes and churches being destroyed by Mr. Smith and his people." The security guard kept repeating, "No comment," as two police officers watched from Smith's lawn. Later, Smith's neighbors complained that reporters had damaged the edge of their lawns while photographing the interchange.

The same day a *Detroit Free Press* story reported that most of the looters in Poletown came from the suburbs. Police officer Chris Wilson said she and her partner arrested seventy people in April and forty-two during the first nine days of May. "Most of them are from the suburbs and very, very far out," Wilson said. She added that two couples from the exclusive Farmington Hills suburb were apprehended in a vacant house. "It was like they were shopping," Wilson said. Items routinely stolen were heavy doors, stained-glass windows, fireplace mantles, storm windows, carpeting, plumbing, and furnaces.[5] Of course, arson continued to escalate as well. The Detroit Fire Department reported that during the first half of 1980 there were only thirty-three fires in Poletown, while during the first half of 1981 there were a hundred.[6]

On May 10 over 1,600 people came to the Immaculate Conception Church to participate in its last mass. Sandy Livingston was touched by Karasiewicz's consideration that morning. She came to take photographs and quickly realized she was going to be uncomfortable in blue jeans. When she saw "Fr. Joe," her "heart sank. I thought he'd probably tell me to leave. Instead he offered me a chair on the side of the altar, told me to make myself comfortable and told me he had no qualms about my taking the pictures. Needless to say, after about ten minutes of extreme discomfort, I went home and changed. I was struck by his consideration—especially since it was the last mass and he must have had a great deal on his mind. Although he was very conservative, he gave no hint that my jeans were inappropriate."

Karasiewicz preached at both services and was applauded when he said it was a sin to destroy "a house of prayer. This is not a supermarket. This is not a dance hall. This is a building dedicated to Christ and to prayer—to our blessed Lord and blessed Mother."[7] Karasiewicz told the congregation, which included a number of Polish Catholics and other well-wishers, that he had great respect for the Nader team. He commented on their hard work motivated by love and by principle, even though none of them were Polish or Catholic. He said he would like to kiss their feet. Fr. Skalski attended, as did the Polish dancers in full dress. There were flag brigades and honor guards. During the afternoon a vigil began and Karasiewicz suggested that they "would storm the gates of heaven with prayer." He said he'd raise the issue with Bishop Szoka after his May 12 installation as archbishop following Dearden's retirement.[8] Some of the vigilers decided to stay the night. Gene Stilp trained Carol Dockery, Nick Kubiak, Bernice and Harry

Kaczynski in nonviolent resistance. He explained ways of going limp when placed under arrest.

Monday May 11 dawned cold and damp. While lawyers for the city and for Poletown prepared to square off over the proper eviction date for the ICC, Poletown residents were barricaded in the church basement. Walter Duda guarded the door, determining if visitors could be trusted by peering through the tiny glass window in the basement door. A two-by-four was wedged in the handle to make the door secure. Waiting inside the church were Walter and Josephine Jakubowski, Carol Dockery, Ann Giannini, John Saber, Barney Topolewski (the organist), George Smiley, and Bernice Kaczynski. Harry Kaczynski decided to leave because he said he knew that if the police laid a hand on him he would react violently.

By 9:55 A.M., according to Sandy Livingston's journal, there was still no word from court. Stilp called everyone together and explained the possible scenarios, and then Duda told stories about his union days, particularly times when they stopped scab labor by parading women and children in front of the plant at starting time. Two filmmakers waited upstairs in the rectory watching for police.

At 10:30 A.M. Mokhiber called Wayne County Circuit Court Judge Richard Kaufman's court and learned that the hearing was still in progress. Then Hodas called again and learned that Kaufman had ruled that Karasiewicz could remain in the church until June 17, as originally indicated in the letter Karasiewicz had received from the city. However, Kaufman said that the Poletown Neighborhood Council and the Poletown Support Team would have to leave within forty-eight hours.

Livingston's notes indicate that by 1:00 P.M. "things have died down and as traditionally happens this was signified by Mrs. Jakubowski bringing out the perogies and white bread." Skalski came by in the afternoon to join the vigil and to pray. Emmett Moten told the press that the city would not move to destroy the church until June 17, since it was attached to Karasiewicz's rectory.[9]

That afternoon Chuhran and Robinson came by and told Karasiewicz they wanted to know when they could pick up the church records. For a moment they seemed to indicate that they would take the rectory furniture with them. Karasiewicz argued that since the Albanian congregation which worshiped at Immaculate Conception needed their records separated from the whole, he would retain custody of them. Robinson said the archdiocese could separate the records, but Karasiewicz refused. Robinson promised to be back the next day and added that Karasiewicz could no longer use church funds to pay the utility bills or other church expenses. Robinson said Karasiewicz's checking account would be closed out. Any collection plate money coming in also belonged to the archdiocese, Robinson warned.

Archdiocesan officials told the press that the suppression of the church meant that "Immaculate Conception no longer exists, that all sacred vestments, communion vessels and other church objects are to be removed and that no public masses or other services may be held in the church."[10]

At 8:30 P.M. Livingston wrote: "What an outpouring of support. Over forty people are upstairs praying. I don't think the church has been empty since the vigil began yesterday afternoon. Not just Detroit, but from surrounding suburbs and townships miles away. And there's the phone calls coming fast and furious. The man from Santa Barbara [California] who read Ralph Nader's column in the paper and wants to be sure we have a working knowledge of homesteading law. The man from outside Detroit who knows of a church in Detroit preserved while a waste water treatment plant was built around it. And reports from a Jewish attorney who knows canon law, summaries of her calls to Rome, to the apostolic delegate, to the Chancery office. . . . While new faces pray upstairs, old familiar ones strategize and rehash over beers at distant tables. . . . The media returns periodically to check up on the vigil, measure our resolve and take a few pictures—some are incredulous, others sympathetic, few leave these days without confiding that they think (just between you and them) there must be some sort of compromise that can be discussed. . . . "

Just after midnight there were twenty-two people upstairs in the church praying, despite the fact that bulldozers were outside destroying seven houses nearby, including the house immediately next to the rectory. Gene Stilp and Paul Stern, two of Nader's staff, stayed the night. Olechowski's car was egged. Sometime during the night a city employee parked outside the church and sat watch all night.

On May 12 the *Detroit Free Press* published an editorial by Joe Stroud, headlined "Pain Is Real, But Can the Church Be Saved?"[11] Stroud aired, in a somewhat maudlin manner, his own feelings attending the last mass at Immaculate Conception Church. Stroud's position and that of the *Free Press* had been explicitly pro-demolition, so it was frustrating to some residents when Stroud presented an editorial, grounded in pure emotionalism, which argued for saving only the church.

". . . on Sunday at Immaculate Conception, I found myself stirred by the sobbing of Polish women near me," Stroud wrote in the editorial. "I found myself angered at the ravages of time and the impersonal forces of change in the city. Much of the service was in Polish, but the language of pain is universal." Stroud didn't know what made him go to the service; he'd had a visit from Karasiewicz a few days before but would have gone to the service anyway. He said he helped close his own United Methodist church when it consolidated with another, despite the pain involved in change. But Stroud added, "At the service I found myself thinking, 'What if this were my church, my neighborhood?' I would hurt, and it would heal no wounds to speak of the greater good, the need to preserve jobs and rebuild the city. It would not really comfort me for someone to say the neighborhood was already near death before the process of building this plant ever started. It would not comfort me to be reminded that death is sometimes a part of renewal."

Stroud concluded by saying that he would be placing some calls to the principal decision makers to see if the church couldn't actually be saved. "The choices the politicians or the community leaders or the church hierarchy made weren't easy. I'm sure they have thought, as I have, that what had to be done had to be done. But is there no room now for the healing gesture, the compassionate response? Is there no magnanimous act that could take the curse off this process? I really don't know. I only know that on Sunday I found my heart with those who wept and prayed at Immaculate Conception."

(It was tempting to ask where Stroud's heart was when Poletown residents first read the relocation information delivered to them by the police in July, or when the public hearings on the project erupted into shouting matches, or during the countless vigils which were just as evocative and which occurred early enough that an appeal from a *Free Press* editor might have made a difference.)

At 10 A.M., May 12, Chuhran returned and requested the church files. Fifteen residents who had been praying in the church went up to the rectory to greet him and to ask him to appeal to the cardinal, because they wanted to retain the files until Archbishop Szoka was installed. Karasiewicz later said that Chuhran was polite and professional during the interchange, but Stilp complained that Chuhran withdrew his hand abruptly when Stilp introduced himself.

That evening 200 people gathered for the Poletown Neighborhood Council meeting. Olechowski announced that 1,600 signatures had been obtained for a petition asking for the preservation of the church. He also praised the Nader team for conducting "themselves in an orderly fashion. When some of us have been all too inclined to push for quick and even violent solutions, they have calmed us down." Fr. Karasiewicz told the group about his morning exchange with archdiocesan officials. "I was elated that it was a very amicable meeting. I see hope for continued good relations with them. We're seeing more and more light. It's a battle for principle—to protect the places where we pray, where we live."

Some people present volunteered to start a boycott against the archdiocese, but Olechowski interjected that the archbishop "knows of our problems; he doesn't need to be rudely reminded of them." Olechowski also made reference to the possibility of a suit based on a 1983 Act, an act primarily invoked when a state deprives one of one's civil rights. The suggestion was made, as was so often true at PNC meetings, without any bearing on feasibility, expense, or likelihood of success and was never mentioned again. Someone else at the meeting proposed nationalizing Ford, GM, and AMC, recalling the city council, and building a whisky plant on the site of the old Dodge Main.

At midnight Karasiewicz and two parishioners were alone in the sanctuary. But soon thereafter a dozen elderly parishioners from St. Hyacinth's, including one woman who could barely walk, arrived to join their prayers.

The following day, on May 13, Pope John Paul II was shot. The Pope's cousin, John Edward Wojtjlo, who had been on the Hamtramck City Council for twenty years, came to pray at Immaculate Conception Church for the pope's health and for the future of the church. He took the liberty to call the press before his arrival.[12] The vigil continued with Duda still at the door with a two-by-four. Early morning was marked by the arrival of Josephine Jakubowski, Ann Dolence, and Jane Vogt, who went first to the sanctuary and then to staff the kitchen for all the others who would arrive.

On May 14, Cardinal Dearden's last day in office, Roger Smith called a press conference and announced that, partly as a result of Joe Stroud's editorial, GM was prepared to move the Immaculate Conception Church off site.[13] The corporation would spend millions refurbishing it, provide a parking lot, and give it back to the archdiocese. Smith told the press that his offer "may seem late in the proceedings. If you want to say we're bowing to public pressure, fine. We'd like to believe we're being socially responsible."[14]

When Fr. Karasiewicz heard the news, he ran from the rectory to the sanctuary, where five women were singing. He genuflected and kissed the tile in front of the altar, then clapped his hands for attention and said: "I just got the news. The church has been saved. Yes, it has been saved. Praise God."[15] The women fell to their knees in tears. Within minutes the church bells were ringing and continued ringing for two jubilant hours. Topolewski, the organist, celebrated more quietly by taking the Nader Support Team up into a room off the balcony to toast the victory with blueberry brandy.

By noon the cardinal and the mayor had rejected Smith's offer. The top officers of GM, the archdiocese, and the city met at the chancery and then called a press conference to announce that GM's offer had been refused. Plans were being laid instead to preserve artifacts from ICC for use in an honorary chapel in some existing church. "The modification to our proposal, as suggested by Cardinal Dearden, is a good one," Smith commented. "We'll continue to work with all concerned toward an equitable solution."[16] A press release quoted Dearden as saying about his last official act in office: "The prospect of relocating the church does not solve the basic problem of a congregation limited in numbers. Immaculate Conception parish no longer exists. For years, its membership has steadily declined. The Polish people who still reside in the area of the present church can readily be served by four existing Polish Catholic parishes all within a moderate distance from the project site."[17]

The whole interchange was a "charade, fabricated to counteract the bad publicity the automaker has been receiving over the Poletown issue," Walter Jakubowski told the *Michigan Catholic*.[18] "GM doesn't publicize anything without first clearing it with everyone involved, but in this case they never bothered to inform the cardinal or the parishioners about their proposal. It's just a 'fine gesture,' a way to save face. As for the modified proposal we couldn't agree to that. Wreck the church and assemble the pieces of it somewhere else? Never."

Press reports the next day indicated that Smith had not consulted the cardinal before holding the initial press conference. "They [archdiocesan officials] said the soonest we could get together was 11 o'clock to talk it over," GM's Donald Postma explained later. "For some scheduling reasons here, we said we were going to go ahead and make our announcement and see how it came out." Asked why GM hadn't waited for the cardinal's approval, Postma said: "It seemed to us it was better to get a specific proposal out there and then let them talk about it . . . rather than spending a lot more time chewing around eighty different ideas. We felt that it ought to get resolved one way or another, because it certainly was dragging on and it was not a good situation. This should lead to a resolution of some sort."[19] However, by May 16 a *Free Press* story made it clear that the cardinal *had* known in advance that GM planned to hold the press conference. According to reporter

Harry Cook, Postma called Dearden's office at 6 P. M., May 13, and told
the cardinal's secretary about the plan. Dearden's secretary, the Rev.
Dale Melczek, drove out to the cardinal's house, where dinner was
being prepared for the new archbishop and several other bishops.
During spirited discussion the church officials decided to refuse the
offer.[20]

Stroud, clearly shaken by the twist of events, wrote an editorial
which challenged some of his own original assumptions about the use
of eminent domain to clear the area. He wrote that he had visited ICC
after the GM press conference and felt joy after speaking with Karasiewicz. Driving back to the Free Press, through the rain he reflected:
"So often we miss what is there: the people, the neighborhoods, the
relationships, the institutions. We think in terms of planning maps and
middle-class values and how we wish it all looked. And we miss the
reality. 'Why has this church come to matter so much?' I asked myself.
My answer was equivocal and tentative. 'Because people feel powerless before the bulldozer. Because one fanatic with a gun and a passion
can pump bullets into even the pope. Because with all the big decisions
and big economic considerations, someone ought to care about the
small matters, like an old Polish church and a defiant priest. Maybe
because eminent domain carried this far does bother me more than I
have admitted.'"

Stroud noted that "the GM action put the public relations burden
on the archdiocese," then concluded: "I thought of Poland, of how
many times the warring armies of Europe have swept across Poland,
and of Poland's struggle to remain herself. I thought of all the neighborhoods we have torn up in this city for good reasons and bad. I thought
of the sense that city people have of being 'swept along by confused
alarms of struggle and flight.' And I was sorry we didn't save that
church."[21]

Residents said they would appeal to Archbishop Szoka as soon as
he was installed, but as Hodas explained, they did not want to assault
him. "We're trying to give him some breathing room," he said. "We
don't want to come on too strong, too fast. He needs to find out the facts
before he does something that's irreversible."[22] Olechowski added that
some people were considering a boycott of church coffers if the archdiocese didn't take some sort of positive stand.[23]

In mid-May an elderly woman who had owned Smigalski's Funeral Home across from the ICC died. Her son asked Karasiewicz to
arrange for her to be buried from ICC, where she had been a parishioner for fifty-five years, but the archdiocese refused.

On May 15 Szoka was made spiritual leader of the archdiocese at

Detroit's Blessed Sacrament Cathedral. His official installation was scheduled two days later in the city's Cobo Hall, which could accommodate thousands. On the same day the *Free Press* published an article lauding Karasiewicz as the "Iron Priest of Poletown." The next day the *Detroit News* ran an article titled "Defiant Priest Had No Choice." In the latter, Karasiewicz said he refused to give the records back to the archdiocese in an attempt to help people in his parish. "This is what Christ taught," he said. "There were times when He even disobeyed the sabbath in order to cure somebody. He was concerned about individuals. If I had done this simply to show some kind of force, simply to be disobedient, I would be wrong. But we have to have some compassion for the people who belong to this church. We have compassion for dogs, we ought to have compassion for people. I've worked downtown as assistant chancellor and there is a danger when you get away from the people. You get into an office and it's easy to forget you're dealing with human beings."[24]

During the early morning hours of May 16, forty people continued the vigil. Topolewski played the organ and the rest, including former parish council member Stanley Stachelski and his wife Helen, sang. At 10 P.M. that night a house at Trombly and Joseph Campeau went up in flames, followed by another directly behind the Kaczynskis' house.

The following Sunday, for the first time since its dedication, no mass was celebrated at the Immaculate Conception Church. That afternoon Szoka was installed as head prelate. Ironically, the pope's selection of a Polish archbishop did little to help Poletown. Just prior to the ceremony Szoka told the press that Dearden's decisions concerning Poletown would stand. "I've been in Detroit four days," he said. "Cardinal Dearden has been here over 20 years. I have to respect his judgment. I'd be foolish to do anything else."[25]

Mayor Young visited the flower sale at the Farmers' Market just south of Poletown that afternoon. When he returned, his car was plastered with red and white "Poletown Lives!" stickers. On May 20, Martha Knablack, wife of ICC's custodian and usher, died of a massive heart attack after moving away from Poletown. On the same day Olechowski met privately with GM's head counsel, Otis Smith, who told him that GM was embarrassed by the city's handling of things and particularly by the fiasco about moving the church. Olechowski told Smith that if the church were destroyed it would become part of Polish folklore in America with long-term reverberations.

The next day Kris Biernacki's house was vandalized. Guns, jewelry, a TV, a radio, and money were all stolen. Police at the scene commented that it was open season for vandals in Poletown, and Biernacki repeated, "I'm so tired, so tired. I can't fight anymore." Biernacki said she was worried about her sister, who lived alone next door in the house they had grown up in. Their parents, old-time Poletown residents, had died a few years earlier, so they were family to each other.

That afternoon Karasiewicz met with Archbishop Szoka for two and a half hours. Karasiewicz was excited by the meeting and pleased that Szoka wanted to meet with him again in one week. "He was most gracious! No bishop has ever been that gracious to me. He said he offered his mass that day, that Thursday when I saw him, for my intentions. And he said, he repeated this a number of times, that honestly he had not made a decision now."

On May 22 GM held its annual stockholders' meeting, but procedures were slightly altered due to the Poletown demolition. Executives were taken to the meeting via an underground tunnel, and security personnel had vans available in the event that demonstrators tried to block the tunnel. Inside, the chief executives sat behind a bulletproof table and spoke from behind a bulletproof podium.[26] Nearly fifty Poletown residents picketed peacefully outside, carrying their GM Mark of Destruction signs. They passed out flyers that said: "GM WANTED for Attempted Murder." About ten Poletown residents were able to attend the proceedings, using proxies that the Nader team had lined up.

MACO (Michigan Avenue Community Organization) members were also there in force. They had borrowed money to buy $10,000 worth of stock in order to have some say in whether the two older Detroit Cadillac plants would close. They had been assured by GM that they would have a chance to speak, but when it became apparent that MACO members were not going to be given the floor, the group ripped up GM's annual report, threw the paper scraps into the air, and left.

Poletown residents did manage to reach the microphones. Carol Dockery told stockholders that three Poletown women had already died as a result of the Cadillac project and insisted that the plant was being built "on the blood of good Christians." Roger Smith attempted to cut off Hodas before his full minute was up, but a chorus of protest went up from every corner. When Bernice Kaczynski complained that this was the second house she was losing to GM, Smith told her he didn't want to hear anything more about Poletown, that the issue had been sufficiently addressed. Kaczynski attempted to continue, but her microphone was shut off. Her unamplified voice rose in protest and others joined her cries, but Smith moved on to the next mike. Smiley took a turn in line and said simply and repeatedly: "I am not your dog. I am not your dog."

One supporter addressed the question of good citizenship, a subject Smith had referred to often during his opening statement. She said it was hardly good citizenship to refuse to even hear out the complaints of a woman like Bernice Kaczynski, who was losing so much to GM. Smith moved to cut her off, but she added that it also seemed odd that although GM counted on its employees receiving the benefits of city services the corporation was still resisting paying taxes, not only in Detroit but in Kansas and Oklahoma as well.

Eventually, the Poletown protestors went across the street to join a MACO demonstration which was attended by councilpeople Mahaffey and Cockrel. Cockrel told the group that the mayor and city council "relinquished all responsibility. . . . Before they gave GM that 12-year tax abatement on the new plant, they should have demanded that GM do something to protect the jobs at the old (Cadillac) plant. Don't rely on elected politicians. Don't count on us. All we want is to get re-elected and keep driving our free cars."[27]

In late May the hearings for Hodas's objections to the taking were in full swing. Councilman Cockrel testified in the circuit court that the council had approved the project without adequate information because the financial arrangements weren't even complete before May.[28] Young testified that everything was done properly and in response to extreme need. Young admitted that the city had proceeded with demolition despite the fact that it had no written guarantees that GM would even build the plant. "If we waited for all the silly guarantees you're talking about," the mayor said, "nothing would ever get built and nothing would ever get done." He added that he was content with the word of former GM chairman Thomas Murphy for assurance that the plant would be built.[29]

When the mayor left the court room, he entered an elevator with Nader staffer Russell Mokhiber. Young looked at Mokhiber and said, "You come from outside the city and don't know your ass from a hole in the ground. This city is fighting for its life and you guys come in and mess with something you don't know anything about. You motherfuckers come in and don't have an interest in the city." Mokhiber responded, "You're saying the same thing that Southern mayors said to civil rights workers—take your principles back where you came from." Undaunted, Young called the four lawsuits launched by Poletown residents "technical trivialities attempting to sabotage an almost $1 billion project. Poletown presented a convenient headline, a convenient sob story. And the people from Poletown realized that they were media events."[30]

On June 1 the *Washington Post* ran a lengthy, front-page story headlined "Polish Resistance, Detroit-Style." The article reviewed the struggle and depicted Karasiewicz as the unlikely dissident priest. "I'm no fighter," Karasiewicz told the *Post*. "But it's a basic thing. It's wrong to cooperate with this type of law in any sort of way. We're fighting the quick-take law behind it all. This is an evil law and we have to fight it. This is the first time it was ever applied on this scale." Residents, Karasiewicz said, are being forced out "by hook and by crook—a crooked law, crooked judges, and to a certain extent a crooked cardinal. You can't establish some kind of crooked law and then say you did it legally. This has national implications and national scope. It sets a bad precedent. No one is safe except the man who has the money, to put it bluntly."[31]

Sandy Livingston's June 5 journal entry was bleak. There had been four fires the night before. As she walked the neighborhood, she ran into Mrs. Cornelius, who lived next door to the relocation office. "She is very frightened, especially after the fire at the corner of Piquette and Elmwood last night. She also said that she and her husband have a garage that they have been trying to get their money for since February. She said that the city is supposed to be out of money by the 20th of June. Many people are not getting their money—she hears them go to the relocation office daily, screaming, insulting people who work there, and threatening to bomb or fire the office if the money doesn't come through soon. Sunday the statue dedicated to the Polish millennium, that stood outside the Immaculate Conception Church, was pushed off its pedestal and broken in three places."

Resistance continued on several fronts. The Nader team helped Hodas affix a huge banner that read "Boycott GM" to an apartment building Hodas owned. The banner faced the corporate world headquarters. Police interrupted their work, saying that the city owned the building. Hodas objected and showed his July eviction notice as proof of current ownership. Livingston wrote: "It's strange that property owners in Poletown only have eviction notices now as proof of former ownership. We weren't arrested, but the police will look into it on Monday. . . . The view from atop Hodas Main [the building's nickname given by the Nader team] is amazing—it's the first time you begin to realize how vast 465 acres are, and how large the Dodge Main plant was—though now there is just the one building remaining. In terms of demolition of homes, the northwest corner . . . is almost gone. There are about three houses remaining in the approximately four-by-three block area and they've even begun tearing up the streets. St. John's has a police officer stationed round the clock right inside the open front door. From the top of Hodas Main the rest of the neighborhood looks good— you see tops of houses rather than broken glass and stepless, windowless homes." Meanwhile Karasiewicz prepared himself for his upcoming encounter with Archbishop Szoka. He told a friend, "I think I will have to take a stand, something like a Dutch uncle. I'm older than he; not more important, God forbid that. But to let him know how much it means. He could make or break himself by this decision; there's really no other way to go—except to do everything possible to save the church. There's no other way to go. It's not a decision, where you have to be thinking a lot this or that way. To my mind, there's no thinking."

Karasiewicz was disappointed when he did finally meet with Szoka again. The new archbishop said that he would not do anything to prevent demolition of the church. On June 9 Karasiewicz told the Nader team that he had explained to Szoka that this was like World War II, because no one was trying to prevent the holocaust that was happening in Poletown. Apparently Szoka was aghast at being compared to Hitler, but Karasiewicz said he wasn't calling the archbishop a Nazi. He was merely declaring that the hierarchy was at fault. When Karasiewicz asked why the archbishop had decided not to fight for the church, he received no answer. The elder priest, who had hoped to speak with the voice of a Dutch uncle, said that he had approached the city, GM, and the archdiocese for answers to no avail. Now he wanted an answer. Szoka responded that he had prayed until he knew the right thing to do. Karasiewicz responded in agony, "No, no, this is the wrong decision. It is wrong." Livingston said later she had never seen Karasiewicz so angry or so gaunt as he was after this conversation.

The neighborhood continued to take assaults. Two Poletown residents were held briefly by the police for allegedly trying to set fire to the Turner Construction office with gasoline and rags. Ironically, they were two of only twelve arsonists apprehended during the first six months of 1981, despite the fact that there were 607 fires during that time, all but this one directed against the homes of Poletown. During the first Friday in June there were two fires at Joseph Campeau and Milwaukee. Residents went to sleep to the sound of constant sirens. There were more fires the next night. Kris Biernacki's family moved out over that weekend. Biernacki said that they were moving into a white, middle-class neighborhood but found it unfriendly. Her sister said that when she picked up the keys to the new house, she had the same feeling she'd had when entering the funeral home to see her father laid out.

Dockery reported to the Nader team that a woman from the relocation office told her that if the Kaczynskis didn't start readying themselves to move out soon Turner would bulldoze Mitchell Street so that they'd get the message. Congressperson Conyers visited Immaculate Conception Church on the first Sunday in June to discuss the possibility of holding hearings about abuses in Poletown. Houses continued to fall to bulldozers, even as the abandoned rose bushes began to bloom. On June 9 the parish council voted to ask GM to honor its commitment to move the church. But within days GM responded that the church belonged to the city, so the council should negotiate with city officials.

By mid-June more Poletown residents had died. Mrs. Wisnewski told *The Bulletin* that eight people had died in the area of Craig and Trombly, including one neighbor who had opposed the project. Her voice competed with a bulldozer's whine next door as she explained that her neighbor "had a heart attack because of the stress. She didn't want to leave. Now they're putting sand on it [the foundations of her old house]. It's all torn down. Nobody wanted to move. This is my third home but the first one I owned. I'm afraid to move because I want to find happiness here but I don't know what will happen. So many have died—I'm afraid I'll die too. It's frightening. A person can't sleep at night. You think someone will come into your home. I had to take something to sleep because I couldn't stand it. My nerves are so gone."[32]

Wisnewski complained that none of her sons, all auto workers, had jobs now and that the GM plant won't change that. "The rich are going to get richer and the poor poorer. Why raise children in this world if you don't know if they'll ever get a job. Honest to God, I'm not going to vote anymore. I voted for everyone, thinking we'd have a better life and it all backfired. When I saw them burying the sand on the lot next door to my house I just started to cry and I asked myself—why this? It is breaking up families and scattering everyone."[33]

On June 12 Karasiewicz managed to meet with Mother Theresa, who had just won the Nobel prize and was visiting the Motor City. She assured him that the church had already been saved and instructed him to say the memorare nine times in thanksgiving to the Blessed Mother. From that day forward Fr. Joe and many of the women who continued to pray daily in the church never failed to repeat the memorare.

Two days before Karasiewicz's June 17 eviction date the city blew up the nearby sugar factory. The Nader team found it increasingly difficult to work in the church basement because former parishioners and Poletown residents were taking everything that wasn't nailed down out of the church.

On June 16 the Poletown Neighborhood Council met to discuss the game plan for the next day. The meeting opened with a prayer. "Holy Mary, Mother of God, pray for us sinners now and at the hour of our death." Fifty or so people sat in a semicircle on pews. The tables were gone. Most of the folding chairs were gone. The piano had been removed. The only remaining decoration was a cardboard American flag stuck on the wall above where the clock had been.

The people present argued about how to pursue their effort to buy the church, as Karasiewicz's little black lap dog cavorted beneath the pews. At issue was Emmett Moten's claim that he had never received a letter from the Poletown Neighborhood Council asking to buy the church, even though the PNC had a receipt proving it had been received. People spoke hopefully about the possibility of a congressional hearing.

Ann Locklear suggested that people occupy the church, hold an illegal vigil. Olechowski opposed the idea, recommending instead that the PNC surrender gracefully. Stilp jumped in and said he would hate to see the church destroyed without a fight. When it became clear there was strong sentiment for occupying the church, at least until the city responded to their offer to buy the church, Olechowski became anxious about logistics. They would need food and sanitation supplies. When Olechowski spoke about money needs, an engineer from suburban Troy jumped up and handed him a check for a thousand dollars (which days later proved invalid). Narayandas (nicknamed Nanu) Ashar's offer was greeted with wild applause, which gave him an open opportunity to take the floor at will, even though this was his first visit to a PNC meeting. Ashar, who came with his wife and two children from India, was irrepressible. He bounded around the basement, speaking of Ghandi and mass resistance. For reasons known only to himself, Olechowski focused on the need for milk. He suggested that since the church's stove and refrigerator would be moved out, the solution would be to get slightly radiated milk from Canada that doesn't sour without refrigeration for two weeks. To this, Ashar yelled out "Holy cow!" A couple from southern Poletown left immediately for neighboring Windsor, Ontario, to buy the milk.

The following day, June 17, Walter Duda and Nick Kubiak, whose aunt lived in Poletown, guarded the basement door, which was jammed shut with the two-by-four. Vicar Robinson arrived at the rectory at 10

A.M., with the police, two workmen, and a truck. Television cameras caught the men loading the rectory furniture onto the pickup truck, but Robinson carefully moved out of range of the cameras. He waited until the loaded truck was around the corner from the church before taking the wheel.

Karasiewicz was called down to the chancery that afternoon. Szoka was irritated that the resistance continued and put the burden on Karasiewicz to empty people out of the basement, lock the church, and call to say that everything was done. Szoka also informed Karasiewicz that he was forbidden to speak to the press. The priest's last words to the press, spoken before the archbishop's gag order, appeared in the *Detroit News* the next day: "It's not simply saving a shrine. The seventh commandment says, 'Thou shalt not steal.' There's a semblance of legality here—when a corporation gets together with a city—but it's stealing. It's a mystery to me why the archdiocese went along."[34]

The evening of the June 17, when Karasiewicz entered the sanctuary to say goodbye to the eighty people there, the TV camera crews respected his desire to be off camera in order to be faithful to the archbishop's order and kept their kleig lights out. Karasiewicz said that a resounding victory had been won because the message of the community had been delivered to authorities who needed to hear it. He said he hoped his bond with parishioners would continue and added that he hoped no one was bitter. It had been a good fight and everyone should feel proud.

Stanley Stachelski, a former member of the church council, responded by reading a letter that indicated people's resolve to stay in the church.

> Dear Father Joe:
> A good priest makes Christ visible; this is how we the people of Immaculate Conception Church will always remember you. We understand that you had to communicate the message to us from your superiors that we should leave . . . the Immaculate Conception Church. We also understand that the archdiocese no longer owns the building and that you are no longer our pastor. Therefore we must decline your request that we leave and do so while respecting most deeply the great leadership that through your priesthood has made Christ visible in our midst. In our hearts this is a struggle of religious, cultural, and historic values as opposed to secular, bureaucratic, and materialistic values. You know which side we must choose to live with, regardless of the consequences."[35]

Karasiewicz responded that he had been ordered by the archdiocese to clear the church and that his attempt to do so was more than a mere formality. He honestly believed that people should leave, since little could be accomplished by staying. He thanked everyone and returned to the rectory to pack last-minute things. Topolewski rose and cried out that Karasiewicz had done his duty but that they would stay.

At 11 P.M. the WDIV news team was shooting live as people in the church filled large garbage cans and all the rectory bathtubs with water so that the toilets could be flushed even if the city shut off the church's water. About forty people remained at midnight, including Fr. Skalski, who went upstairs to pray. At that moment Karasiewicz came downstairs with a twinkle in his eye. "Get out of here, you lawbreakers," he said before hugging everyone goodbye. Many people wept as he climbed into his ancient Olds stationwagon loaded with things and drove away.

About a dozen people stayed the night. Hodas went up into the rectory to watch for police while the rest made decisions about what to do if the police attempted to seize the church. People agreed that they would prefer to be in the sanctuary if the police arrived. A spokesperson would speak to the police through the locked basement door, saying that the church address was the return address for their letter inquiring about purchasing the church and that they were waiting for a reply.

At 1:15 A.M. Josephine Jakubowski pulled on slippers and crawled onto a wrestling mat which had been laid out in one corner of the basement. Other women nestled there with her. One elderly woman chuckled later, "I haven't slept with my husband in ten years, and here I was sleeping within ten feet of a young man I had never met." Half the Nader team stayed the night. *Free Press* reporter Maryann Rzepka joined the all-night crew now spread out through the church and rectory. During the night Olechowski, who was unwilling to join the occupation, called to say that the elderly people should sleep near the bathrooms for their own convenience.

The following day some of the night crew left but were replaced by others who returned to vigil. Karasiewicz came back with Skalski to help remove the statues from the sanctuary. People were delighted to be reunited with their priest but wept bitterly as the marble work was removed. By mid-afternoon a huge scaffold stood behind the altar. Workmen stood on it roping and chaining the central statue of the Virgin Mary.

Livingston wrote: "The contrast is overwhelming. The scaffold is up and the women are singing away with the organ in the background. 'Ave Maria' and directions for how to rope and chain the Blessed Mother mingle in the sanctuary. . . . As each slab is pulled out you can see how deeply it affects the residents and parishioners who sit and watch and continue their unanswered prayers. What did those workmen of the twenties think? Perhaps they thought that they were building an immortal monument to Polish culture and Catholicism that would outlast generations. Probably, they had no idea that it wouldn't even outlast their own children."

After the statue was down, it was placed on a dolly. The women in the church crowded around it and followed it in a funeral procession down the aisle, sobbing. The statue was loaded into a pickup truck and taken away for eventual use in some chapel shrine to the ICC.

On June 19 a man arrived at the church to shut off the water. Stilp met him at the door and said, "Thanks, not today." After consulting a police officer, the utility man drove off. But that evening a Michigan Consolidated employee shut off the gas from the outside. Later in the evening Karasiewicz called to speak with everyone and to make sure they were alright and in good spirits.

Two days later, the chief of the seventh precinct stopped by the church and told Paul Stern, a member of the support team, to call if the group at the church experienced any harassment. Women from the group later took a pie to the police at the precinct in appreciation and also let them know that complaints about lack of police protection were not aimed at them, but at city hall. Karasiewicz stopped by that Sunday after saying mass at St. Hyacinth's. He scrupulously avoided entering the church, but residents and supporters flooded out to greet him on the sidewalk.

On June 22 Judge Vokes ruled against Hodas's objection to the taking. Back at the church the basement phone lines were suddenly cut. When Jakubowski, the PNC's treasurer, called to complain, the phone company agreed to resume service by 6 P.M. The disconnect had been ordered by Chuhran, of the archdiocese. The next day all the utilities except the phones were shut off. Candles in coffee cans and red glass vigil lamps were placed on the two remaining tables, in all the sanctuary windows, and across the basement floor. A suburban private-school child volunteered to collect candles from his classmates to help supply the occupation.

The PNC meeting that night was held in the sanctuary so that people could sit on the pews. Olechowski spoke to the group with a flashlight in hand. His voice penetrated the darkness, and his light periodically flickered over the crowd. He recommended that the church be surrendered "with honor." Everyone could leave, but they could form human chains around the church, putting their bodies between

DAVID C. TURNLEY

The mood was funereal when members of the archdiocese came to Immaculate Conception Church to remove the statues, the altar, and the marble work. The statues were laid on a dolly and paraded throughout the church before being loaded on a truck. Josephine Jakubowski (center) followed behind with her niece and great-nephew, Ann and Doug Locklear.

A Poletown child approaches St. Francis during the stripping of the church.

the building and the bulldozers. People in attendance grew irritated, pointing out that most nights there were ten people spending the night in the church and that others came and went during the day. How could he expect them to completely ring the church twenty-four hours a day? Olechowski's plan was vetoed, but Stachelski admitted that after nearly a week in the church, he was growing tired.

Smiley, who had provided the flatbed truck for the bulldozer demonstration, was invaluable during the occupation. He had and could craft tools for nearly any purpose. After the water in the church was shut off, Smiley fashioned a wrench on a twelve-foot extension and reached it into the outdoor connector to restore water service to the church. Then he and others filled the narrow pipe that shielded the subsidewalk faucet connection with pebbles so that the city could not return and shut it off again.

On June 24 the PNC lost phone service again. People had to trek to the Jakubowskis' house to make calls. The absence of utilities made everyone wary of a police move against the church. But people took some comfort in a generator that two men brought to the church after seeing the occupation on TV. The generator was kept on the rectory's second floor porch next to the "GM Mark of Destruction" sign that hung on the outside wall. Phone service was restored the next day at noon without explanation.

On June 25 a chimney crashed through the window of the Caldwells' house on Mitchell. The crew taking down a neighboring house had miscalculated and caused the accident. Neighbors on Mitchell were concerned, remembering that the relocation office worker had threatened increased demolition on their street to drive the Kaczynskis out.

Phone service was in and out on June 26. Increasingly, the people staffing the occupation were outsiders. Sigrid Dale came for the evenings to sing hymns over a beer with her new friends. Smiley, in his colorful tie-dyed T-shirts, brought his brother or his kids to do whatever odds and ends needed doing. An Emergency Medical Service driver came and slept nights at the church. Tony and Cele Kirkegaard were constantly available to help out, and former parishioners Ted and Mary Krukierek made a point of attending meetings and demonstrations. Jim Lemire, an architecture student at the University of Detroit who had spent a year in Poland, rode up on his motorcycle and stayed the night. When the mayor began to complain about "outside agitators" in Poletown, Lemire did what he had seen Polish dissidents do— he adopted the epithet and silkscreened T-shirts with a city skyscape and the words "Boycott GM" on one side, "Poletown Outside Agitator" on the other. Deb Choly, a Wayne State law student, spent days and nights helping out. Kate Stritmatter jeopardized her health and her job by spending so much time at the church. Marie Grucz, from Hamtramck, helped out. Chris Kujowski would come to the church after closing down the west side bar she tended. Cliff and Sandy Poshadlo and their son, Cliff, Jr., helped occupy the church. (The right-wing conservatism which allowed them to support Donald Lobsinger, founder of an anti-Communist vigilante group in Detroit called Breakthrough, also motivated them to protest the demolition of a church.) Sharon Bohls, who was a resident of a wealthy suburb and was going through a divorce, spent more time at the church than almost anyone. She was fanatic about cleanliness and safety precautions. Because of her influence, bags of fire retardant were placed next to each candle. Her scrupulousness was often helpful (although some people grew suspicious of her motivation when she jotted down the names of everyone entering the church, copied over all the phone numbers on the office wall, took down the posters critical of GM, including the exterior Boycott banners, and spent time in friendly conversation with police.) Nancy VomSteeg, a teacher at Cranbrook private school, often attended vigils at the church and assembled a photo album, which she made available to residents.

On the last Saturday evening in June, six large fires broke out. At one point one fireman, who had fought thirteen fires throughout that day, was forced to choose which of three fires to go to next. On June 28, there were eleven more fires, and the house next to the Jakubowskis' was bulldozed. One whole block on Trombly was completely gutted. Over the weekend the Famous Bar-B-Q Restaurant closed. Carl Fisher put a hand-lettered sign next to the register reading: "As you know we must close (under duress) Saturday June 27 our last day. Thank you for your past patronage—we wish you all the best and may God bless you all. Till we meet again. Carl."

On June 29 the Nader team announced that they were leaving for Washington the next day. During their going-away party that night the Parke School caught fire, lighting up the entire sky and filling the air with the now familiar smoke and dampness. Fourteen other buildings burned that night. One firefighter shouted from his passing truck that he hoped the church would be saved. Karasiewicz came to the party but couldn't enter the building, so the Nader team and everyone else ran up to the sidewalk to hug him. In the basement forty people sat on mats and pews around a Coleman lantern learning civil rights songs which had been rewritten with Poletown lyrics by one supporter. CBS national TV crews were there shooting for a documentary they planned to make. The cameras caught folks singing a song which would become a favorite and could be heard under Bernice Kaczynski's breath for weeks.

> Paul and Silas bound in jail
> had no money for to go the bail
>
> Chorus: Keep your eyes on the prize
> Hold on. Hold on. Hold on. Hold on.
> Keep your eyes on the prize, hold on. Hold on.
>
> The only thing that we did right
> was the day we begun to fight.
>
> General Motors, change your plans;
> we'll stay here 'cus it's our land.
>
> Coleman Young, we've this to say:
> we'll be here from day to day.
>
> Hey, archbishop, it's in your hands;
> it's up to you to change their plans.
>
> All outsiders join the fight;
> it's up to us all to put it right.

The song became a mainstay of demonstrations that followed and often attracted onlookers on Detroit's streets who remembered the tune from former struggles.

The Nader team said goodbye to their Mitchell Street neighbors the next morning. They took bottles of champagne to the Kaczynskis, the Dockerys, and the Crosbys and asked them all to toast the fight in a year or two. The day they left, the *Free Press* carried a story that was headlined: "Fires in Deserted Poletown up 250% since February," although of course the neighborhood wasn't entirely deserted. In the article Earl Berry, president of the Detroit Firefighters Association, said that his men had responded to more than thirty Poletown fires in less than three days. He complained that vandalized houses were dangerous to enter because they might be missing stairways or other fixtures, and he said he would sue if any of his members were injured.[36] Berry told the *Detroit News* that one unit responding to Poletown calls had more fire service than "any fire company has had since the 1967 Detroit riots."[37]

The occupation continued after the Nader team left. Choly and Stritmatter were available to coordinate things, but their faces were less familiar than the Nader team's, and residents were also increasingly tied up with trying to relocate their possessions before they burned to the ground. New supporters arrived full of advice about how to stop the project, oblivious of the measures which had already been pursued. It became harder to turn up an adequate number of people to stay in the church at night, and some began to wonder if the city's strategy was to wait everyone out.

On July 6 Walter Jakubowski signed a request for a Wayne County or federal grand jury investigation of the arson, selective bulldozing, and diminishing of city services. Two days later the *Village Voice* carried a cover story about Poletown, focusing on the church occupation. And on July 10 the *Free Press* ran a story by Marianne Rzepka, who had been very present throughout the occupation.[38] Whether it was the media attention, the grand jury request, or some other factor is still unknown, the city decided to move on the church.

In the extremely early hours of July 14, a woman stopped by the church basement and yelled through the locked door that she worked for the police department and that they were going to seize the church the next morning. Later, while it was still dark, a uniformed officer came and said the same thing. By 5 A.M. police were setting up metal barricades blocking off the freeway service drive and all the streets in a four-block radius around the church. They brought in the Special Weapons Attack Team (SWAT) and police dogs. People inside the church began to ring the bells in an appeal for help. Folks at the St. Hyacinth's rectory heard the bells and began to ring their own bells to alert their parish. Soon a collection of people gathered on the sidewalk. Residents watched in sleepy horror as the police, who had been refused entrance, attached a tow truck and chain to the sanctuary side door and ripped it open. Some of the sixty officers on site swept into the sanctuary with flashlights. They peered under pews and behind the remains of the altar. In time, they mounted the stairs to the balcony and found the people who had been frantically ringing the bells. The bell ringers fled to the basement, and the two officers, who admitted they didn't want to be on this duty, let them slip into the basement and lock the doors behind them.

Soon the exterior basement door was ripped open with a tow truck. Twenty police officers lined the near wall and folded their arms. Several others, with flashlights, searched the rectory. Deputy Chief Richard Dungy stood beside city official Russell Chambers as he read

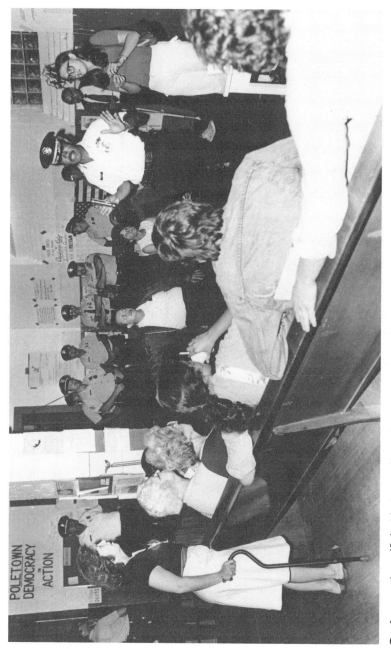

On the morning of July 14, sixty police officers cordoned off the area with steel fences then ripped their way into the church by tearing the doors off with a tow truck. Photo by Taro Yamasaki.

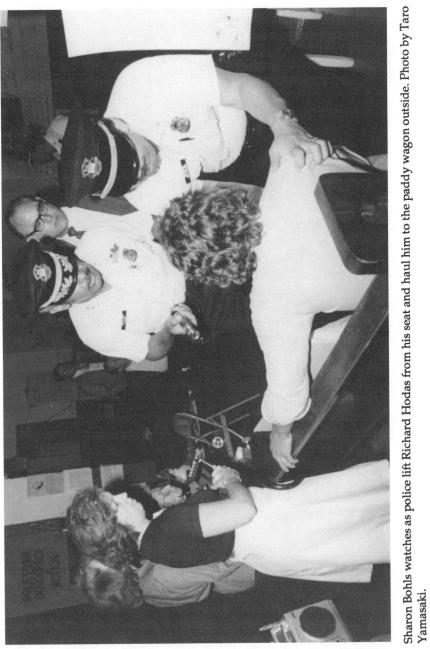

Sharon Bohls watches as police lift Richard Hodas from his seat and haul him to the paddy wagon outside. Photo by Taro Yamasaki.

the trespass act. During this period Josephine Jakubowski, Helen Krupa, Marie Grucz, and Sandy Poshadlo held hands, praying the Hail Mary. Smiley clicked on a tape player that generated loud revolutionary reggae music, which was an expression of his faith. Others smoked cigarettes and were restive. Some took turns on the two phones, which surprisingly were working, and called most of the media organizations in the city and some national ones as well.

When George Corsetti interrupted Chambers to say that the eviction was illegal under landlord-tenant law, Dungy grew angry and placed him under arrest. Hodas remembers objecting, and then "the white deputy pulls me by my shirt and says, 'You're next.' A young white cop got my hands, put them behind my back and handcuffed me, but he was nice and gentle. He wasn't like the big buffoon that pulled me up by the shirt." Angry voices could be heard yelling in chaos. Police voices yelled, "You got one choice. You either leave or you're under arrest." Ashar, who had been tape recording the whole morning's events, started yelling at the top of his voice, "Gestapo! Gestapo get out!" Police grabbed all the men, one by one, yelling, "Are you leaving? Are you leaving? You either leave or you're under arrest." Barney Topolewski, George Smiley, Nanu Ashar, and Jim Lemire were handcuffed and put in the waiting paddy wagon with Corsetti and Hodas.

Then the police told the women to leave. They were much gentler with them, perhaps because several were in their seventies. However, the women were adamant that they would not leave the church unless they were under arrest. Three times they were told they were under arrest. Finally, two ascended the basement steps, and once assured they were being put into the paddy wagon, the others followed (including *Free Press* reporter Marianne Rzepka).

At the seventh precinct all twelve were held in the waiting area. They were locked in but had access to a pay phone and to the two officers who staffed the back desk. A sliding wooden door separated them from the front office, where a crowd of supporters and TV cameras waited. Ashar had brought large color posters of the pope and of Ghandi, which he had people hold while he took photos. People's spirits were generally high. Some had a media phone list and started calling out on the pay phone. "This is collect from Poletown in jail," the operator repeated to surprised news room reporters. There would be a pause and the charges immediately accepted. Hodas conducted a live radio interview straight from the precinct.

In time the police separated the men and the women. They took away the men's property and fingerprinted and booked them. Then they placed them in the back cell. The women were kept in the holding area. During the interim three of the women—Jakubowski, Poshadlo, and Grucz, all over fifty-five years old—made friends with the young male police officers. They approached the desk and said sweetly, "We know you don't want to do this. You must hate this." And they reminded them about the pie they had brought to the precinct earlier.

To the women's dismay, the police moved the men to the downtown jail and told the women they were free to go. The women had repeatedly told the police that they wanted to be treated just like the men. After consulting, they agreed to refuse to leave the holding area. Several of them gathered in the corner closest to the sliding door and whenever it opened, they chanted to the TV cameras, "Coleman Young took the men, take us too." The women called a friend and asked him to relay their position to their supporters and to the media. It had now been nearly six hours since the police move. None of those jailed had eaten breakfast or lunch. Josephine Jakubowski's expectations had been raised to great heights when someone reported over the phone that 400 priests had gone to Poletown to try to stop the demolition, but she was doubly disappointed to learn subsequently that it was untrue. Finally, she subsided into tears, sitting on the wooden bench in the holding area, leaning against the cinder block walls, weeping unendingly.

At noon officers informed the women that the men were being released. All charges were dropped. The women ended their sit-in triumphantly, walking out of the precinct and into the arms of their friends and onto live noon news shows. They quickly learned that Gene Stilp and Sandy Livingston had flown back from Washington and would greet them at the church.

At the church things were less jubilant. An eight-foot fence was being erected around the church. The police were there in force. The K-9 units, with their dogs, were still there, and police helicopters provided surveillance overhead. The pews and the masonry were being stripped from the building.

Karasiewicz returned to the scene and violated the order forbidding him to speak to the media. He strode up the sidewalk, accepting the embraces of his parishioners, and then said sternly, "These people responsible for this are worse than the Communists in Poland. That is the message I gave them before, and I guess they couldn't understand it before. They might as well get it straight now." "Including the archdiocese, Father?" a reporter asked. "Absolutely!" "Because of how fast everything was done?" "Because it is a criminal act," Karasiewicz responded. "To go down to a very basic definition of stealing, it is simply taking someone else's property against their will. That's all it is. So, this property was taken away from them, the people, against their will."

Gene Stilp, an attorney for Ralph Nader, joins residents in the occupation of the church, which began when the city and the archdiocese evicted Fr. Karasiewicz from the rectory.

Hundreds watched in disbelief as the church was stripped of its stained-glass windows, masonry, and pews. More than sixty police officers were on site to protect the demolition process.

A crowd of 200 gathered around the church to watch. Many wept as the pillars in the bell towers were smashed and the bells removed. They saw the cross at the peak of the roof chiseled loose and lowered upside down to the sidewalk. The stained-glass windows were carefully extracted and swung to the ground on ropes, still intact for auction. The organ came out. The light fixtures.

There was a pall on the crowd for most of the morning. The police presence was strong, the dismantling in full swing. Occasional instances of tension flared up. Five people—Gene Stilp, Karasiewicz, Sigrid Dale, Nick Kubiak, and Ann Dolence—climbed onto the truck that was to remove the bells. For a moment demolition was halted. When threatened with arrest the five stepped down. People gathered at the fence by the front door of the church and wove flowers through it, just as Poles who supported Solidarity were doing outside the gates where workers were on strike. Residents hung banners on the fence that read: "Help Us Detroit," "Save Our Church," "Boycott A.D.F." (Archdiocesan Development Fund). They knelt and prayed the rosary. The Jakubowskis' home was open to everyone who needed a meal, a place to make a telephone call, somewhere to wash. Their kitchen table was crowded with people, some of whom laughed that they were drinking "Polish tea," a spiked tea that they liked comparing to Irish coffee.

That night Gene Stilp slept outside the church. A few demolition workers had remained all night to remove the remaining windows. At dawn demolition resumed under the protection of sixty police officers. When young Cliff Poshadlo, a computer analyst, noticed a bulldozer nearing the church, he knelt in its path. Others joined him. When the bulldozer backed up and changed direction, the people moved into its path again and knelt. But when an officer said the driver was just going to park it, people let it pass. Later, to their chagrin, the wrecking crew expanded the fence to include the bulldozer, so it couldn't be blocked again. Later in the morning Jerry, an EMS worker, dashed into the demolition area and climbed onto the bulldozer. When he refused to leave, he was taken to jail.

Poletown supporters kept hearing police officers confide that they didn't want to be there. One officer told Corsetti he considered the demolition fascism. Another told Hodas an anti-GM rhyme that he had made up. Carl Fisher remarked later that he'd gotten to know a lot of the officers at his restaurant. "I think you're reaching into something beyond a uniform," Fisher said. "They have a job to do. But their inner feelings, sometimes they hide them. And they bare them after they're off duty, if you know them personally. They're religious. They're humanitarian. The men, in general, they got a lot of kindness and they understand what's going on. They know that this is a people's church. They know that it represents some of these people's families dropping nickels and dimes in the coffers, going without a loaf of bread or something like that. But they have a duty. It goes higher than just the individual policeman or the officers in charge—it goes higher than them."

But as the afternoon wore on, the mood was more tense. At ten-foot intervals all around the fence, beside each police officer, people knelt and left red vigil lights. Finally, at 5:30 P.M., in front of cameras shooting live, the Homrich Wrecking crew began to prepare the wrecking ball. People hollered through the fence, "You don't have to do that. Why would you destroy our church?" A small group clung to the fence and began singing, "Keep your eyes on the prize, hold on." Unconsciously, they started rocking the fence. Soon, others—mostly outsiders—joined them and the fence began to rock in long sweeps. The poles were coming loose. Police jumped into the fray and ripped people off the fence, throwing Stritmatter to the ground and bruising Ann Locklear's arm. Instantly men in their fifties and sixties, including Karasiewicz, interposed themselves between the people who had been swinging on the fence and the police. In anger they lectured the police that they had no right to treat people like that. Stilp intervened and asked Karasiewicz to lead everyone in prayer. Fr. Joe did that. People collected in a half circle on the ground, kneeling with their faces toward the church.

As they knelt, the wrecking ball grazed against the upper story of the rectory, then swung away and returned, smashing into and through the brick wall. In one gasp people emitted a twisted, anguished cry, and Josephine Jakubowski in her kitchen nearby knew what it meant and began to cry. Within ten minutes the rectory garage was destroyed and the top floor of the rectory was torn wide open. On the fence waved a banner saying: "Save Our Church."

People asked each other what they could do, each wanting to do something. Finally, several arranged a plan to have a diversion at the back of the church so that Gene Stilp could slip under the fence and into the church to stop or delay demolition as long as possible. At 7:30 P.M. several people began swinging on the fence and singing again. They clung to the fence until the police pulled them off, this time more gently. The officers pleaded with people not to do this, saying they didn't want to hurt anyone. But each time the group returned to the fence until there was a crowd of officers. Meanwhile, Stilp was strolling up Trombly with an elderly parishioner who had been at the church often during the resistance. Suddenly, and to her surprise, he ducked under the fence and ran into the church. Cries of "Man in the church!" went up from the construction crew and the wrecking ball stopped.

For a few minutes Stilp searched the church for a hiding place. It was dark and full of plaster dust. The pews were missing and the layout seemed foreign to him. Quickly, he hid in a closet at the west end of the church—the end closest to the demolition and probably the least safe. Stilp had planned to handcuff himself to something but could find nothing remaining that would serve. Police found Stilp within minutes and dragged him from the church. A crowd gathered, chanting and clapping and shouting. Spontaneously, they surrounded the squad car in which Stilp had been put and started hammering on the roof, demanding his release. Police came up behind the group, pulling some people off the car by stretching their billy clubs across bodies and pulling. The car peeled out suddenly in reverse. The chants continued until an uneasy calm descended. Dungy and his superior officers, embarrassed, reviewed the police and made sure they were stationed all the way around the fence.

More than a dozen people, including Karasiewicz, went to the seventh precinct to support Stilp. He was charged with illegal entry of a vacant building and possession of stolen property worth less than $100. The stolen property charge, which was later dropped, stemmed from a police belief that Stilp had stolen his handcuffs from an officer.

Finally, after midnight Stilp was released, pending a hearing the next day. He went with friends to a restaurant in Hamtramck, where they had an early breakfast. In the early morning hours Stilp and his friends arrived home and found three squad cars waiting in front of the house. None of the police said anything or even got out of their cars, just hovered there and watched. In time the squad cars left.

Meanwhile, back at the church demolition continued under floodlights. Toward dawn the demolition crew, in a move reminiscent of the police tow truck tearing the door off the church, toppled the foundation pillars by chaining them to a tractor that backed away from the building. The preparations were slow, the process excruciating to watch. At last the pillars collapsed and the entire fresco-covered church roof collapsed in a cloud of dust.[39]

In these predawn hours Nanu Ashar instructed his wife to crawl under the fence with him and their two children. All four of them, including an infant, scrambled under and tried to reach the destroyed church. Police converged on them. There were few onlookers present, and the police were more abusive than at any other time during the

Gene Stilp, of the Nader staff, was arrested when he dodged under the fence and into the church. Observers cheered when they heard "Man in the church!" and instructions to stop the wrecking ball. Photo by Taro Yamasaki.

Nanu Ashar, an engineer from India, was arrested at the site of the demolition of the Immaculate Conception Church when he tried to save the building by crawling under the fence with his wife and two children. He and his wife (on the left) were held overnight in the Detroit jail. The two children were suddenly placed in the hands of a Poletown supporter (the woman holding the baby) whom they did not know.

week. Ashar's wife's sari was torn and her glasses trampled. Police handcuffed her abruptly, shouting, "Goddamned woman" and threatening that her children would be taken away from her. Mrs. Ashar, who spoke very little English, was thrown in a squad car with the five-year-old and the baby, who lay crying in her sister's arms. Nanu Ashar, who was forced into a second car, spread his arms and cried, "I am not a criminal. I am not a criminal." He wore an "I love the USA" T-shirt which he had proudly shown Poletown residents earlier with the jubilant comment "Dress for success, dress for success." The Ashars were not released until the next morning. The young couple from southern Poletown who had gone to fetch the radiated milk for the occupation a month earlier took the children home with them for the night.

The next morning Stilp was arraigned before a magistrate who dropped the charges on the grounds that the law was designed to protect vacant buildings from destruction. "But in this case, Mr. Stilp entered a vacant building that was being destroyed to try and save it. I, therefore, drop the charges."

At 10 A.M., seventy people were milling around the remains of the church. A large portion of the front wall was all that remained and that was only there because the steel reinforcements within it were hard to demolish with a wrecking ball. Rubble, bricks, and dust were everywhere within the fence.

People gathered, as they had for the last two days, at the Jakubowskis. Josephine was distraught, tearful, unable to sleep. She fussed over her guests and wept as she made food or served tea. Plans were laid that afternoon to take an old GM car to the corporation's world headquarters and destroy it. During the negotiations the Jakubowskis' phone went out. When queried, Michigan Bell said the demolition must have taken a line down, but the Locklears' phone downstairs was still in perfect service.

At 4:00 P.M., a crowd gathered outside the GM office building. Soon a car appeared and double parked outside the building. It was spraypainted with messages reading: "Boycott GM" and "GM Destroys Churches." Nick Kubiak and Jack Smiley picked up crow bars and picks and began shattering the windows and denting the metal. The tools were passed from hand to hand: elderly women, students, parents, Poletown residents, and supporters alike took their turns. Jerry climbed onto the roof and jumped on it before smashing in the windshield with his heels. Cliff Poshadlo, Jr., approached the car and gathered a handful of broken glass. He leaped onto the vehicle and shouted, "Here's your church! Here's your stained glass windows!"

The church roof fell at midnight.

The glass flew into the air. "Here's your altar," he said pointing at the exposed and destroyed engine. The tires were pierced with a pick. People spoke of burning it but finally just left the hulk in the street. One squad car and three uniformed police officers watched the demolition but did nothing to prevent it nor to detain the crowd. Security personnel watched nervously from within the GM building. Most of the crowd went from GM to the Catholic cathedral ,where they picketed on one of Detroit's main thoroughfares.

In a brutally ironic twist the Poletown Neighborhood Council had arranged to have a booth at a Polish fair in Macomb County that week. They had hoped to raise people's awareness of what was going on in Poletown and to raise money to save the church at the same time as they sold sauerkraut and kielbasa. After demolition of the church, no one had the heart to pursue the project, but over $800 was invested in nonrefundable deposits for the booth and the meat. So Josephine Jakubowski slaved over huge vats of sauerkraut while four supporters tried to find companies that would donate the necessary catsup and mustard and napkins. With immense effort, on top of tearful and sleepless nights, the booth was opened and staffed all weekend. The take was $840.

Chapter

8

Poletown Priest Buried
with Its Past

We've got to do more of this, not less of it. How else are cities going to
survive? I understand some people are going to be inconvenienced, but if
that never happened you would never build a freeway, you would never
build a hospital. Some things have to be done that are in the best interest
of everybody. . . . And what's the best thing? To have the (Poletown)
plant built here. . . . I'm hopeful that justice, truth and good things will
triumph.

—GM Chairman Roger Smith
Detroit News, March 13, 1981

The demolition of the church took the heart out of the Poletown
resistance. The PNC held meetings at Hodas's house, but they regularly
subsided into angry quarrels. The voices of those who yelled "I told
you so" blurred with those who said their proposals had never been
listened to from the start. Olechowski took the brunt of people's anger,
partly because he had been the leader of the defeated PNC but also
because residents felt that Olechowski's main concern had always been
the unaffected part of Poletown on the south side of the freeway.

At what proved to be the last meeting of the PNC, people voted to
send a scathing letter to the archdiocese, the mayor, and General Motors. But Olechowski objected, saying the letter "would be a slap in the
face of the establishment." The group was shocked. The church was
destroyed. The neighborhood had been terrorized and burned to the
ground. What did they have left to lose? When they approved the
letter, Olechowski protested that this body couldn't use the PNC signa-
ture because there weren't enough original members present. Henry
Michalski, who lived next door to John Saber on Kanter Street, lost his
temper and screamed that he and his friends had nothing left, while

Olechowski still had a neighborhood and probably still had plans to rehabilitate it. The letter was signed, mailed out, but the PNC name was left off it.

Another group, the "Friends of Father Joe," formed spontaneously that fall. Fifty to 100 people, who usually met now for worship at St. Hyacinth's, gathered at a Polish hall on the city's west side under the leadership of Bob Gianinni and Christine Kujawski. Members wore pins with pictures of the ICC and T-shirts that read: "I'm proud of Father Karasiewicz." Some put "Boycott GM" stickers on their purses. The agenda usually revolved around Karasiewicz's status with the archdiocese and the immorality of the quick-take law.

Supporters and residents agreed that it was hard to continue the Poletown resistance without a central headquarters and symbol like the church. Drawing public attention to one individual house wouldn't have the same symbolic value. But people did promise that if they were notified they would form human chains between the police and families that were being forced to leave. As it turned out, most remaining residents finally signed purchase agreements during August and September. There was a brief flurry of activity when the city petitioned Judge Martin for the right to evict people prior to the date on their ninety-day notices, but that was resolved out of court.

The Jakubowskis moved into a large house with an enormous backyard in Shelby Township. Technically it was a nicer house than their upstairs flat in Poletown, but Walter sarcastically remarked that it would seem like home in seventy years. "I was exiled from Poletown," Walter told the *Detroit News*. "They destroyed our roots, our home, everything. It's like taking a sixty-year-old tree and transplanting it." Josephine added, "I have a beautiful home but every time I try to say a prayer, I cry. We lost our friends. Many moved to Warren, East Detroit, Sterling Heights. They're so far away. It's hard to take. You're supposed to forgive and forget but how can you forget? . . . I don't know if I'll ever get over it."[1]

The Dockerys moved to suburban Warren, a few miles away from the Gianninis, Crosbys, and Kaczynskis, who were scattered throughout northeast Detroit, but since Carol hadn't learned to drive it was hard to keep in touch with her family and friends. Ann Giannini's rose bushes survived the transplant and Andy opened a candy store on Seven Mile, but neither of them were happy. "Something goes out of you when you put so much effort into one home and they come and tear it down," Ann said. "If we were forced to move, why weren't we able to go together? They had all that empty land in Hamtramck. Why couldn't they put up homes for people who want to stick together? We don't have any new friends yet. The people are nice but it takes a long time to be able to talk and visit like we did."[2] Gianinni added that the new neighborhood was too quiet. "Nobody sits out on their porches. I ask my husband, 'Where is everybody?' He says they're watching TV. Who can watch that much TV?"[3]

The Crosbys moved into a pleasant little house, but George Crosby never adapted. He became disoriented and repeatedly asked to be taken home. Finally, after he had wandered away from home for three hours in bitter winter weather, he was put into a nursing home, where he died shortly thereafter. Louise Crosby learned soon after that she had cancer. Barbara Sokol didn't find a new home or make preparations to move. The city finally brought moving vans to her door, loaded up her stuff, and put it in storage. Sokol went to live with her sister and brother-in-law, Ann and Frank Dolence.

The Kaczynskis moved into a brick home with a fenced-in yard but soon discovered that their neighbors were transient. When Pat Barszenski paid a visit to them, her car was stolen from the street in front of their house. Four years after they moved in, Bernice was unsettled by the appearance of police lights. When she went outside, she discovered that a nude woman's body had been dumped out of a car just up the block. Both Bernice and Harold were bitter about the move and unhappy in the new house.

"The corporations have lost all respect for the young as well as the elders," Bernice said. "Right now it's just money, whatever they can get. They are forgetting about principles and human lives. Of course the elderly are suffering, but what's in store for our younger ones? I've got grandchildren married and right now I've got a son-in-law making a career out of the Marine Corps. If war breaks out, I say let General Motors go fight the war. Why should our children go out there and get killed, and we brood and feel sick over it? I don't feel I'd want him to go and I think I'd be just ornery enough to go out there and protest the draft and everything that goes along with it and what it stands for, because they aren't fighting for a free America. They're fighting for corporations to gain money. That's the way I feel."[4]

Ben and Ethel Feagan relocated their business on the far east side. The home they bought, in the Kaczynskis' new neighborhood, pleased them, but the business languished. For three years, they said, they had hardly any clientele. "This eminent domain . . . they can take it and shove it," Ethel Feagan complained. "If they can take my business from me, honey, they can do it to anybody."

Carl Fisher, sixty-three, who never tried to relocate his Famous Bar-B-Q Restaurant, said he missed the people. "They're dispersed, and

I don't feel I can find them any more," he said. "The cops [who used to visit Fisher's restaurant] still stop by my house in Highland Park if they're passing through. My neighbors all wonder when I'm going to be arrested," Fisher laughed. But his biggest regret was that the city could have multiplied the 1,700 indigenous jobs in Poletown with just a fraction of the money it sunk into the GM project.[5]

John Saber, sixty-eight, was finally left by himself in Poletown. Although his neighbors' houses had been bulldozed, he remained. He was endlessly engaged in preparing his own legal defenses, which were based on little more than anger and slurs against the mayor. But he would type them on legal paper, observing the exact margins. He told all who would listen that he was going to sue and win big. His sister, Helen Schuster, a seventy-two-year-old seamstress, lived in the upper flat and waited with him. Outdoors, Saber built a cinderblock wall around his home to protect it from the bulldozers. He told stories about his years in the military when he was a recruiter for World War II and later an officer in Italy, appropriating peasants' homes for his own use. He expected his military training to stand him in good stead when it came time to fend off the city with his .22.

At the end of the summer of 1981, Eddie Niedbala, the owner of the Chene-Trombly market, died of a heart attack. His widow reopened the Chene-Trombly market, keeping its old name, on Mount Elliott just south of the freeway. Stanley Danieluk, ninety-two, also died a few months after leaving the neighborhood. Danieluk was one of the last to leave, staying on even after his family moved his furniture out. Two months after moving in with his daughter, who had selected a larger home she hoped would allow him enough room to feel independent, he died of a bleeding ulcer.[6] Joseph Gorno, sixty-six, who had founded Gorno Steel and Processing in Poletown in 1963, died after leaving Poletown. In his obituary, his son is quoted saying that Gorno fled to Florida rather than watch the demolition of the seventeen-year-old steel processing plant. "That was a crusher," Gorno, Jr., said, "but he bounced back from it, like he always did. He fought for it, tried to delay the wrecking crews as long as possible."[7] Mattie Bailey's husband died of a broken heart, according to his widow. "He knew our house (in Poletown). It was old but it was no trouble," Bailey told the *Detroit News*. But their new house on Detroit's east side had a leaky roof and wet basement. "He was always running, trying to get this house fixed up. It was too much. He was my all and all. It's just me and the Lord now."[8]

Szoka met with Karasiewicz at the end of the tumultuous summer

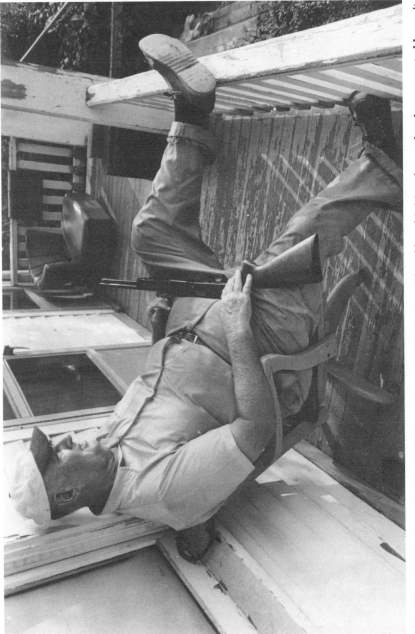

DAVID C. TURNLEY

John Saber, the last person to leave Poletown, guarded his home with a .22 and initiated countless home-created lawsuits against the mayor.

and told him not to say mass at St. Hyacinth's any more because people needed to disperse and find new parishes. Karasiewicz agreed. He was sent to St. Helena's in Wyandotte to temporarily replace a parish priest who needed a sabbatical to convalesce. But just two months later, Karasiewicz was abruptly told to leave St. Helena's. He said later that he had the impression that the rector was angry at him for being called back from his convalescence. No one knew why the archdiocese removed Karasiewicz, but some speculated that he was being punished for the media splash that greeted the celebration of his thirty-fifth anniversary in the priesthood just five days prior.

On October 18 the Friends of Father Joe had sponsored a huge dinner to celebrate the thirty-fifth anniversary of Karasiewicz's ordination. More than 400 people attended, including the Nader team, which flew back for the occasion. The Polish dancers, who had practiced in the basement of the ICC, performed during the meal and afterwards everyone joined in dancing. The food, the praise, the drinks, and the dance flowed freely, culminating in a Grand March during which everyone had the opportunity to kiss everyone else twice. There was a sky-high quality to the evening, which was widely reported in the media. Karasiewicz seemed delighted and was looking forward to a three-week vacation trip, beginning October 26.

But Karasiewicz's spirits were dampened by his knowledge that no appointment awaited his return. He traveled east during his vacation and took time to visit Gene Stilp's parents in northern Pennsylvania. While he was away, the newspapers broke the news that GM would postpone opening its Poletown plant for one year. Instead of opening in 1983 to produce 1984-model-year cars, the plant was projected to open in 1984 to produce 1985 cars. (Actually the plant would be delayed a second year, causing Frank Runnels of UAW Local 22 to complain that Detroit Cadillac workers at the older plants would have to be laid off instead of transferred as originally promised.)[9] Former residents bitterly pointed out that they could have stayed in their homes an extra year. Some, including mayoral challenger Perry Koslowski, suggested GM was going to abandon its commitment to build the plant altogether.[10]

Karasiewicz returned home November 13. One week later the archdiocese called him and said he should contact a deacon about being a hospital chaplain. The Friends of Father Joe reported that he was staying with his brothers and was discouraged that his future depended upon arrangements to be made by a deacon whom he had been unable to reach by phone.[11] Karasiewicz had nowhere to say mass, no word of an appointment, and had been told not to return to St.

Hyacinth's. Fundraisers were planned for Poletown's priest, who was apparently very low on cash, since he was without a position, but also very private about his grief and need.

At the end of the month Skalski asked the archdiocese to assign Karasiewicz to St. Hyacinth's to assist him, because he was recuperating from an accident. This was done and Karasiewicz moved back into Poletown. On December 4 a friend told Karasiewicz that on December 8 the archbishop was meeting with other bishops to discuss an appointment for him and that word would come soon. Karasiewicz took a brief retreat, but when he returned the promised word had still not arrived.

On the feast of the Immaculate Conception, fifty Poletown residents and supporters bundled up and made their way back to the site of the church. The area was a vacant, frozen mass. Residents could place the church by judging the distance to Saber's house, one of the only houses remaining. Ironically, one of the only other remaining landmarks in the entire project area was the 1,100-grave Beth-Olem Cemetery. People gathered with candles by a wooden cross that Bob Giannini had fixed in the ground where Immaculate Conception's main altar had stood. After prayers and hymns, many former residents complained that they were not looking forward to Christmas. Many hadn't looked for new churches. Some said they couldn't muster a sense of tradition from old ornaments hanging in new homes. Bernice Kaczynski threatened to deck her tree with "Poletown Lives!" stickers.

But soon thereafter everyone's sense that things could get no worse was hopelessly overwhelmed by word that Fr. Karasiewicz had died alone on Dec. 14 at the St. Hyacinth's rectory. The fifty-nine-year-old priest had a heart attack in the early morning while reading his devotions. Everyone who had been attending meetings of the Friends of Father Joe speculated that their "iron priest of Poletown" had died of a broken heart. Many wondered if anticipating Christmas, normally one of the busiest times of the year for clergy, was more than Karasiewicz could bear without a church.

Karasiewicz's body was laid out in vestments at St. Hyacinth's before the funeral on Dec. 17. People met there to pray and weep. The death of their priest made news, but to former Poletown residents and supporters the tearful regret of television reporters rang hollow. In the *Free Press* account of Karasiewicz's death, the priest was found at dawn with a book in his hands in which he had underlined the words, "My hour has come." The obituary included predictable quotes from Dearden and Szoka saying that Karasiewicz had been "a very good" and "conscientious" priest. But Vicar Robinson said, "During the time he was

Fr. Joseph Karasiewicz stands before the remains of his church. "This is worse than the Communists in Poland," Karasiewicz said. "To go down to a very basic definition of stealing, it is simply taking other people's property against their will, and this was taken away from them, the people, against their will."

going through the business at Immaculate Conception, he . . . had become a hostage to Nader's group. They had completely brainwashed Father Karasiewicz. It was . . . unreal. He got so caught up in that kind of continual pressure that he did not know what was really going on in the last three or four weeks over there." A GM spokesman said, "We are terribly sorry to hear about it . . . genuinely sorry."[12]

Preparations for the funeral were difficult. Karasiewicz's brothers, who had supported him during the last six months, did not want Szoka to officiate. Yet Catholic protocol required that as many clergy as possible attend the funeral, and it was normal for the archbishop to perform the service. The family asked Skalski to preach and friends and Poletown residents to read scripture and serve as acolytes and pallbearers. The archbishop, because it was required, was to participate in the consecration of the eucharist.

The Nader team flew into town the evening of December 16. Sandy Livingston noted: "It was difficult not to recall Vicar Robinson's warning of May 7 in the basement of the church: 'This guy, when he ends up in the nuthouse and this building is down . . . you think about him . . . you catalyzed him, you motivated him.' Such a statement did a disservice to Father Joe. Yet, by virtue of the fact that the organizing effort was based in his church I think he took a more active role than he might have otherwise." Members of the team arrived at St. Hyacinth's the next day, feeling ill and looking pale. The church was packed. The aisles were flanked by the Polish honor guard who had attended the last mass celebrated at the ICC and Karasiewicz's anniversary party. The Polish dancers were there, as well as parishioners from other churches Karasiewicz had served. Poletown residents and supporters could be heard complaining about the presence of the archbishop, whom they called a traitor and a murderer. When the clergy processed in, a whole section of people at the front of the church turned their backs to Szoka. The sermon cut to the quick of the issues. There was an ironic tension in the church as Skalski, with the archbishop seated front and center facing the congregation, preached: Karasiewicz "was no armchair liberal. He was no stooge of the Nader people. He was no pie-eyed radical. He tried to slow and stay the heavy hands of corporate, materialistic, economic objectives, masking themselves as the common good, while in actuality it would seem they were serving the rich."[13]

During the distribution of communion, many Poletown residents avoided the archbishop by crossing the aisle in order to receive the bread and wine from another priest. One man, a member of the Friends of Father Joe, went up to the archbishop to receive, extended his hands, and when Szoka offered him the bread, shook his head and turned to receive the host from the other priest. A woman accepted the host from Szoka and then asked, "Why did you let Father Joe die of a broken heart?" The archbishop blanched and took a step back in silence.

Neither the archbishop nor most of the clergy joined the funeral procession, but hundreds of others did. The route to Mt. Olivet Cemetery was altered to include a trip through Poletown. Car after car passed down Trombly through snow-covered fields of vacant land. Where the church had once stood, Bob Giannini erected a sign reading: "Rest with God Father Joe, Until we meet again." It was decorated with a wreath and flanked by the cross that marked where the altar had stood. The crowd at the cemetery huddled together against the wind and recited Polish prayers by the bronze-colored coffin. At the conclusion people circled the casket and laid their hands on it, some stooping to kiss the lid. One lone "Poletown Lives!" sticker was reverently placed at the head of the coffin, and many people's fingers lingered on it as they walked by.

Back at St. Hyacinth's, Chris Kujawski passed out a flier she had written. It concluded: "Over the past seven months, Father Joe was ignored, humiliated and mistreated by the hierarchy of the archdiocese of Detroit, by the very people who stand in the pulpit every Sunday calling for brotherhood, fellowship and extolling the value of human rights."

In late January of 1982 Roger Smith and Coleman Young met at the GM plant site to witness the raising of the first structural column for the new plant. The forty-two-foot beam would mark the center of the plant. Mayor Young commented that GM had been the victim of "vicious and unreasonable assault" for the project, adding "I don't know— it's like shooting Santa Claus."[14]

In the spring of 1982 Saber's lively and unusual court hearing came to a predictable conclusion. Saber represented himself, talking endlessly and eloquently about things often extraneous. He was allowed latitude because he was a layperson and the hearing continued for weeks. Saber railed and bared his soul in court, shocking supporters one day when he announced: "I am not a homicidal maniac." No one in court had implied he was, but Saber went on to state that although he had shot at people in the abandoned house next door to his, he had thought the people were vandals. How, he asked, was he supposed to know they were Turner Construction people?

The court ordered Saber's eviction and on March 22 five police cars pulled up on Kanter Street. Officers wrestled Saber to the floor, while Roger Saber, John's adult son, handed the police the .22. Saber, yelling, "This is worse than what's happening in Warsaw," was taken away in a squad car.[15] A moving company filled three vans with Saber's possessions, which included reels of World War II aerial film that he had shot, a train set, and boxes of news clippings. Everything was put into storage. Helen Schuster stood by, sobbing, "I don't want to go, please don't make me go."[16]

Immediately after their eviction Saber and his son stayed at St. Hyacinth's rectory, but in the months to follow Saber moved back and forth between his sister's Pearl Beach cottage and the Detroit bus station. By 1984 Saber was gaunt, having been hospitalized several times for malnutrition. He claimed to all who would listen that he was suffering from "mental anguish" resulting from the GM project.

On the first anniversary of Karasiewicz's eviction from the Immaculate Conception Church, Poletown residents and supporters returned to the site. Traffic into the area was slow, because construction crews were blocking lanes to take down the pedestrian overpasses which Fr. Cendrowski had fought to have built for schoolchildren in the 1950s. Surveyor stakes marked out the land which had once held the foundations of 1,362 homes but now was flat and vacant except for the steel skeleton of the plant rising to the north. Ann Giannini brought roses from her new garden to put at the foot of the new white cross erected at the spot where the original one had stood for nearly a year before being broken down in the spring. Fifty people convened in the mud to pray and to talk. They still speculated about whether they could buy the plot of land from the corporation.

GM officials gave permission for the people to gather on the site on condition that the media not be alerted to the anniversary. The ceremony was solemn, but afterwards Bernice Kaczynski and Ann Giannini began yanking up surveyor sticks and throwing them to the wind.

In his 1984 state of the city address, Mayor Young described the acquisition of Poletown and construction of the GM plant as his "most significant accomplishment." Many had hoped that the Poletown resistance would teach city hall never to repeat that sort of demolition. But in 1986 the mayor announced plans to condemn and destroy 1,000 Detroit homes and businesses for a Chrysler expansion project. The project was projected to preserve 4,000 jobs. It would cost no less than 195 million public dollars, and quite possibly more. During the course of the project it became clear that the City of Detroit had been landbanking in the area since 1975.[17]

Chrysler told UAW members that it would only commit to the

Josephine Jakubowski takes a moment to pray at the cross that marks the place where her church once stood.

DAVID C. TURNLEY

By fall of 1981 nearly all of Poletown had been destroyed.

expansion project if the union made significant concessions. The corporation wanted the number of job classifications dropped from ninety-eight to ten, which some workers worried would make them interchangeable and even more expendable. Chrysler also insisted on acceptance of the team concept, which encourages the breaking down of adversarial worker-management relations but may also fatally weaken the unions.

The union leadership agreed and sold the concessions to the workers, who ratified it overwhelmingly. But Stephen Smith, who had worked at Chrysler for fifteen years, told the *Detroit News*, "The union leaders at the top level have completely betrayed us; they're working for the other side. They're not working for us."[18]

The city council approved the project and the media gave space to claims that the neighborhood was deteriorating anyway. The mayor boasted that even people who had said they opposed the project were scurrying down to city hall to collect their checks. But Lutchia Gray, who grabbed the microphone at the conclusion of a public hearing on the Chrysler project, accused the mayor of allowing the neighborhood to deteriorate in order to make property acquisition easier. "This thing has been planned all along and we were made to suffer," she yelled.[19] As in Poletown, property owners were represented by condemnation lawyer Alan Ackerman, who had helped draft the legislation that was now depriving them of their homes and businesses.

Fr. Nicholas Farina sent a letter to the editor of the *Free Press*, saying he was shocked both by news of the Chrysler expansion project and by how rundown the city's neighborhoods had become during his six-month absence. "It seems clear to me that the city has great interest in creating a beautiful downtown area and pleasing Big Business, but little interest in preserving the neighborhoods. . . . The poor and people of modest means are running out of places to live. I wonder whether the ultimate aim of the city administration is to have not only the most mega-plants in the nation, but the fewest viable neighborhoods."[20]

And, in fact, many of Detroit's remaining viable neighborhoods were under threat. People near the Detroit City Airport, where the Kaczynskis and Feagans relocated, learned that the mayor was considering sacrificing their homes and perhaps part of a cemetery for an expansion which would make it possible for 747s to land at the city airport. In addition, the city planned to take more land in northeast Detroit for prison construction. Residents of the Detroit's Cass Corridor learned that in 1983, the director of city planning, Corinne Gilb, wanted to attract a World's Fair to the area by first leveling forty acres and planting tulips to attract a horticultural fair, followed by a high technology fair. The Cass Corridor neighborhood was labeled the "technology crescent" by city planners. When residents, mostly single renters and elderly poor, complained, Gilb responded: "This isn't Poletown, for God's sake, this is tulips."[21] People north of Tiger Stadium got nervous when it was rumored that the new owner of the Tigers, Tom Monaghan, offered millions of dollars for St. Peter's Episcopal Church, probably in an attempt to get the Catholic Worker soup kitchen out of the neighborhood.[22] Land speculation was felt in earnest when Monaghan and others tried to give the area "a facelift" by opening a new pizza store, replacing an old-time auto parts business with a Tiger bar, and razing old houses for parking lots. Also, in southwest Detroit plans were discussed which would involve building a tourist center at the foot of Detroit's privately-owned bridge to Canada, which would require demolition of thirty acres of homes.[23]

Meanwhile, the City of Flint had agreed to destroy 400 homes for construction of "Buick City," a $250 million GM manufacturing area. At about the same time the *Free Press* reported that Hamtramck might take title to the homes just north of the Poletown plant (the same homes Poletown residents had hoped might be sacrificed in place of theirs for the GM plant) to build an industrial park.[24]

The Millender Center (prefabricated in Ohio) was constructed in 1985, and it still stands partially vacant, across from the partially vacant Renaissance Center. Track was laid for a $147 million people mover, an elevated minisubway which would connect downtown offices, retail centers, and hotels so that the clientele need never set foot on Detroit's sidewalks. By 1985 the People Mover was $73 million overbudget.[25] Patches of the riverfront were closed off for private developments which were often heavily subsidized with public money. The *Detroit Metro Times* drew the mayor's ire when it revealed that the administration had plans to encourage construction of gambling casinos on Belle Isle, the city's beautiful and already over-used river island park.[26]

In 1985 the mayor received a 44 percent raise, giving him a salary of $115,000 and making him one of the best-paid city officials in the nation. But Young was not without critics. At a 1987 National Conference of Black Political Scientists, Linda Williams reported that the mayor's "corporate-centered development strategy serves the same masters which ruled Detroit before 1973, that is, Detroit's historically powerful business elites." Williams added that Young's only contribution to Detroit's poor, black residents may be his integration of the police department, because the city's residents are increasingly poor and welfare-dependent. "While Young governs," Williams concluded, "business magnates still rule."[27]

News columnists began to raise the same concerns. "There is a trickle [of new residents] into the city, drawn by lofts and expensive apartments that encircle the reinvigorated downtown," George Cantor wrote in the *Detroit News.*

"But people continue to pour out of Detroit's neighborhoods as through the sluice gate of a dam. These residents did not run when the great exodus of the middle class reached its peak in the late 60s and early 70s. . . . These people stayed then and would prefer to stay now. [But] they all echo the same theme. The arsons and break-ins and abandoned hulks that scar every block are more than residents can take. Virtually all of them refuse to believe that this vandalism is random. Instead, they discern a pattern. [After reading a news story that said the city was planning three new industrial corridors, one correspondent told Cantor] "As soon as I saw that story, I knew we'd had it. It was right after that when the arson started. You can't tell me this isn't being deliberately ignored . . . or even worse . . . by the people downtown." Over and over again I heard references to Poletown as an explanation as to why this was happening. "The city ran into a buzz saw there and it wants to make sure there's nothing left to oppose its plans here," one businesswoman on Van Dyke told me."[28]

Chuck Moss wrote a column that was even more damning:

"We're rebuilding a new city," says Mayor Young, and he ain't kidding. . . . What is the Detroit that Mayor Young destroyed, and what is he building? Make no mistake, the city government is indeed a conscious destroyer. When that cancerous "abandoned" rat-filled, junkie-infested house on your block is owned by the city, and your land is mapped out for a casino or a politically favored big corporation, the decay of your neighborhood is no coincidence. The city he is destroying is summarized in one word: "Poletown." It's a city of neighborhoods, churches and parochial schools, of local grocery stores and tiny corner bars. It's a place of fierce traditions and loyalties, resistant to mayoral power. It's small-scale and human. What city is he building? Renaissance Center, Joe Louis, Riverfront, GM Poletown: big, ugly, brutal concrete projects which have no relation of scale to anything human. Young's Detroit is a place of mammoth construction with equally vast contract fortunes to be dispensed and a strangling indifference to everyday, street level life. Coleman Young, the old socialist, is building a Brave New World. And it isn't working. Humans don't like to live that way."[29]

Little rebellions began to surface around the state. When residents of Detroit's Third Street noted that Burroughs Corporation was buying up options on property in their area, they fought back immediately. They speculated that Burroughs was probably buying the land to provide parking areas for its new $40 million office complex. And they guessed, rightly, that if Burroughs were public about its intentions, it would either have to forego the federal grant it was seeking or agree to pay $4,000 to every resident it relocated for the parking area. Instead, Burroughs pursued the Urban Development Action Grant while vigorously denying any plans to turn the neighborhood into a parking lot. Its land purchases were done quietly and went largely unnoticed until the community started to fight back. Protestors from the area watched the film *Poletown Lives!* and tried to learn lessons from the fate of that community. When they picketed outside Burroughs Corporation, they carried signs reading "No More Poletowns" and "What Good Is a City with No Communities?"[30] A coalition of community groups came together, calling themselves SOS (Save Our Spirit). Their agenda was to try to get some control of the city budget, which they did by designing their own budget, agreed on by all members. In this way the mayor could no longer count on redirecting funds by having community groups squabble and compete among themselves. Likewise, in 1988 a coalition of thirty neighborhood groups discussed the possibility of organizing a city property-tax strike to protest the city's cavalier attitude toward their communities.[31]

The summer of 1988 provided Young with a number of defeats. First, a retirement pension increase (which hiked the mayor's pension from $20,000 to $80,000 a year) was protested by citizens who circulated a petition demanding that the increase be subjected to ballot approval. To preempt the ballot action, the city council rescinded its action authorizing the pension increase for the mayor and for council members. In the August primary, voters rejected the mayor's gambling proposition three-to-one. They also approved financial allocations to neighborhood development, while refusing to support allocations for further downtown developments. Then, in the fall of 1988, the city council passed, seven-to-one, an ordinance which could require the mayor to get council approval before he could pursue the plans he had made public to move the Grand Prix race onto Belle Isle. The next day, Young announced that the race would stay downtown.[32]

In 1988 Emmett Moten, who had directed the CEDD, expressed disappointment that the Poletown plant had not generated the new feeder plants that he had anticipated. The plant opened two years late, when 1,500 workers completed training, in July, 1985. At the employees' entrance the corporation posted a sign reading "This property is monitored by closed-circuit TV cameras and security personnel. Trespassers will be prosecuted."

James Hocker, a GM worker since 1952, had mixed feelings about working at the new plant because of its policies. Hocker, who had worked as a janitor at the Conor Avenue Stamping Plant, said in a NOAR (National Organization for an American Revolution) newsletter:

> Poletown is totally different. Most people coming to this plant have no concept of what they're getting into. You go through two weeks of training school, minimum, which is designed primarily to train you in group dynamics and inform you about the personality of the people you'll be working with. Then they bring you into the plant and introduce you to the job. In our case, we had to go through eight weeks of school, because of the technical training. I am what they call "tech support"— which includes those workers supporting those workers in production. They have put janitors on a pedestal compared to where we were before. They say we have to become people who take initiative and responsibility because of the character of our job. The slogan is "Work Smart, Not Hard!" We have all the equipment to do the job. We don't sweep the floors, we have machines to wash them. We only use brooms to get the corners clean. For example, I have been working in the powerhouse driving a scrubber which is a huge machine with brushers underneath that you can let down to the floor, brushes in the center which are constantly moving and scrubbing, and a squeegie at the back with a vacuum which sucks up water and cleans the floor. The big scrubbers cost about $20,000, the little ones about $1,200.
>
> You [also] have a tremendous amount of automation in the body shop. They have a machine called the "Robogate" which does in one action what it used to take numerous workers to do. They have cameras which show up bad welds. Each car is on a skid from the beginning, so before a car gets out of the department, they can shift it to one side for repair. Meanwhile other cars can keep going down the line. Whenever a worker has to work under a car, the car goes up and stays up until it gets to the station where it has to go down.

Hocker said most workers were amazed by the technology and the amenities at the new plant. No expense had been spared. An outside contractor was hired just to keep the lawn pretty. The cafeteria was lavish in comparison to the ones at the old plants. (Ironically, despite the mayor's projection that several hundred street sandwich vendors would thrive near the plant, most workers were likely to eat at the cafeteria.) The restrooms were nicer. And for the time being, Hocker said, workers were pacified. But he wondered if labor issues would eventually flare up. Already, skilled workers were being put into eighteen-month training courses to pick up other skills. Traditionally, the union would protest this, because a millwright skilled as a welder might cost a welder his job. But in 1985 members couldn't be sure what the UAW would do. The leadership at Solidarity House seemed most interested in following GM's lead and diversifying by making aggressive takeover bids at other shops, including the 21,000-member Michigan State Employes' Association.[33]

There were other concessions in the works as well. Workers were given less than twenty-four-hours notice for forced overtime at the Poletown plant. "The role of the union has become limited or irrelevant compared to the past in relation to everyday problems in the plant— like working too hard or not having the tools you need," Hocker said. "The union used to take care of these problems, but now if you have a problem at work you don't call a committeeman to take it up with the foreman. You take it up at the team meeting." Hocker had been elected a team leader. "Some workers come to the job with the lackadaisical attitudes of the past, and it shows up quickly at our team meetings which meet once a week on company time," he said. "The workers bring their complaints or problems to the facilitator or team leader before the meeting and they go on the agenda. Everybody participates in the discussion because that is what we were taught in [GM's training] school, how to work as a team. That is how you find the contradictions that are developing among workers. The supervisor sits in our meeting. He is the resource person; he knows who to see to solve a problem."

Hocker seemed pleased by the responsibility GM was giving workers but tentative about the effect of the corporation's new policies in the long run. He pointed out that GM was unlikely to pay much in property taxes and, since most of the workers in the plant lived in the suburbs, workers' income tax contribution would be minimal. "We need to see that we are not getting what we thought we would get by using public monies to create the Poletown plant. Poletown is a small oasis compared to the reality around it. Instead of the city and community being bolstered, what we are seeing is a shrinking number of privileged workers on the inside who don't see the deterioration and destruction taking place on the outside because they don't want to see it, even though in the long run it is going to jeopardize all of us."[34]

One person who visited the Poletown plant and did see the toll GM's progress had taken on the community was *Free Press* editor Neal Shine. Shine toured the plant in early 1985 and felt haunted by the anguished faces of Poletown residents. Although he was impressed by the plant and its technology, Shine wrote that he kept wondering what part of Poletown had been located beneath the plant. "I wondered if anybody had ever suggested to GM that the location of some of the

Poletown landmarks, great and small, be honored with a stenciled marker on the new cement floor. Things like: 'On this spot, Stella Borowski operated her grocery store on Kanter for 50 years,' or 'This marks the location of the *Famous Bar-B-Q Restaurant* on Chene near Grand Blvd. where Roman Karolewski and Al Azar played their last game of gin rummy in 1981.' A city that loses part of itself, Shine wrote, "loses a part of its humanity."[35]

The public heard less and less about Poletown's former residents. Some of them still gathered informally for mass at St. Hyacinth's, particularly on the anniversaries of Karasiewicz's eviction, the seizure of the church, and the priest's death. Bernice Kaczynski and Ann Giannini kept the issue alive for a while by petitioning the city council to name the ring road at the new plant "Poletown." It was their hope that no one would be able to enter the plant without remembering the struggle and the pain that went into its construction. In a sense the name the council gave the central freeway bridge leading to the plant does acknowledge the multiple curses uttered by Poletown residents and the haunting loss of the community. The sign reads "Lucky Place." (See Appendix D.)

One of the unresolved questions in the city's lore about Poletown is whether or not Poletown's residents are content in their new surroundings. City officials claimed that the majority of residents received more money for their homes than they could have otherwise gotten and took the opportunity to move into a better neighborhood. This appeared to be refuted by the deaths, Citizens District Council complaints, and court suits, but a $31,500 study conducted for the city by Leon Pastalon, a gerontologist at the University of Michigan, confirmed the city's view. Pastalon indicated that 87 percent of 100 randomly selected, elderly subjects found their new neighborhoods quieter and safer.

"The evidence is very strong that a most difficult and potentially explosive situation was handled very sensitively and skillfully by the Community and Economic Development Department," Pastalon concluded.[36] The fact that respondents liked their new homes proved that: "(1) elderly people can successfully adjust to a new residential setting very readily despite long residential tenure in one place and (2) the relocation program did an excellent job of facilitating the match up between need, preference and the 'practical.'" (This last point was made despite the fact that only 6 percent of those interviewed said they relied on the city's relocation program.)

Pastalon did not stress that his data revealed "the large majority of respondents," said they missed their former neighbors, friends, churches, and stores, adding that "they were glad it was over and never wanted to have anyone experience that kind of trauma." Nor did he dwell on the fact that about one-half of the respondents thought the move "made their health worse," complaining of nervousness, depression, fatigue, and illness. Sixty-two percent of the respondents also complained that the city payment did not cover the full cost of their new houses.

Five months later a companion study, which interviewed former Poletown residents under sixty years of age, came to the same conclusions. Using the same survey questions the Relocation Unit of the Neighborhood Service Organization found that 84 percent of those relocated thought their new housing safer, more spacious, and more comfortable. Forty-four percent indicated there was nothing they disliked in their new neighborhood and that there were fewer abandoned houses, unleashed dogs, and incidents of crime.

However, in his results Joseph Gorham notes that the questionnaire did not allow for distinctions between whether the signs of neighborhood deterioration in Poletown preceded or followed announcement of the GM project. Only a small percentage of this sample, which included three times as many renters as homeowners and was 57 percent black, felt their health had suffered from the move. But, surprisingly, this survey turned up more respondents who were dissatisfied with the move, even though 44 percent of them had lived in Poletown for five or less years.[37]

Some of the central issues in the Poletown struggle have been clarified. For instance, the fear of robotics expressed by Harley Shaiken proved to be premature, since GM's robots were unable to perform as hoped. The *Wall Street Journal* reported in 1986 that "so far, the Hamtramck plant, instead of a showcase, looks more like a basket case. Though the plant has been open seven months, the automated guided vehicles [AGV's] are sitting idle while technicians try to debug the software that controls their movements. In the ultra-modern paint shop, robots at times have spray-painted each other instead of the cars. Some cars have been painted so badly that GM had to ship them to a 57-year-old plant to be repainted."[38]

Reliance on machines gave way to reliance on the team concept, which one employee at GM's Poletown plant described as follows: "During two weeks of classroom training we played psychological games to make us more outspoken and friendly. The team tried to figure out, if you were in the middle of the ocean on a sinking boat, what you'd throw overboard—a pocket-knife, raft, etc." A team concept handout read in part: "Expected Behaviors: Level with each other. Do more than your share. Volunteer to help others." She added: "People bent over backwards to do their jobs. If someone comes in late, others will cover their work." But when the plant was reduced to single-shift production, GM required that people double up on jobs and morale fell. "Everyone was so disappointed. Everything's chaotic."[39]

The public also learned GM decided to truck supplies in and cars out of the plant. The acreage set aside for railmarshalling, which was pivotal in Poletown's suits, was not used. In fact, GM had the initial track that was laid buried and covered with landscaping. In addition, Larry Brown, the project economist at CEDD, conceded that Poletown residents' demand that GM build a parking structure had been reasonable. Brown said GM officials met with city realtors at least once a week. "We worked with them trying to minimize their use of the land," Brown said. "They could have done anything they wanted to do, but they're the experts in producing cars efficiently" and they demanded the land.[40]

In addition, Poletown residents' suspicions that the state eminent domain law had been altered primarily in order to enable the city to take their homes proved to be well grounded. A 1985 *Detroit News* spread on Detroit's development and future indicated that GM had offered Detroit a shot at coming up with land for a plant in 1979, but Young couldn't act quickly enough.

"I had been through that first experience with Murphy, when we couldn't move in time," Young said. "It was over a Cadillac transmission plant. Indiana was bidding for it, as was some place further south, along with Livonia [Michigan]. When we were out of it, I joined in to persuade GM to build in Livonia. If a plant is in Livonia, it helps Detroit. A plant in Indiana obviously doesn't help anyone. So we settled that, then we got ready for the next time GM came around. We had the state law changed to provide for quick-taking of land by local government—which was used for the first time when we put the Poletown thing together."[41]

Observers noted a frequent confusion of pronouns which blurred corporate and public roles. Comments Roger Smith made to the *Detroit News* in an article about city development clearly reflected this. "One of these days," GM's chairman said, "I believe we'll get around to knocking down the trash that's left on Woodward Avenue, put up a few things, and we're really going to find a beautiful city there."[42] Smith's willingness to pass judgement on Woodward Avenue and to volunteer to knock it down horrified some members of the 4C's, a community group striving to rehabilitate that area for the low-income people who already lived there. It also rang familiar in the ears of some who had lived in the housing near GM's world headquarters and in Poletown.

In the mid-1980s GM started demanding reassessments of their plant properties in Michigan, arguing that they were paying 70 percent too much in property taxes. School districts throughout the state started fretting when a study compiled by Ralph Nader's associate Jim Mussleman revealed that the total value of the tax challenges requested by GM in July 1985 was $50 million annually. In Grand Blanc, the reduction requested would cut $1 million from GM's $1.46 million in property taxes. School superintendent David Fultz complained that the schools would be devastated and that the township could ill afford to hire the lawyers and appraisers to fight back in court. GM's challenges were handled by the Honigman, Miller, Schwartz and Cohn firm, which had represented the City of Detroit's interests during the demolition of Poletown for GM.

Pontiac, where 40 percent of the tax base is paid by GM, was likely to sustain severe losses. Ironically, GM also pursued an assessment reduction at its brand new, highly modernized Orion Township plant, despite the fact that the plant had already received a sizeable tax abatement when the city of Pontiac gave the permission for the suburban replacement facility. GM argued that its Orion Township plant, which had been assessed at $121 million, should really be assessed at $75 million.[43]

Then in 1987, when GM topped the Fortune 500 list for the second year in a row, the corporation announced that it was closing nine plants and laying off 29,000 workers, 17,450 of whom lived in Michigan. Standard & Poor's analysts predicted that this loss would cost Detroit $10 million in income tax revenue. Members of UAW locals 15 and 22 approached the Detroit City Council for help, asking the council to prevent repossession of workers' homes and cars. The union members said GM had misled the city when it implied that the Fleetwood and Clark plants would remain open until 1989 and that workers had expected to maintain their living standard until then.[44]

After opening two years late the Poletown plant was open sporadically. In February 1987 its second shift was laid off indefinitely, and by summer the first shift was laid off, because GM was selling 25 percent fewer large, luxury cars than it had the year prior for the same period. One Wall Street analyst told the *Free Press* that "the dealers are just choking on cars now. There are too many cars out there now." The only car production that continued at the Poletown plant was for the

Allante, a new $50,000 GM car that offered only one option—with or without a mobile telephone.

Belatedly, members of the city council expressed anger at GM for taking advantage of city help in construction of the plant and then offering only 3,400 jobs (and even those were on again, off again). "GM has slapped Detroit in the face," Councilman John Peoples complained.[45] By 1988 the one shift that was on line was forced to work involuntary overtime, working six-day weeks. By 1989 unemployed UAW members and area residents circulated petitions, asking GM to discontinue overtime so that others could work a second shift.

Worst of all, J. T. Battenberg III, manager of the Flint Product Team of the Buick-Oldsmobile-Cadillac Group, told the *Automotive News* in 1987 that its Poletown-style plants were too big. "If we had it to do over," he said, "we would build them smaller."[46]

Meanwhile, UAW president Owen Bieber complained to Congress that in 1987 GM was expected to open twelve new plants in Mexico, where workers earn less than $1-an-hour. At the same time, Bieber said, GM was increasing its joint venture plants in Korea, where wages are low and "workers' rights were severely limited under martial law." Bieber also noted that GM was saving hundreds of millions of dollars because of worker concessions and then giving $30,000 bonuses to 6,000 of its executives. Apparently not lacking for capital, GM spent more than $7 billion purchasing Hughes Aircraft and EDS, Bieber added.[47]

Not surprisingly, unemployment in Michigan stayed high. The year the Poletown plant was originally slated to open, one out of every five workers in Michigan was looking for a job. Michigan's unemployment, officially figured at 17.6 percent, was the highest it had been since the federal government started keeping those statistics in 1956. Unemployment for black people was twice as high as for whites.[48] On the same day GM's record profits were reported, another article indicated the mayor would beef up his fight against crime and his reliance on undercover police.[49] By 1985 crime in the city was so prevalent that Young—whose first mayoral platform protested police murder and racial brutality—defended a homeowner who shot and killed a teenager who tried to break into the house.[50] Within a matter of days a second homeowner shot a burglar, this time after chasing him out of the house and onto the sidewalk. City observers began to express concern about a vigilante spirit.[51] Throughout the 1980s each year's crime statistics topped the last. The police chief gave talks to his officers, cautioning them not to "become paranoid." Twenty surveillance cameras were placed on downtown buildings. A special police team was put together that was capable of "surgical, precision shooting." The police department purchased a military tank. And when the city council passed an ordinance that curbed police surveillance powers in an effort to protect the rights of demonstrators, the mayor vetoed it.[52]

Meanwhile, the debts incurred by the city of Detroit for the GM project came home to roost. The $100 million Section 108 loan was originally slated to be repaid in six years. Detroit agreed to repay an average of $5 million a year between 1984 and 1987 and, at the end of the decade, to make balloon payments of $37.5 million and $41.6 million. The interest due on each portion of the $100 million drawn by the city ranged from 9 percent to 15 percent. The city monies which had been offered to the Department of Housing and Urban Development as collateral for the loan were Detroit's Community Development Block Grant (CDBG) monies, which were originally legislated for neighborhood development. However, there was no doubt that the balloon payments due for 1988 and 1989 were going to exceed the city's block grant allocations. Therefore, Detroit floated $54 million worth of revenue bonds in 1984 to repay part of the Section 108 loan.[53]

However, covering the costs of the Poletown plant would prove to be a further burden. Court awards exceeding the "just compensation" paid to home and business owners in Poletown began to roll in early. And, of course, the new quick-take act provided that the city pay attorney fees totaling one-third of the difference between the court award and the city's original payment. Within two years it was clear that the city would be at least $80 million dollars overbudget for its land acquisition in Poletown.

As early as October 1981 the Citizens District Council, which authorized the condemnation in Poletown, reversed itself and complained bitterly that the city's taking of land amounted to a "brutal confiscation." The Rev. Arkles Brooks, co-chair of the CDC, said the city "failed to provide even the minimum of assistance towards a successful relocation of businesses displaced from the project area, and has failed to live up not only to verbal commitments but also to written contracts." In a resolution of censure the CDC said the city "in effect destroyed numerous businesses and deprived the property owners not only of their (property) but also their livelihood."[54]

Councilperson Mel Ravitz reported in 1984 that in at least five cases the court award was ten times the amount the city offered. Property values were hiked from $723,000 to $7,509,000 for parcel 1662 (Great Lakes Steel), and from $356,955 to $4,200,000 for parcel 717. Ravitz reminded the council that the quick-take law provided for city payment of all attorney fees in order to penalize municipalities that did not operate in good faith when assessing the land in question. In the case of parcel 717, the attorneys representing the owner received $958,000. Attorney fees for parcel 1661 would be $2.3 million.

"Clearly, the project isn't going to be as good for the city of Detroit in the long run as was anticipated and we may not even come out whole," Ravitz said. "It will be a very advantageous thing for GM, but I am doubtful whether the city will find it equally bright and smiley down the road."[55] Ravitz added that the award for St. Joseph's Hospital was likely to be $30 million above the city offer of $11 million, which could entail attorney fees of $9.7 million. [Current predictions are that it may be a $100 million award.] Ravitz also complained that CEDD was generally uncooperative and kept information from the council, pointing out that the council still didn't have access to the city's out-of-court cash settlement figures.[56]

Among those who took the city to court were Charles Mistele and Kenneth Colbert. Mistele sued because he was unable to relocate his eighty-six-year-old coal business with the $357,000 the city offered for his property. Mistele told the city council that the city wouldn't honor its agreement to reappraise his property and that he couldn't get a bank loan to provide for the move because he couldn't offer the title to his property as collateral. Mistele said his company had provided the city with seventy jobs and had provided coal to the Detroit school system for $1 million less than the company which took the bid when Mistele closed.[57] Kenneth Colbert, who managed a gas station at Chene and I-94, sued because he lost his livelihood. Colbert, who did not own the Boron gas station, said he had increased its profitability dramatically but had to go on welfare when it was taken for the GM plant. A jury awarded him $30,000 plus $20,000 in interest in April 1985.[58]

When James Shively filed suit for 110 homeowners in April 1985, he said: "It became quite evident that there was no intention . . . to follow the necessary rules to make sure that the citizens were protected and getting housing that was adequate."[59] Federal regulations required that the government ensure that people relocated into "decent, safe and sanitary" housing with a comparable amount of space, in an "area not less desirable," and accessible to place of employment.[60]

Most of the homeowners' complaints alleged inadequate city inspection of the new homes. Residents said that after purchase they discovered defects in the plumbing, wiring, appliances, or basement and sidewalk masonry. The CDC noted 530 complaints, only six of which had been resolved by CEDD. In a report to the city council, Minnie Pearce of the CDC wrote: "Once the land was cleared and the blue-print drawn, bricks in place, CEDD felt as though the project had been completed with success, not giving a *?** about the citizens. Now let it be understood we are not appearing before you just for jobs but for some relief for the relocatees. It's indeed a great sorrow that this Project went down in history as being the largest and fastest relocation Project ever; on the other hand, the Citizens were left in the cold with no statistics to give them. We as a city can afford to give General Motors a twelve-year tax abatement and not give the taxpayers a $300 furnace. Once again, the scales of justice have been tipped where the 'haves' keep getting and the 'have nots' never do."[61]

The 560 complaints included lists of grievances from all the former Poletown residents who had fought the project and relocated in the city of Detroit, but from many others as well. City officials suggested that businesses and residents alike sued for money because they were solicited by condemnation attorneys who saw an opportunity to make millions of dollars. Whether people's complaints were entirely legitimate, or whether they represented a resentment of their new surroundings or a basic sense that they were owed more for the inconvenience of moving, can't be easily determined, but their decisions to sue certainly would seem to provide some caution to the government about whether to pursue projects of the same scope.

"By the time this is done, it [the city] will be four times over budget for relocation and acquisition," predicted Bert Burgoyne, an attorney who represented a number of Poletown businesses. Had the city honestly estimated the costs of acquiring and clearing the land for the GM project, Burgoyne said, the federal government would never have approved the project.[62]

But city planner Larry Brown sees it differently. "We'd do it again," declared Brown, the principal development economist for the Central Industrial Park Project. "There's no question about it. The city didn't have a choice. We'd have to do it again. If we had not been able to accommodate General Motors in the city, then we would have had no credibility with any other companies in terms of being able to deliver buildable land or financing. We were just really lucky that General Motors gave us a year's notice."[63]

Epilogue

Some will consider this book too harsh. They will suggest that there are mitigating factors which have been given, at best, short shrift. They will point to more positive aspects of the mayor's administration and argue, rightly, that he has played a vital role in helping to develop and empower a black middle class in Detroit. Others will defend Cardinal Dearden, saying that he had a tremendous commitment to the inner city. Still others may have kinder words for the media, the courts, the Left, GM.

It's my intention, however, to put the story in high relief. I don't want it obscured by mitigating factors, which, like a veil, can distort reality, making it appear complicated—a morass for which no one is accountable. This book is not intended to be an apologetic for the powers-that-be.

Readers whose sympathies are with the Poletown residents may feel that the story is too relentlessly depressing: people whose lives were composed of their union loyalty, their tenure in the auto plants, their patriotism, and their willingness to fight in U.S. wars were rejected, ignored, and robbed by the very institutions through which they claimed their identities. But there is a hopeful twist to the story: these same people broke free of the illusion of civility that these institutions carry as trappings. I remember clearly when Bernice Kaczynski went to the microphone during the 1981 General Motors stockholders meeting. All the weight of the place was against her. The aura there was orderly, well-educated, well-paid, powerful; everyone seemed to be following the rules politely. But when GM chairman Roger Smith cut Bernice off in mid-sentence, telling her he had heard enough about Poletown, there was an outcry. Poletown representatives could see clearly that GM's power was being used to deprive this woman of her home, her community, her preferred way of life, and now her voice. The rules in the place were skewed. The winners of the game were predetermined. So historically law-abiding Poletown residents felt free to cry out and to disrupt that meeting. In exactly the same spirit, Poletown resisters learned to interrupt reporters' interviews, to raise placards at the mayor's inaugural dinner, and, ultimately, to go to jail when the city's police force moved on the church.

Poletown residents knew at the outset that GM's and the city's voices were more powerful than theirs. Had they all yielded to the "sense of inevitability" which Justice Ryan described, the Cadillac project would have been put in place relatively easily. The apparent impact of the story would have been mild.

But by deciding to speak the truth, even as their homes and community and much of what they were fighting for was destroyed, the Poletown resisters managed to force the powers to expose the full brutality of which they were capable. If residents had not pressured GM to save the church, Mayor Young and the cardinal would never have had to act out the charade of refusing GM's offer to move the building; their full complicity might not have been revealed. Likewise, observers would never have witnessed the overwhelming police power present at the time of the seizure and destruction of the church. By holding vigils and demonstrating at every turn, Poletown residents made the forces at work visible.

Many people who learn of Poletown say, "This can't happen in America!" But the story makes it clear that it can, and by inference we can believe that it also happened to the Indians, to the slaves, to those whose family farms are being swept into corporate ownership.

The creative, resilient, outraged spirit of those in Poletown who fought the GM project is their gift to the future. It is a spirit mixed with irreverence and humor. I picture GUCCI banners flying from the church ramparts. I remember older women taking a pie to the police officers at the seventh precinct and later placing red vigil candles next to the feet of each police officer stationed at the demolition of the church. The garden flowers woven through the fence surrounding the demolition stand out too. I remember Bernice, Harry, and Carol laughing as they rode their bikes around the neighborhood—the Poletown Patrol trying to keep things safe from the destructive power of GM and the city. And there was laughter on Mitchell Street when residents tacked "Mitchell Creek" signs on the trees, making a joke out of the fact that the city allowed a broken water main to flood their street.

The spirit is a human one. It is alive in every culture, focused in small acts of courage. In Poland, people erected a cross on the site where a demonstrator had been killed by the government. The government removed it. The people replaced it and left flowers. When the cross was removed again, people laid flowers in the hole where the cross had been, and the act now served a double purpose—to show reverence for the one who had died and to serve as a reminder that the government wanted to destroy all such symbols. We have many symbols like these, from the Passover meal and the cross itself to the trail of tears, the underground railroad, and Ghandi's fasts.

"There is another Polish community under strife in Poland," Tom Olechowski told Poletown's residents at the beginning. "They have tanks ringed around the country. They are under threat of death, and they are standing up to tremendous power and pressure from their own government, from their own police, and from Russian tanks. If they can stand up to that kind of pressure, I think we too can deal with pressure. I want to remind you of a saying that there is in Polish: 'Jeszce Polska Nie Zginela'; that means 'Poland still lives!'"

Poletown lives! It lives in the hearts of those who lost their community and way of life in 1981. It lives in this book and in the film called *Poletown Lives!* It lives in college classrooms and among community groups where these events are discussed. It lives in the fact that the new Cadillac plant is known as the Poletown plant. It lives, too, among those who wonder if they will have the courage to act in freedom when they face such powers.

We can be thankful for the story. It is the best of our heritage.

A

How Eminent Domain Has Been Used Nationally

Historically, the power of eminent domain was vested in a sovereign who could take a subject's land at will. When American revolutionaries declared themselves free from the claims of the English king and drafted the constitution, private property rights were central. Colloquialisms, unfortunately sexist in nature, developed which indicated that "a man's home was his castle," that he "was lord of his household." There was a presumption that what went on within one's home was private and free from the grasp of the state. The house itself was the shelter of this freedom.

The states' earliest power of eminent domain enabled officials to take title to private property solely for construction of public projects or the development of natural resources. The standard of review imposed by the courts was whether land condemnation served a "public use"— for instance, the construction of schools and hospitals.

With the advent of industrialization in the nineteenth century this prerogative was broadened so that the government could use eminent domain to take private land for private corporations eager to construct bridges, canals, highways, and railroads. The courts' rationale was that although private land was being forfeited to another private entity, the resulting benefit would be for public use and accessible to the public. Even so, as early as 1837 some courts began to rebel against this broad reading of the state's power of eminent domain. Judges began to insist that eminent domain be restricted to projects designed for the public's actual use and in which the public maintained some control of the property, as in the case of public schools. In 1877 the Michigan Supreme Court ruled that nothing short of "necessity of the extreme sort" should justify the state's usurpation of private property rights.[1]

The tension between broad and narrow interpretations of eminent domain continued into the twentieth century. "Throughout the nineteenth century and into the twentieth, the courts were divided on the meaning of the public use clause; a narrow reading required a guarantee of public access to the property taken, while a broader reading merely required a tangible public benefit," writes Laura Mansnerus. "The conflict was generally resolved in favor of the broad reading, under which 'public use' came to mean public advantage."[2]

By the mid-1930s state courts permitted the condemnation of private property in order to eliminate slums. Even though the condemned land was often turned over to private developers, the courts interpreted slum clearance as a public good in and of itself, a good that would improve the public health and welfare. Michigan endorsed a slum clearance law in 1939. (The only state insisting that the elimination of slums did not constitute a public use was South Carolina.[3])

Twenty years later when a department store owner in Washington, D.C., protested the condemnation of his store, which was located in a blighted area, the U.S. Supreme Court ruled against him. The court declared that "it is within the power of the legislature to determine that the community should be beautiful as well as healthy, spacious as well as clean." In that Berman v. Parker decision, the court ruled that it had very little discretion in such matters when the projects were consistent with public legislation.

By the 1970s state legislatures had expanded economic development legislation to allow for land condemnation for the creation of industrial parks and encouragement of commercial developments. Legislatures and courts began to write about "public benefit" and "public purpose" as the criteria for condemnation, instead of "public use." This interpretation of the state's power is convenient for municipalities which, in recent years, have been less able to clear massive tracts of land by resorting to slum clearance projects. A "public advantage" or "public purpose" rationale better supports public agencies' appetite for prime land in the center city which does not necessarily overlap with blighted areas. The standard of review for this application of the law becomes whether there is a "clear and significant" public benefit and whether or not the public benefit is primary or incidental.

The broad interpretation has become so dominant that Stephen Lefkowitz, general counsel to the New York State Urban Development Corporation, said: "It's hard to imagine an economic development program that is structured in a serious way that would not survive a 'public purpose' challenge." Lefkowitz added that the court limits its role to guarding against "the aberrant, the unfair situation, the clear case of overreaching."[4] Only "an out and out give away" could prompt the courts to interfere with a state's use of eminent domain, according to University of Minnesota law professor Alan Freeman.[5]

But critics suggest there needs to be a more exacting review imposed than the only one written into the law, which is an examination of whether government officials acted in bad faith. Certainly municipalities can act within the law, in good faith, to condemn land for a highly questionable development project.

In a *New York University Law Review* article, Laura Mansnerus listed several reasons why the courts might anticipate that application of eminent domain would require review:

> A condemnor of urban property typically is an economic development corporation that invests time, expertise, and money in designing public projects. Considering that such a program will often take on a life of its own, the parent agency cannot be expected to assess its own plan soberly, much less to account for a condemnee's interests. Yet the condemnee usually has no umpire comparable to a benefits review board or even to a zoning board. In the issue of whether property may be condemned in the first place, there is often no impartial reviewing authority but a court. Nevertheless, the fact that economic development corporations usually have good and honest intentions leads courts, as a general practice, to sanction their plans without detailed inquiry, and thus to foreclose any effective check on institutional self-interest.
>
> [Another] reason to scrutinize the decisions of local officials, at least more so than those made by larger bureacracies, is that they are especially vulnerable to powerful private interests. Judicial deference in these cases amounts to abdication exactly when the individual most needs protection from political—and not necessarily majoritarian—forces. . . . Industries and developers have obvious interests in enlisting municipal government to help effectuate their plans, and local governments have few reasons not to comply. . . . A public use must be shown to exist, not merely declared to exist.[6]

Wheelings and Dealings by GM Elsewhere

At the time that the Poletown plant was announced, the only plant of this design in operation was in Oklahoma. However, another was under construction in Orion Township, Michigan, and others were slated for Wentzville, Missouri, and Kansas City, Kansas.

Oklahoma

In Oklahoma GM's way of conducting business landed it in the state supreme court. The local school district and the attorney general, Jan Cartwright, sued GM for avoiding paying property and sales taxes by engaging in what Cartwright labeled "subterfuge." In a unanimous decision, the court ruled against GM.

Lana Tyree, an attorney who worked on the case against GM, described the corporate maneuvers. In the mid-1970s, the Oklahoma Industries Authority (OIA) floated $1 million worth of bonds and placed the money in an account for GM. GM then channeled its construction monies for the $350 million plant through that account. GM did not pay any sales tax on the materials it bought through that account, because the Oklahoma Industries Authority is tax exempt. The state of Oklahoma lost an estimated $14 million in that process.

In addition, GM transferred the land surface rights of its site to the OIA for twenty-four hours. Thereafter GM claimed property tax exemption. Tyree said that GM claimed to have an agreement with the state exempting it from property taxes but couldn't "tell us who made the agreement and they can't come up with it, but they claim there is an agreement. It's all done in executive suites behind closed doors without the public ever knowing it's going on—it's the fastest game in town." [7]

Officials at the OIA—top executives of the OK Gas and Electric,

Bell Telephone, the First National Bank, and the publisher of the *Okla-homa Daily*—closed the OIA's records to prevent examination of their transactions with GM, Tyree said. During the same time, the *Oklahoma Daily* published thirty editorials criticizing Jan Cartwright.

GM also managed to avoid pollution restraints on its new plant by borrowing the pollution rights of another firm. In itself, that is common practice in Oklahoma. Each plant gets a designated pollution allowance; unused allowances can be purchased by other companies, which accommodates them both without raising the overall pollution level in a municipality. What made GM's maneuver unusual was that it borrowed the pollution rights of a company in a completely different city.

GM's method of acquiring land was also criticized. While it was not at all illegal, some observers were angry that GM relied on other land-holding companies to purchase the land for it. By the early 1970s GM was able to take the land over from companies in Virginia and Texas which had acquired the parcels without much notice.

Kansas City

GM's land acquisition in suburban Kansas City was also criti-cized. The area selected was not zoned for industry, and area residents had paid an average of $75,000 a home in order to live in a semirural environment. But GM was able to purchase its site from a development company called the Minnesota Avenue Inc. Area residents question whether that site had been secretly designated for industrial develop-ment for some time since it was peculiarly annexed in 1975.

The fear of the Piper Area Association, which formed to combat the plant's construction, was that their middle- and upper-middle-class homes would be isolated between an industrial urban area at one end and the GM plant at the other. Rail lines and a highway spur would likely extend on both sides of the community from the city to GM's new plant. Residents anticipated that eventually the whole area would be-come an industrial corridor.

Richard Rosenthal, head of the neighborhood group, said that negotiators for the Missouri Pacific Railroad visited home owners be-fore the GM project was even approved by city leaders and told them that if they didn't sell voluntarily the state would condemn their land anyway. Residents allegedly received a letter, signed by the president of the railroad, which claimed that "the constitution prohibits against interference with interstate commerce."

When residents learned that the Kansas City Port Authority had agreed to issue $500 million worth of bonds for development of the GM site, they filed suit. They argued that the port authority's jurisdiction was restricted to the operation of levy lands and waterways. The site in question was eighteen miles from the nearest waterway.

In March 1981 the state supreme court confirmed the residents' view and prohibited the port authority from proceeding with its bond issue. However, within two and a half weeks legislation was drafted, introduced, and passed by the state legislature changing the domain of the port authority. The port authority was newly authorized to "foster and promote the development of industrial districts." This was done in part to satisfy GM's demand that all the necessary arrangements be in place by May of 1981.

The chairperson of the state senate committee which drafted the new legislation was Norman Gaar. Gaar was also the city bond attorney. Press reports indicated that since the standard counseling fee was 1 percent, Gaar stood to gain $5 million as a direct result of his legislation. The Piper Area Association referred to the new law as the "Gaar retirement bill."

"The pattern is the same in every city," Rosenthal said. "GM holds a gun to the head of the city. It doesn't give them time to consider sound plans, forcing them to act prematurely, to grant what GM demands. Then, GM stands aside, letting the the city officials take all the heat, saying 'the city needs us and we want to be good neighbors.' GM puts politicians in an untenable position."[8]

The area school district sued to protest GM's request for a twenty-year tax abatement and residents sued to protest the rezoning of their single family, agricultural-use area.

Rumors of racism plagued the Piper Area Association's efforts to block the GM project. Rumors began to circulate in black neighborhoods that the project was being fought because the area's homeowners didn't want black people crossing their land on the way to work at the plant. The Piper Area Association confronted the rumors directly by going to the black community and explaining their objections. When a black community group went to the city to demand more fire protection, the Piper Area Association went too and backed it up.

In April 1981 GM announced that it was going to postpone its Kansas City plant project. Piper Area Association members greeted this as a victory, but Kansas City media reports indicated that the local politicans felt stung but were still unwilling to criticize GM.

A *Kansas City Times* story explained that local financial investments had already been made for the GM plant. A $13.6 million UDAG had been secured for road construction, a fire station, and other support facilities; Missouri Pacific had already begun its $20 million rail extension to the plant site; the UAW had started laying plans for construction of a union local near the plant; and Jack Cooper Transport had already researched construction of a trucking facility at the site. "GM's decision came after nine months of scrambling by city officials to get things ready for the giant carmaker. The city had to rush through rezoning of a plant site, fight battle after battle in the courts, struggle with the state Legislature, and fend off a committed citizens organization." Nonetheless, the *Times* story continued:

> City officials made one thing apparent Wednesday, no matter how hard GM's decision was to accept, they will be back next year—and with smiles on their faces. The reason is because of the enormous impact the plant would have on the area—the kind of industrial development city officials everywhere dream of constantly but almost never get.
>
> "This is the biggest plum ever," [Port Authority chairperson Clifford] Nesselrod said last week when it looked as if the city would still be given the green light. A glance at the figures given on the plant is enough to reveal the tremendous impact not only on Kansas City, Kansas, but on the entire metropolitan area. The plant carries a $500 million construction tag with maximum employment at 6,000 people. Added to that is the annual $125 million payroll, which is expected to fertilize citywide growth indefinitely.[9]

Media reports like the one above infuriated residents because they contributed to the myth that GM could only bring great opportunities to the region. It is small surprise that the Piper Area Association was chastised for being obstructionist—media reports would seem to indicate that when GM decided to delay the plant the millenium had been postponed.

Orion Township

GM's construction in Orion Township involved many of the same controversies that were at play in Kansas and Oklahoma. GM told Orion Township that everything had to be arranged between January 1980 and June 1, 1980, or the corporation would reconsider. News of the plant project was leaked to the press in January; GM indicated it had planned to announce the project in March, which would have given the township three months to respond. GM demanded a $7.2 million annual property tax abatement, $16 million in public monies for road construction, environmental waivers, and rezoning.

GM's chairperson Thomas Murphy told the press, "If the necessary arrangements can't be worked out, then we'll have to continue to look elsewhere." This increasingly familiar GM threat may have carried extra weight in Michigan since no automaker had built a new plant in the state for twenty-three years.[10]

Land for the GM plant was acquired by Grand Trunk Western Railroad two months before the project was made public. Grand Trunk executive Michael Niemann was quoted as saying that an unnamed automaker was buying the land. He added "I don't know why they want to be so secretive."[11]

There was a land struggle in Orion Township as there was at each of the other sites. Orion Township, like the Piper Area, was zoned for residential use. Its water, gas, sewer, and electrical hookups were inadequate for industrial use. It had only a small police department and a volunteer fire department. Home owners in the area, including residents of a trailer park adjacent to the new plant site, opposed construction of the plant.

Gordon Judd, a Roman Catholic priest whose Basilian order had a retreat house in Orion Township, attended the public meetings on the project. Judd commented on how GM's representatives were always well dressed and smooth, but "all along they would concede nothing and reveal nothing. I didn't want the jobs to leave the area, but what GM was saying was that they wanted the plant but would concede nothing."

To attain the tax abatement it wanted, GM had to get permission from Pontiac's City Commission, because under Public Act 198 corporations which move from one Michigan city to another are ineligible for property tax abatements unless the original host city gives its approval. The City of Pontiac did propose that GM take over 500 acres within the city limits—the land which housed the Clinton Valley Hospital—but GM refused. So, despite the fact that Pontiac would suffer considerably because of the plant's removal, the commission okayed the transfer.

"The fear that GM would go to Alabama was very, very real," James Bush of the Eastern Michigan Environmental Action Council explained. "The people of Pontiac were in a panic. There were attempts to intimidate trustees, almost a lynch mob psychology. Workers were afraid of losing their jobs. Real estate interests wanted to turn the [Orion Township] area into subdivisions and plant sites. There's really no one around who's really up to understanding it, let alone managing it."[12]

An article in the *Pontiac-Waterford Times* noted that five of the seven Pontiac commissioners either worked for or had previously worked for General Motors.[13] As in every other community invited to scramble for a GM plant, fabulous promises were made about the opportunites the plant would provide. GM projected that it would employ 6,000 workers; community business people were told to expect a retail boom; retail interests argued the entire area would profit.

But hindsight offered a clearer perspective. A 1984 *Detroit Free Press* article traces the disappointment of Orion Township officials and GM workers, who complained that GM's new plant opened late and then went off and on line repeatedly.

"There's been so many promises made regarding that plant— what it would mean to this community, the increased employment, the increased housing demand, and it just hasn't materialized," said Orion Township supervisor JoAnne Van Tassel. "Today we work, tomorrow we don't. Hey, we're up and running, isn't this super? The next day, thousands on layoffs. The layoffs cast a pall over everything. You just begin to feel good and you get laid off again."[14]

GM postponed opening the plant twice then finally called 1,200 workers back in January 1984 just to shut down again and lay them off. GM spokewoman Laurie Kay explained that false starts in the production time table are indicative that GM is committed to producing cars that are "up to snuff . . . the commitment has been made that this plant is going to build cars that are ready to go, or they're not going out to the public."[15]

In the process, however, GM was wreaking havoc in the lives of its workers. Some of the GM employees who had joined the UAW's door-to-door campaign advocating construction of the plant felt cheated. Partly through their efforts, a referendum was passed that made it legal for GM to build in the township despite the complaints of residents.

UAW local treasurer Bill Spencer said that many of the workers laid off in 1980 had scattered throughout the country by the time GM issued its recall in 1982. "They've migrated everywhere. They've picked up jobs in Florida, Oklahoma, Arizona. GM called for these people, sending letters and mailgrams all across the country. They gave notice at their jobs, moved their families, came back to report for work that week, just to find that the job was going to be delayed again. Now they're in a mess. They've quit their jobs, picked up moving expenses, I had a guy come in here that day that had his family sitting in his car. They drove all the way from Oklahoma."[16]

As a result, Orion Township has not seen the predicted swell of business in the community. "So far, for the business community, it's the case of people not having the disposable dollars," Van Tassel said. "They don't have the money to go out and spend on a new dress, new suit, night on the town, stove, dishwasher, microwave, stereo, whatever."

Ironically, Orion Township started production with GM's most elite vehicles—1985 front-wheel-drive Olds 98s and Cadillac DeVilles. The cars are, of course, among GM's most profitable.

Appendix
C

An Optimistic View of the Plant

From the Associated Press, 17 October 1985, printed inthe Menominee *Herald Leader* under the headline "Poletown in GM's High-Tech Masterpiece":

High technology begins here when truckers hauling parts pull up to the loading docks. Instead of a traditional bill of lading, their paperwork consists of bar codes, like those carried on packaged food at the supermarket.

One swipe of a light pen reads the code and notifies the plant computers and assembly line workers that the latest shipment of windshield wipers, engines or headlights has arrived.

At once, one of 60 automated guided vehicles, computer-controlled and driverless, is dispatched to fetch the parts and take them to appropriate work station, following metallic wires buried in the floor.

In an effort to improve quality, there will be no warehouse at Poletown. The industry has been switching to delivery of parts on a 'just in time' basis, which cuts down on defects and inventory and labor costs.

Supply companies are patched in to the factory's computer network, knowing when to send out the next shipment of parts and when to order another shipment of materials from its own subcontractors.

Most parts arrive here only four hours ahead of assembly.

To get the cars started, sheet metal pieces are shipped to a subassembly point by conveyor and fitted together loosely with tabs, much like a toy car is assembled.

These shells move to the body shop, where 150 electric welding robots zap the pieces into place. Some robots are programmed to wheel and turn and perform a dozen welds.

Although highly sophisticated, welding robots have been around for years. What's new at Poletown is the proliferation of automated machines that can "see." They will help blind robots place the doors on the cars.

Another computer vision system makes sure the parts are aligned properly by examining the metal, making a computerized profile, then comparing that with a model of a perfect car body stored in one of the plant's computers.

Robots also will install the windowshields and rear windows, squirt waterproof sealer around glass and joints, install the rear wheel housing and rear axle bushing and put on the tires.

The paint shop will be almost totally staffed by robots. Like welding, robots have done this task before. But at Poletown, the paint shop robots also will be programmed to open and close doors so other robots can spray inside.

Computers and automation get together for another high-tech trick—tracking the cars by computer chip.

When a customer orders a car from the plant the body style, paint color and options desired are stored on a computer chip placed under the nose of the raw body shell.

Computers read this chip information as the shell winds through the plant. Parts for optional equipment such as a sunroof, special seat or tinted glass are dispatched to meet the shell at an assembly station.

The chip tells the painting robots what color to apply. If a two-tone is desired, the shell is looped through the paint shop for a second time.

Appendix
D

"Name Shame"

Wall Street Journal, 26 July 1985, B-23.

Would anyone name a ship "The Titanic"? Would anyone name a dirigible "The Hindenburg"? That's about how General Motors Corp. feels when people call its new Detroit car-assembly plant "Poletown"— a name that recalls the outrage many felt when the city destroyed a Polish neighborhood in 1981 to make room for the GM facility.

The correct name, as GM public relations people take great pains to explain, is the Detroit-Hamtramck Assembly Center. But the local press constantly refers to the facility as Poletown and they aren't the only ones. Some crates of parts shipped to the plant are labeled "GM Poletown" or "P-town." A recent issue of the plant's internal newsletter even had a story headlined "Poletown Dawg," about a plant mutt.

The name Poletown was "coined by the dissidents who were opposing" the plant, says a GM spokesman, "so of course we don't want to be reminded of that." But GM's efforts seem futile. Overcoming the name Poletown, says the spokesman wearily, "is like carrying water uphill."

Interviews

Andrews, Barbara, Poletown resident. By Information Factory, Detroit, Mich. Spring 1981.

Brown, Larry, principal development economist for the City of Detroit, Community Economic Development Department, Central Industrial Park project. By Jeanie Wylie. 9 Feb. 1984.

Bush, James, City of Detroit Human Rights Department and Southeastern Michigan Environmental Action Council. By Jeanie Wylie. 9 Feb. 1984.

Cendrowski, Alexander, retired rector of the Immaculate Conception Roman Catholic Church in Poletown. By Jeanie Wylie. 3 July 1981.

Conyers, John, U.S. Congressperson. By Jeanie Wylie. 10 Jan. 1983.

Crosby, Louise, Poletown resident. By Information Factory, Detroit, Mich. Spring 1981.

Cunningham, Helen, aide to city councilperson Mel Ravitz. By Jeanie Wylie. 6 February 1984.

Desantis, Maggie, Warren Conner Coalition in the Chrysler plant area. By Jeanie Wylie. 1986.

Dockery, Carol, Poletown resident. By Gene Stilp for the Center for Study of Responsive Law (hereafter CSRL). 1981.

Duda, Walter, Poletown resident. By Ron Brownstein for CSRL. 7 June 1981.

Feagan, Ethel and Ben, Poletown businesspeople. By Jeanie Wylie and CSRL. 1981.

Featherstone, Arthur, aide of U.S. Congressperson John Conyers. By Jeanie Wylie. 1982.

Fisher, Carl, Poletown businessperson. By Ron Brownstein for CSRL. 6 June 1981 and 14 July 1981.

Gallio, Christian, Economic Development Corporation of Wayne County. By Jeanie Wylie. 14 July 1982.

Garrett, Joyce, Detroit public relations and mayoral press secretary. Telephone interview with Jeanie Wylie. 7 April 1981.

Gianni, Ann, Poletown resident. By Jeanie Wylie. 1981 and 1984. By Gene Stilp for CSRL in 1981.

Hodas, Richard, Poletown resident. By Ron Brownstein for CSRL. 5 June 1981.

Homrich, Loretta, co-owner of Homrich Wrecking. By Jeanie Wylie. 7 July 1981.

Immaculate Conception Church demolition tape. By CSRL. 14 July 1981.

Jackson, Wallace, CEDD project planner. By Jeanie Wylie. 31 August 1981.

Jakubowski, Walter. Poletown resident. By Gene Stilp for CSRL. 1981.

Judd, Gordon, Roman Catholic priest. By Jeanie Wylie. 6 August 1985.

Kaczynski, Bernice and Harold, Poletown residents. By Jeanie Wylie. 1981, 1984, 1985, 1987, 1988. By Information Factory, Detroit, Mich. Spring 1981. By Ron Brownstein for CSRL. 5 June 1981.

Karasiewicz, Joseph, rector of the Immaculate Conception Church. By Ron Brownstein for CSRL. 4 June 1981. By Information Factory, Detroit, Mich. 14 July 1981.

Kuhn, Maggie, director of the Gray Panthers. 8 March 1981.

Lucero, Teofilo, Poletown resident. By Jeanie Wylie. 4 April 1981.

Luria, Dan, UAW researcher. By Jeanie Wylie. 13 November 1981.

Lyte, Alice, director SemiQuois community group and CDC member. By Jeanie Wylie. Fall 1981.

McDonald, F. James, president, G.M. By Jeanie Wylie. 4 April 1981.

McClain, Brenda, staffer at the Michigan Avenue Community Organization. By Jeanie Wylie. 27 August 1981.

McClary, Robert, Detroit Police Department, captain in arson investigation. Telephone interview with Jeanie Wylie. 14 Dec. 1981.

Maloney, Malcolm, rector of St. John's Roman Catholic Church in Poletown. By Jeanie Wylie. 7 July 1981.

Nader, Ralph, organizer. By Information Factory, Detroit, Mich. 10 March 1981.

Nanu Ashar. Immaculate Conception Church arrest tape. 14 July 1981.

Niedbala, Eddie, Poletown businessperson. By CSRL. 10 June 1981.

Olechowski, Thomas, president of the Poletown Neighborhood Council. By CSRL. 25 June 1981.

Reosti, Ron, lawyer. By Ron Brownstein. 26 June 1981.

Riegle, Don, U.S. senator. By Jeanie Wylie. 4 April 1981, University of Detroit.

Roesler, Walter, president of the Brightmoor Business and Community Association. Telephone interview with Jeanie Wylie. 19 August 1981.

Rosenthal, Richard, president of the Kansas City Piper Area Association. By Jeanie Wylie. 14 April 1981.

Saber, John, Poletown resident. By Ron Brownstein for CSRL. 5 June 1981.

Skalski, Francis, rector of St. Hyacinth's Roman Catholic Church. By Ron Brownstein for CSRL. 8 June 1981.

Snider, David, consultant on social justice issues, By Jeanie Wylie. 21 August 1981.

Thomson, Bill, CEDD. By Jeanie Wylie. 9 Feb. 1984.

Tyree, Lana, Oklahoma attorney. By Jeanie Wylie. April 1981.

Voydanoff, Daniel, vice president of the National Bank of Detroit. By Jeanie Wylie. 13 August 1981.

Wollard, Steve, staff at MACO. By Jeanie Wylie. 1981.

Notes

Chapter 1

1. John Bukowczyk, "The Decline and Fall of a Detroit Neighborhood: Poletown v. General Motors and the City of Detroit," *Washington and Lee Law Review* 41, no. 1 (Winter 1984) p. 51.

2. Jack Bayerl, "Rediscovering Our Heritage," *Ethos* 8, no. 26 (17 April 1975) : 7. Czolgosz added, "I would like the American people to know that I had no use for priests. My family are all Catholics and used to go to church until the bad [economic] times of 1893. We had been taught by the priests that if we would pray God would help us along, but it did no good."

3. The Central Industrial Park Environmental Impact Statement, prepared by the City of Detroit, Community and Economic Development Department, December, 1980, pp. M–8-10,

4. Ibid., B-1.

5. Joseph Wytrwal, *Behold the Polish American* (Detroit: Endurance Press, 1977).

6. Steve Babson, *Working Detroit* (New York: Adama Books, 1984), p. 39.

7. Bayerl, "Rediscovering Our Heritage" : 8.

8. Babson, *Working Detroit*, pp. 78-80.

9. Stanley Nowak, an early UAW organizer, recalls how prevalent his work was in the Polish community: "I spoke twice a week on a Polish radio program in Polish. I wrote leaflets that were distributed on Sunday mornings in front of the Polish churches; I organized meetings in Polish halls, and even some open air meetings in parks and playgrounds." For more information, consult Babson, *Working Detroit*.

10. Ibid., p. 16.

11. Marco Trbovich, "Ethnic Detroit/Polish Life," *Detroit Free Press*, 25 March 1973, A-1.

12. Leslie Woodcock Tentler, "Who Is the Church? Conflict in a Polish

Immigrant Parish in Late Nineteenth-Century Detroit," *Comparative Studies in Society and History*, 25, no. 2 (April 1983) : 249.

13. Therisita Polzin, *The Polish Americans/ Whence and Whither?* (Pulaski, Wis.: Franciscan Publishers, 1973), p. 84.

14. St. Albertus' Church was organized in 1870 by Fr. Dominik Kolasinski, a priest imported from Poland by Bishop Caspar Henry Borgess. Kolasinski lavished time and money on the church but was sent to the Dakota Territory after the bishop learned that he was accused of sexual immorality and money mismanagement. When Kolasinski's successor attempted to say mass, parishioners packed the church and disrupted the service. Fourteen people were arrested, and the new priest left under police protection. The bishop closed down the church for nineteen months. When Borgess failed to reopen the church at Christmas time, several thousand people began a spontaneous march to the bishop's house, prompting Borgess to flee out the back in a carriage. Angry parishioners returned to Poletown and began throwing rocks at the home and store of one of Kolasinki's antagonists. Shots came from the house and a young Pole fell dead. In 1888 Kolasinski returned and began construction of another church, even bigger than the first. Sweetest Heart of Mary, begun without diocesan consent, had huge cost overruns which forced the parish to default. But Kolasinski rallied the parish to take a loan from a Canadian bank to buy it back. During that process the church established a board of lay people with the authority to hire and fire their own priest.

Nine years later, sometime after Borgess's retirement, the archdiocese recognized the parish and accepted Kolasinski. The church was able to hold onto its title until 1960, when the archbishop required it in exchange for a loan to fix the roof. For more information, consult Tentler, "Who Is the Church?" and "The History of Detroit's Polonia,"*Hamtramck Citizen*. While other ethnic groups sometimes experienced similar isolation within the church, Poles were the first to set up a splinter group, called the Polish National Catholic Church in 1898. Trbovich, "Ethnic Detroit."

15. Cited in James M. Anderson, "A Socio-Historical Study of Poletown, Preliminary Draft," University of Michigan, 19 Nov. 1980, p. 16.

16. Ibid. p. 5.

17. Babson, *Working Detroit*, p. 71.

18. Ibid. pp. 72-73.

19. Ibid. pp. 81-82, 85.

20. The cigar workers' strikes were sparked in January 1937 when twenty-five women were fired for demanding higher wages. The Webster-Eisenholer Cigar Company was the first struck, when 500 women sat in. But by the end of February 2,000 women had taken control of five plants. The issues went beyond wages. The women complained that the high humidity and the heat maintained to preserve the tobacco were damaging their health. The women who fed the tobacco machines said the tobacco dust was accumulating in their lungs and prematurely aging their faces.

The women were represented by the UAW. Organizer Stanley Nowak, who was recruited by the women because the AFL's Cigar Workers Union had abandoned organizing efforts in Detroit, set up strike kitchens and organized committees for negotiation, recreation, sanitation, and security. "They won the complete support of the whole neighborhood," Nowak recalled. "Churches and priests supported it, small businesses supported it, Polish newspapers supported it, everyone was in sympathy with these women." Babson, *Working Detroit*, pp. 76-77.

21. Anderson, "A Socio-Historical Study," p. 13.

22. John and Horace Dodge started manufacturing the "Old Betsy" at Dodge Main in 1914. Sometime after their deaths in 1920, Walter P. Chrysler bought it in a move the *Wall Street Journal* called "a minnow swallowing a whale." The purchase increased Chrysler's manufacturing capacity by five times, making it the third largest automaker.

23. Joseph Serafino, *West of Warsaw* (Hamtramck, Mich.: Avenue Publishing Co., 1983), p. 111.

24. Babson, *Working Detroit*, p. 86; Steve Babson, Dave Elsial, *Union Town* (Detroit: Detroit Labor History Tour Project), pp. 20-21.

25. Babson, *Working Detroit*, p. 91.

26. Environmental Impact Statement, I-33.

27. Polzin, *The Polish Americans*, pp. 84-85.

28. In a 1980 Poletown study University of Michigan historian James Anderson noted that "several people spoke of the stability achieved in the 1970s, and what is striking about the area is its resiliency—the strenths it exhibits. Chief among these strengths is the strong, sometimes fierce attachment for the area. This is not unexpected from the elderly Poles who are still a significant element of the population—and the elderly in general. But, the sentiment is found in a variety of quarters. . . . The area has been and continues to provide a home for a variety of groups while they have sought a place in American society. This has been true of the blacks who came in the 1950s and who are now oldtimers. The community tends to divide not along lines of race but between long time residents (whether owners or renters) and transients who have no attachment to the community. The emphasis on owning and maintaining a home which is so strong among the Poles seems to have become a part of the territory."

29. In fact, Detroit Mayor Coleman Young would tell Studs Terkel in 1980 that "the Poles had been the last group to migrate to Detroit, so they were at the bottom of the ladder. The blacks and the Poles were fighting for a hold on the bottom. . . . Even though the black community had been bulldozed out, the Poles haven't moved. Home really means home to them." *American Dreams: Lost and Found* (New York: Pantheon Books, 1980), p. 359.

30. For a compelling account of the League of Revolutionary Black Workers, read Dan Georgakas and Marvin Surkan, *Detroit, I Do Mind Dying*, (New York: St. Martin's Press, 1975).

31. In the film *Finally Got the News* DRUM member Chuck Wooten explains that during a union election "the Hamtramck police department began to move in a much more open way. They gave us tickets on our cars and just generally

harassed us. One day about fifty of us were in the union hall, which is right across from the police station. The mayor of the city and the chief of police came in with guns in their hands. They told us to stop making trouble, and we said all we wanted to do was win the election. While we were talking, a squad of police came through the door swinging axe handles and throwing Mace around."

32. In 1970 a black worker at the Chrysler Eldon plant killed two foremen and a job setter. Eventually, a Wayne County jury acquitted him after touring the plant. Ken Cockrel, who represented him, claimed he would put Chrysler on trial. And, in fact, the judge ended up calling conditions at the plant "inexcusably bad" and "abominable." Faulty equipment and forced overtime were constant worker complaints throughout the industry.

33. Jeanie Wylie, "How New Malls Corner the Market," *Detroit News*, 29 June 1982, A-1.

34. Interoffice correspondence of the City of Detroit, Subject: Central Industrial Park Relocation Information, held by Center for the Study of Responsive Law (CSRL), Washington, D.C.

35. Census data, City of Detroit Planning Department.

36. Patricia Chargot, "A Portrait of Poletown: Framed by the Past, Its Spirit of Survival Has No Boundaries," *Detroit Free Press*, 23 June 1980, A-3.

Chapter 2

1. In the early 1980s, Officer Frank Siemion, thirty-nine—the first Detroit police officer killed while on duty in seven years—was shot by three teenagers stealing food from a party store.

2. Melinda Grenier, "Wayne County loses 100,000 Auto-Type Jobs," *Detroit News*, 9 Feb. 1982, B-5.

3. Melinda Grenier, "'You're Out!' Outplacement Helps Jobless Pick Up Pieces," *Detroit News*, 7 Nov. 1982, E-1. The closing of Hudson's downtown retail store was a particularly crippling blow to Detroit: the eight-story building, which filled an entire city block, was considered an anchor for a planned $235 million Cadillac Square redevelopment project. Joe Hudson, Jr., had promised to keep the store open. However, Hudson's was sold to a Minnesota family department store chain, which decided to sell the downtown store. Ironically, Hudson's had helped precipitate the demise of downtown Detroit when it built the nation's first covered suburban mall in the late 1950s.

4. Walter Guzzardi, Jr., "A Determined Detroit Struggles To Find New Economic Life," *Fortune*, 21 April 1980, p. 74.

5. David J. Snider, "Commercial Disinvestment from Detroit," an unpublished study, 1981, based on census data.

6. Al Stark, "Where Is Pride If We Lose Our Cultural Gems?" *Detroit News*, 5 Feb. 1984, A-3.

7. Susan Watson, "Crimes Against the City, Where Are the Stats?" *Detroit Free Press*, 2 March 1984, A-3.

8. Between 1979 and 1980 U.S. car production fell 31.7 percent. Worse, truck production was down 54.8 percent. The slump resulted in a 30 percent rise in

unemployment. To cover their losses, the auto makers raised prices 41.9 percent during the same period. *UAW Research Bulletin*, May 1981, p. 20.

9. *Business Week* observers estimate that GM made a $1,000 profit on each large car sold, but only $300 on smaller ones. *Business Week*, 24 March 1980, p. 79.

10. Harley Shaiken, address at Labor Notes Conference, Detroit, 1981. Shaiken added that "it has become popular to say that there's enough blame to go around; that if we all got into this current situation together, meaning the companies, labor, and government, then we have to look to the future together to get out of it. I think that's a very misleading approach."

11. "U.S. Autos: Losing A Big Segment of The Market Forever?" *Business Week*, 24 March 1980, p. 79.

12. At a University of Detroit symposium GM President F. James McDonald said: "Some of our critics say our present condition is just a symptom of a basic weakness in the industry. They say we're big-car oriented, or that we can't move fast enough, or that we refuse to give customers what they want. That's non-sense." The real cause of the industry's failure, he said, was government regula-tion of fuel, government regulations for minimum gas performance, the government's failure to increase depreciation allowances quickly, the government's imposition of passive restraint requirements, and its failure to "modify" or liberalize the Clean Air Act. McDonald added that "the best and most cooperative efforts" weren't being made by labor to eliminate the Japanese industry's $8-an-hour wage advantage.

13. "Plants That Are Not Kept Up to Date," "Managers Who Are No Longer Entrepreneurs," *Business Week*, 30 June 1980, pp. 74, 78. A Motor City example of this corporate trend was the Bendix takeover, in which Congress criticized the business community for tying up $5.6 billion in the take-over battle.

14. "Union President Ribs Spending for Mergers," *Detroit News*, 5 Oct. 1982, B-7.

15. For example, David Kushma's article, "Michigan Slump Blamed on High Pay/ UM Looks at Economy," *Detroit Free Press*, 13 Oct. 1981, A-1.

16. GM Annual Report, 1981, p. 2.

17. "General Motors Financial Report, First Quarter 1981," *UAW Research Bulletin*, May 1981, p. 13.

18. Donald Woutat, "Auto Money Moves South of the Border," *Detroit Free Press*, 2 March 1980, B-1.

19. Michael Robinson, John Nehman, and Richard Willing, "GM Asks $5-an-Hour Wage Cut/ Almost All Fringes Targeted," *Detroit News*, 14 January 1982, A-1.

20. "Ford Motor Company Financial Report, First Quarter 1981," *UAW Research Bulletin*, May 1981, p. 14.

21. Patrick Fitzgerald, "Ford to Close Flatrock Casting Plant," *Detroit News*, 15 Sept. 1981, A-14.

22. Woutat, "Auto Money Moves South of the Border."

23. Stark, "Where Is Pride?" During the same period Standard and Poor lowered its Detroit bond rating from BBB- to BB, saying, "the rating is . . . reflective of rapidly gathering clouds of yet another potential fiscal crisis.

24. A Johns Hopkins study, by Harvey Branner, reveals that for every 1 percent rise in the rate of unemployment there is a 4.1 percent rise in suicide, a 5.7 percent increase in the number of murders, and a 1.9 percent rise in the incidence of cirrhosis of the liver and other diseases.

25. U.S. Congressman John Conyer's office estimated that 9,000 Detroit households (or 40,000 people) were without centralized heating in the early 1980s.

26. The elderly were major victims of poverty, although many of them failed to contact city services or helping organizations. Joanne Clocke, administrator of a home meals program, estimated that 25,000 senior citizens should be provided home meals, although her program was able to provide for only 2,000.

27. As cited in Jane Slaughter's *Concessions and How to Beat Them* (Detroit: Labor Education and Research Project, 1983), p. 51.

28. "Trimming Down to Revive the Growth Pace," *Business Week,* 1 June 1981, pp. 86-87.

29. *Chrysler, the People and the City,* released by DARE (Detroiters for a Rational Economy), March 1980.

30. Sidney Lens, "Reindustrialization: Panacea or Threat?" *The Progressive,* Nov. 1980, p. 44. *New York Times* reporter Judith Miller noted in *Working Papers* that corporatist rhetoric promises that business, government, and labor "would march off toward prosperity, removing obstacles as they went." She added that this would benefit big businesses that are in a position "to take advantage of the corporate state, but not the small businesses that actually provide most of the new jobs and innovation in the economy." *Working Papers,* 12 November 1980.

31. Jeanie Wylie, Lawrence Walsh, "Remaking the Motor City—and America," *The Progressive,* July 1982, p. 27.

32. "If Detroit Collapses, the State Will Also . . ." *Ebony,* Feb. 1974, p. 35.

33. STRESS killed twenty people and conducted 500 raids (without warrants) between 1971 and 1973. One of STRESS's victims was a Wayne County sheriff's deputy who was shot six times as he stood, hands on the wall, i.d. in his hand. STRESS officers said they chased the man when they saw him carrying what looked like a gun. For more information about STRESS and police/community relations at that time, consult Dan Georgakas and Marvin Surkan, *Detroit, I Do Mind Dying* (New York: St. Martin's Press, 1975.)

34. Young's appearance before the House Un-American Activities Committee was broadcast on Detroit radio. An excerpt follows:

> COMMITTEE COUNSEL FRANK TAVENNER, JR.: Are you a member of the National Negro Congress?
> COLEMAN YOUNG: The word is "Negro," not "Negra."
> TAVENNER: I don't think I said "Negra," but if I did it was unintentional and I am sorry.
> YOUNG: Thank you. I resent the slurring of the name of my race. In some sections of the country it is "Negra" and I resent that.

After Young refused to answer any questions about his activity in black trade unions, Representative Charles Potter, a Michigan Republican, asked, "Do you consider the Communist Party un-American?" Young responded, "I consider the activities of this committee un-American."

35. Reginald Stuart, "The New Black Power Of Coleman Young," *New York Times Sunday Magazine*, 16 Dec. 1979, p. 110.

36. Ibid.; Ken Fireman, "Tax Hike Supporters Spent $427,000," *Detroit Free Press*, 31 August 1981, E-6.

37. *Fortune*, 25 Feb. 1980, p. 45.

38. Coleman Young addressing the Senate banking committee in 1979, cited in *Chrysler, the People and the City*.

39. Noel Grove, "The Two Worlds of Michigan," *National Geographic*, June 1979, p. 802.

40. Daniel Voydanoff, vice president of the National Bank of Detroit, interview with author, 13 August 1981.

41. Andrew McGill, Barbara Young, "The Top 47 Who Make It Happen," *Detroit News*, 17 Sept. 1978, A-1.

42. Andrew McGill, Barbara Young, "Getting It Done, Together," *Detroit News*, 4 Oct. 1978, A-1.

43. Douglas Williams, "GM Spearheads Renewal of Detroit Neighborhood," *Washington Post*, 30 Sept. 1978, E-1.

44. Jack Kresnak, "He's Down But Not Out," *Detroit Free Press*, 28 Feb. 1981, A-3.

45. Robert McClary, addressing a Poletown Neighborhood Council meeting in March 1981 and in a subsequent telephone interview with the author.

46. Tom Lonergan, "GM's 'New Neighborhood,'" *Detroit Metro Times*, 30 April 1981, p. 1.

47. Ibid.

48. Don Tschirhart, "Ahoy Waiter!" *Detroit News*, 22 Nov. 1983, A-3.

49. Felix Rohatyn, "Back from Bankruptcy: New York's Lessons for Detroit," *Detroit Free Press*, 4 June 1981, A-9.

50. Tom Hundley, "Go For Broke: Young Bought The Rescue Plan Then Sold It," *Detroit Free Press*, 30 August 1981, B-1.

51. Ibid.

52. Fireman, "Tax hike supporters spent $427,000."

53. Hundley, "Go For Broke."

54. Jeanie Wylie, "Preventing Another Poletown," *Detroit Metro Times*, 14 Dec. 1981, p. 1.

55. Jeanie Wylie, "How New Malls Corner the Market," *Detroit News*, 29 June 1982, A-1.

56. Wallace Jackson, CEDD project planner, interview with author, 31 Aug. 1981.

57. Ibid.; Jackson, interview with author.

58. Studs Terkel, *American Dreams: Lost and Found* (New York: Pantheon Books, 1980), p. 368.

59. City advertisement, *Fortune Magazine*, 25 Feb. 1980, p. 45.

Chapter 3

1. See Appendix B.
2. City of Detroit, Community and Economic Development Department, Central Industrial Park Environmental Impact Statement, Dec. 1980, 2:4.
3. Colin Covert, "Jobs Don't Salve Their Fears," *Detroit Free Press*, 9 March 1984, B-3.
4. Patrick Fitzgerald, "GM May Build its Own Robot Force," *Detroit News*, 28 Apr. 1981, B-7.
5. GM's 1981 stockholder report, "Quality of Work Life/ Productivity," p. 28.
6. Thomas Murphy, GM chairman, letter to the Detroit Economic Development Council, 8 Oct. 1980.
7. David S. Potter, GM vice president, in *Land Grab* by Harvey Ovshinsky, documentary shown on WDIV-TV, Detroit, Mich..
8. Kathryn Jones, legal counsel for the judiciary committee, memo, 27 Nov. 1979.
9. The primary movers in the two committees responsible for drafting the new condemnation law both had major roles in the Poletown struggle within the year. Jason Honigman, who introduced the law revision commission's draft of the bill, later represented the City of Detroit. The state bar committee's chair, Alan Ackerman, represented Poletown property owners suing for more money.
10. See Appendix A.
11. Paul G. Citkowski to state representative Perry Bullard, 4 May 1981. Detroit attorney Kenneth Hylton also criticized the new law, saying in an October 1979 letter to a legislative subcommittee that "it is my humble opinion, that a respondent would consider the operation of such a legal vehicle in eliminating their interest in private property as coercive and dictatorial."
12. Steve Konicki, Robert Roach, "Quick Talker Sells GM plant—But He Buys Criticism Too," *Detroit News*, 2 Nov. 1980, A-1.
13. Ibid.
14. Thomas Cunningham, City of Detroit, Community and Economic Development Department, court deposition, 30 September 1980. By February 25, 1981, the city's figures were somewhat revised. The block grant allocation rose to $5 million and a Section 108 loan of $60.5 million was included.
15. David Moberg, "GM Retools Detroit, *In These Times*, 4 Feb. 1981, p. 1.

Chapter 4

1. City of Detroit, Community and Economic Development Department, transcript, public hearing at Kettering High School, 14 Oct. 1980
2. *Poletown Lives!* transcript, p. 9. This Poletown documentary was produced by Information Factory and can be previewed by writing to 3512 Courville, Detroit, Mich. 48224.
3. Harry Cook, "Members Rail at Poletown Church's Sale," *Detroit Free Press*, 24 Feb. 1981, A-3.

4. "You Have to Start All Over Again," Workers' League in Detroit, *Bulletin*, 17 Feb. 1981.

5. *Poletown Lives!* transcript, p. 1.

6. Thomas Ewald, "Poletown!" *Michigan Catholic*, 15 Aug. 1980, p. 1; *Poletown Lives!* transcript, p. 12.

7. Sandy Livingston, Poletown chronology, Center for the Study of Responsive Law, 1982.

8. James Ricci, "The Iron Priest of Poletown," *Detroit Free Press*, 15 May 1981, D-1.

9. Stephen Franklin, "GM Protestors Picket Church," *Detroit Free Press*, 29 Sept. 1980, A-3.

10. Thomas Ewald, "Poletown Church Group Hopes to Ease Resettlement Fight," *Michigan Catholic*, 3 Oct. 1980, p. 1.

11. Patrick Steele, Advisory Council on Historic Preservation, telephone interview with Gene Stilp, winter, 1981.

12. Bill Vann, "Protest GM Demolition Plan," *Bulletin*, 17 Oct. 1980, p. 12.

13. Ronald Reosti, statement to the Poletown Neighborhood Council, 3 March 1981 .

14. Ibid.

15. George T. Martin, Findings of Fact and Law, Poletown Neighborhood Council v. City of Detroit and the Detroit Economic Development Corp., 8 Dec. 1980, Third Judicial Circuit Court of Michigan.

16. During this time, Bob Giannini and Pat Barszenski organized a raffle to help provide money for court costs. Residents raised $1,000 by raffling three baskets of liquor.

17. "We're Like a Testing Ground," *Bulletin*, 24 March 1981, p. 13.

18. Patricia Chargot, Luther Jackson, "Big Court Battle Looms over GM Site," *Detroit Free Press*, 9 Nov. 1980, A-3; David Moberg, "GM Retools Detroit," *In These Times*, 4 Feb. 1981, p. 1; and Eddie Niedbala, with CSRL representative, Detroit, 10 June, 1981.

Chapter 5

1. Eventually, the Poletown Neighborhood Council decided to use certified mail so that they could at least prove that their letters had been received.

2. Warren Brown, "Balancing the Pain," a *Washington Post* column printed in the *Minneapolis Star*, 26 Feb. 1981, C-1.

3. William Serrin, The Company and the Union, cited in *Detroit, I Do Mind Dying*, by Dan Georgakas, Marvin Surkin, (New York: St. Martin's Press, 1975), p. 32.

4. Lynda Ann Ewen, *Corporate Power and Urban Crisis* (Princeton: Princeton University Press, 1978), p. 263.

5. Haynes Johson, Nick Kotz, *The Unions*, cited in Georgakas and Surkin, *Detroit, I Do Mind Dying*, p. 33.

6. Andrew McGill, Barbara Young, "Portraits of Power: Seven at the Center," *Detroit News*, 20 Sept. 1978, A-1.

7. William Winpisinger, president of the International Association of Machinists, complains that such alliances "appear to permit workers to participate in shop-floor decision-making processes. In reality, they circumvent the worker control and safeguards at the point of work; open the way for invasion of labor-displacing technology; undermine worker identity and solidarity with the . . . union movement; and set up local trade unions for decertification drives." Quoted in Jane Slaughter, *Concessions and How to Beat Them,* (Detroit: Labor Education and Research Project, 1983), p. 2.

8. Ibid., p. 51.

9. Brown, "Balancing the Pain."

10. Headlines like "GM Demands $5-an-Hour Wage Cut" would rock Detroit during the years to follow. In *Concessions and How to Beat Them,* Jane Slaughter explains that in 1982 Ford reopened contract talks and altered a wage package affecting 160,000 workers, which saved the company $1 billion. General Motors did the same. The concessions, which affected 319,000 workers, were valued at $3 billion.

11. During the time that decisions were being made about Poletown, the UAW was losing up to $1 million a month. The union eliminated one-tenth of its staff and lost 40 percent of its Detroit membership. The union's general fund balance dropped from $57 million to $33 million. New UAW president Owen Bieber said the membership level was the lowest possible for the union to be able to "just break even." (Brown, "Balancing the Pain").

12. Stanley Aronowitz, "In Unionism There Is Fear," *The Nation,* 6 Dec. 1980, p. 599.

13. In June, 1982 a young Chinese man, Vincent Chin, was beaten to death with a baseball bat by a Detroit auto worker who was reported to have believed that Chin was Japanese. The murder was portrayed in a 1987 documentary, *Who Killed Vincent Chin?* by Christine Choy and Renee Tajima, WTVS-TV, Detroit, Mich.

14. Similarly, in a letter to a religious group concerned about events in Poletown, Robert McCabe, director of GM's treasurer's office, wrote: "Mr. Douglas Fraser, the UAW's president, put it quite eloquently when he pointed out that if only a few or even a few hundred jobs were involved, none of us would consider disturbing this neighborhood. But 6,000 jobs are involved and neither we, the community, nor the UAW can risk losing them."

15. Brown, "Balancing the Pain."

16. George Crockett to Bernice Kaczynski, 21 Apr. 1981.

17. John Conyer to Coleman Young, 22 Apr. 1981.

18. Kevin Fobbs, "A City in Demise," *WIN* magazine, 1 May 1981, pp. 11-12.

19. Robert Roach, "Proposed GM Plant Criticized," *Detroit News,* 5 Aug. 1980, A-1.

20. *Poletown Lives!* transcript, p. 10.

21. Detroit City Planning Commission, Report, 20 Oct. 1980, p. 14. The planning commission's report listed the following deficiencies:

—The 6,150 permanent jobs alluded to in the Section 108 loan guarantee application are retained jobs which are vulnerable to automation. The EDC should "make every effort" to require GM to provide at least 6,000 for twelve years.

—The EIS predicts the city will break even in fifteen years. This does not take into account the likelihood of a $60 million tax abatement. In addition, the EIS includes revenue from GM's older Detroit Cadillac plants, as if they were somehow connected to the project.

—Only $63 million of the $199.7 million known to be needed for the project had been secured.

—GM's timetable precluded any expert analysis of whether GM's land demands were, as required by law, "reasonably necessary to carry out the purpose of the Plan." And even if they were not "there is no assurance that GM would revise its criteria even if the specialists found that the project would be feasible on a smaller amount of land."

—GM's timetable required a waiver on the EIS's preparation. Therefore, the council would be unable to hear criticisms even of the abbreviated document before voting on it. "This brings about the potential that all the social, economic, and physical impacts that would be generated by the Project may not be fully addressed . . . or rectified before the project initiation."

—The city's $30 million Urban Development Action Grant was unusual because of its unprecedented size, its assignment in the application for land acquisition and relocation while CEDD proposed using it to repay the Section 108 loan, and because its approval or rejection would occur months after the council had to vote on the project.

22. Patricia Chargot, "A Portrait of Poletown/ Framed by Its Past, Its Spirit of Survival Has No Boundaries," *Detroit Free Press*, 23 June 1980, A-3.

23.Luther Jackson, "GM's Commitment on New City Plant Expected This Week," *Detroit Free Press*, 24 Sept. 1980, A-3. The 1,362 "residents" refers to homeowners. There were 4,200 residents.

24. Patricia Chargot, Luther Jackson, "GM Site a Doomed World/Detroit-Hamtramck Residents Anxiously Await Bulldozers," *Detroit Free Press*, 6 Oct. 1980, A-1.

25. "GM Plant: A Federal Loan Is Just a Small Step on a Most Challenging Project," *Detroit Free Press* editorial, 11 Oct. 1980, A-8.

26. Yamasaki expressed frustration that the *Free Press* did not publish even one of his exclusive July 1981 arrest photos inside the church. These photos showed clearly the overpowering police presence. (See pp. 179-87 in this volume.)

27. Robert Roach, "New GM Factory Won't Add Any Jobs," *Detroit News*, 22 Oct. 1980, A-1.

28. Robert Roach, "State Staffer Disputes Aid for Cadillac Plant," *Detroit News*, 24 Oct. 1980, A-1

29. Robert Roach, Steve Konicki, "Quick Talker Sells GM plant—But He Buys Criticism," *Detroit News*, 2 Nov. 1980, A-1.

30. "HUD's Good Timing," *Detroit News* editorial, 17 Oct. 1980, p. A-8.

31. "GM's Michigan Investment," *Detroit News* editorial, 19 Oct. 1980, A-14.

32. "Poletown Area Deserves Better," *Macomb Daily* editorial, 10 Dec. 1980, A-6.

33. WDIV-TV, editorial, 5 Feb. 1981, 6:28 P.M.; 6 Feb. 1981, 12:28 P.M.

34. WJBK-TV, "Viewpoint," 7 April 1981.

35. WXYZ-TV, 6-9 March 1981.

36. "Continue Poletown Challenge," *Michigan Chronicle*, 21 March 1981, p. 1.

37. Kirk Cheyfitz, "Why It's a Good Idea to Bulldoze 'Poletown,'" *Monthly Detroit*, May 1981, p. 4.

38. Greg Kowalski, "Letters," *Detroit Free Press*, 17 May 1981.

39. Michael Betzold, "Push Comes to Shove," *Detroit Metro Times*, pts. 1 and 2, 13 Nov. 1980, 27 Nov. 1980.

40. James Kelly, with research by Barrett Seaman, "The Last Days of Poletown—A Neighborhood Faces Doom and a New Plant May Rise," *Time Magazine*, 30 March 1981, p. 29.

41. Robert McCabe, director of GM's treasurer's office, to Keith Rolland, director of Community Reinvestment Program at the Riverside Church Interfaith Center on Corporate Responsibility, New York, June 1981.

42. Colman McCarthy, "GM, the Gentle Goliath, Is Winning," *Detroit Free Press*, 9 April 1981, A-9.

43. Jack Anderson, "GM's Mighty Appetite Threatens Poletown," *Detroit Free Press*, 9 April 1981, A-9.

44. William Safire, "Poletown's Wrecker's Ball," *New York Times*, 30 April 1981, A-23.

45. David Moberg, "GM Retools Detroit," *In These Times*, 4 Feb. 1981, p. 1.

46. Jeanie Wylie, "A Neighborhood Dies So GM Can Live," *Village Voice*, 8 July 1981, p. 1. See Appendix B for details of GM's plant construction in those areas.

47. George Corsetti, Jeanie Wylie, Richard Wieske, *Poletown Lives!* released March 1983. For previews write Information Factory, 3512 Courville, Detroit, Mich. 48224.

48. Dan Luria interview with author, 13 Nov. 1981, for a review of his "Rational Reindustrialization" booklet.

49. Ron Reosti, quoted by Larry Tell, "Detroit Fray: Progress v. Property," *National Law Journal*, 1 June 1981, p. 1; and interview with Ron Brownstein, CSRL, 26 June 1981 .

50. NOAR, What Is Good for GM Is Not Good for America, (Detroit, Mich.)

51. "If Detroit Collapses, the State Will Also. . . " *Ebony*, Feb. 1974, p. 35.

52. Dearden laid out his position in a clergy newsletter: "It did not seem proper for the Church to offer positive support to the proposed plan. That would have involved taking sides against some in the local community. . . . At the same time, the Church could not credibly voice concern for the severe unemployment in our community and stand in positive opposition to a proposal which would generate hundreds of jobs. . . . A position of neutrality toward the plan was chosen as the most proper one. Though it is true that many people in the area are

happy at the prospect of being able to go elsewhere, it was evident that some would experience pain at the prospect of moving. In order to lighten that pain, a decision was made to involve staff members of the Department of Christian Services with the representatives of the parishes." *Priests' Newsletter*, 30 March 1981.

53. Harry Cook, Greg Skwira, "Jubilation over Poletown Plant Turning to Worry," *Detroit Free Press*, 2 July 1980.

54. Judith Gaines, "Ethnic Area Losing Fight against GM," *Atlanta Journal and Constitution*, 3 May 1981, A-20.

55. Thomas Ewald, "Poletown Church Group Hopes to Ease Resettlement Fight," *Michigan Catholic*, 3 Oct. 1980, p. 1. In fact, the *Michigan Catholic* article noted that Poletown residents were experiencing "shock and fear" and that feelings of hopelessness were giving way to "anger and a strong-willed determination on the people's part to fight this corporate intrusion into their neighborhood." The purpose of the new archdiocesan committee, it explained, was "to quell some of that tension building within the community."

56. Ibid. Another local spokesperson, Francis Skalski of nearby St. Hyacinth's, told the bishop, "Win or lose the church should take a definite stand for the people just as the church had in Poland. There was a risk involved, a chance he might get burned for it, but I felt it was a risk the church should take. You talk about El Salvador, you talk about other places in the world where the rights of people are being taken away and the church takes a stand. Yet, when it comes to something right here, it seems some officials in the church feel they shouldn't make a decision." Francis Skalski, interview with Ron Brownstein (CSRL), 8 June 1981.

57. James Ricci, "The Iron Priest of Poletown," *Detroit Free Press*, 15 May 1981, D-1. Under the previous cardinal, Karasiewicz had been sent to study in Rome and employed within the chancery when he returned. Dearden removed Karasiewicz to small urban parishes. During Vatican II Karasiewicz felt the devil entered the church and said so. In addition, the cardinal found it difficult to remove Karasiewicz from St. Casimir's, a Polish and Hispanic parish that the priest had come to love.

58. Tim Kiska, "Fiery Priest Dies at 59," *Detroit Free Press*, 15 Dec. 1981, A-1.

59. Joseph Karasiewicz, interview by the Center.

60. Ewald, "Poletown Church Group."

61. Marco Trbovich. "Ethnic Detroit/Polish Life," *Detroit Free Press*, 25 March 1973, A-1.

62. Wladyslaw Gowin, "Description of Cardinal as Insensitive to Poles Is Inaccurate," *Michigan Catholic*, 20 March 1981.

63. David Crumm, "Szoka Moves to Close 43 Urban Churches," *Detroit Free Press*, 29 Sept. 1988, A-1.

64. Joyce Garrett, telephone interview with author, 7 April, 1981.

65. Coleman Young, quoted in Ken Fireman, "Jobs Win, Community Loses in Poletown," *Detroit Free Press*, 7 May 1981, A-11.

66. For instance, city council chairperson Erma Henderson wrote in an 18

Feb. 1981 letter to Robert Selwa: "I take issue with your assertion that it is the city and not GM who is displacing these people. If GM had given us four to six years, we could conceivably have prepared a site in and around River Rouge Park and displaced no one. Make no mistake, we are cooperating with GM but everything that has happened thus far has been at their behest."

67. Gary Blonston, "The Profits, the Loss," *Detroit Free Press Sunday Magazine*, 22 Nov. 1981, p. 57.

68. Corinne Gilb, quoted in *Rural American Women*, a newsletter published in May-June 1981, p. 2.

Chapter 6

1. "MERB Subcomittee Report on Detroit Central Industrial Park Project," *Detroit Free Press*, 2 Jan. 1981, A-2.

2. *Poletown Lives!* transcript, p. 4.

3. Richard Hodas filed suit, challenging Martin's decision when it was made public in April 1981.

4. Bob Giannini, quoted in "This Neighborhood Is My Family's Entire Life," *Bulletin*, 24 Feb. 1981.

5. Gus Speth, of the Council for Environmental Quality, to Moon Landrieu, secretary of HUD, 19 Jan. 1981.

6. Ralph Nader to Roger Smith, 30 Jan. 1981.

7. "Ralph Nader's Mission," *Detroit News* editorial, 3 Feb. 1981, A-16.

8. "Cadillac: The Case for Renewal Outweighs Nader's Argument," *Detroit Free Press* editorial, 3 Feb. 1981, A-8.

9. An editorial in the *Bulletin* read: "These policies represent a deadend and can only hold back the struggle in Poletown. . . . The plans to demolish Poletown and indeed to close plants throughout the country are not some unfortunate mistake but is an integral part of the government's policy to make the working class pay for the economic crisis. Every struggle today to defend housing, jobs, and living standards is inescapably a political struggle against the government." "Beware of Nader's Raiders," 20 Feb. 1981.

10. Hamtramck had forgone all federal grants for twelve years because it failed to resolve complaints by black residents who won a court verdict that "the City of Hamtranck . . . has been conducting a program of 'Negro removal'" by condemning black neighborhoods for new development. The case was finally resolved so that the $30 million UDAG could be received. Joseph Serafino, *West of Warsaw* (Hamtramck, Mich.: Avenue Publishing Co., 1983), p. 50.

11. National Bank of Detroit was founded in 1933 by General Motors and the U.S. government's Reconstruction Finance Corporation. Its president during the 1980s has been Charles T. Fisher III, a member of GM's Fisher family. NBD continues to handle a variety of GM accounts and its president is on GM's board of directors.

12. Harry Cook, "Members Rail at Poletown Church's Sale," *Detroit Free Press*, 24 Feb 1981, A-3; AP report, "Cardinal under Fire over Old Church," *Daytona Beach Morning Journal*, 25 Feb. 1981, B-16.

13. Ibid.

14. Joseph Karasiewicz, rector of the Immaculate Conception Church, to Roger Smith, 19 Feb. 1981.

15. Tom Olechowski, PNC president, to Pope John Paul II, 25 Feb. 1981.

16. Douglas Ilka, "Court Halts Poletown Evacuation," *Detroit News*, 21 Feb. 1981, A-1.

17. Thomas Ewald, "Is Supreme Court Too Late for Poletown?" *Michigan Catholic*, 1 March 1981.

18. Ron Dzwonkowski, "Poletown Council Suit Goes to High Court Today," *Lansing State Journal*, 3 March 1981; "Court Vows Rapid Ruling on Poletown," *Detroit News*, 4 March 1981, A-4.

19. "Rapid Ruling."

20. Dzwonkowski, ""Poletown Council Suit."

21. "Rapid Ruling"; Dzwonkowski, "Poletown Council Suit."

22. Jeanie Wylie, Metro newswire report, 4 March 1981.

23. Pat Shellenbarger, "Top Court Vows Fast Poletown Decision," *Detroit News*, 4 March 1981, A-1.

24. Luther Jackson, "High Court Hears Poletown's Case," *Detroit Free Press*, 4 March 1981, A-3.

25. Ken Fireman, "Trials of Coleman Young: Joy—and Fury," *Detroit Free Press*, 20 April 1981, A-1; *Poletown Lives!* transcript, p. 5.

26. Lou Mleczko, "GM Site Foes Map U.S. suit," *Detroit News*, 11 March 1981, A-1.

27. Emily Gail gained local renown when she hired planes to carry the message "Say something nice about Detroit" over other U.S. cities.

28. Lou Mleczko, Joan Walter, "Ruling Cheers Many; They're Ready to Move," *Detroit News*, 14 March 1981, A-3.

29. Excerpts from the court's opinion, reprinted in the *Detroit News*, 14 March 1981, A-1; Luther Jackson, "Court Paves Way for GM Project," *Detroit Free Press*, 14 March 1981, A-1.

30. Pat Shellenberger, Robert Reach, "Benefits to Public Are Key," *Detroit News*, 14 March 1981, A-1.

31. Ibid.; Jackson, "Court Paves Way."

32. Patricia Chargot, "How Poletown Views the Ruling," *Detroit Free Press*, 14 March 1981, A-1.

33. Patricia Chargot, "Rally in Poletown Celebrates Court Approval of the GM Plant," *Detroit Free Press*, 15 March 1981, A-1.

34. Joan Walter, Bill Clark, "Poletown: Its Spirit Fades as Neighborhood Dies," *Detroit News*, 15 March 1981, A-1; Denise Crittendon, "200 March in Support of GM Poletown Plant," *Detroit News*, 15 March 1981, A-12.

35. Hodas added that "the secret activities of New Detroit also put a new light on the recent strongly worded editorial on WJBK-TV 2 in favor of GM's position and against the residents fighting to save their homes and shops. That editorial was delivered by Bob McBride, another member of your board."

36. Luther Jackson, "Buses Help Swell Ranks at GM Rally," *Detroit Free Press*, 17 April 1981, A-1.

37. Joseph Karasiewicz to Roger Smith, 20 March 1981.

38. Richard Wilcke, president of the Council for a Competitive Economy, address to the Poletown Neighborhood Council, 31 March 1981.

39. Monroe Walker, "Must Get Tax Break, GM Warns," *Detroit News,* 2 April 1981, B-2.

40. Luther Jackson, "Tax Break for GM Unsure, Council Says," *Detroit Free Press,* 2 April 1981, A-3; Walker, "Must Get Tax Break."

41. David Moberg, "GM Retools Detroit," *In These Times,* 4 Feb. 1981, p. 1.

42. Walker, "Must Get Tax Break."

43. Jackson, "Tax Break for GM Unsure."

44. Walker, "Must Get Tax Break."

45. Tim Kiska, Luther Jackson, "Tax Break for GM Approved," *Detroit Free Press,* 3 April 1981, A-3.

46. Ken Fireman, ". . .and the City Council Tempts the Giant with a Hefty Break on Taxes," *Detroit Free Press,* 9 April 1981, A-9.

47. Fireman, "Trials of Coleman Young." A few years later Fireman incurred the mayor's wrath again when he wrote a series exposing corruption in the administration. The mayor cried racism and went on a campaign against Fireman.

48. Hugh Davis, Detroit attorney, interview with author, 31 March 1981.

49. However, Feikens thoroughly alienated many in the black community when he said: "One of the things that we have to give black people the time to learn to do is learn how to run city government, to run projects like the water and sewer plant. Unfortunately, they're still in an era of development, many of them, in which they think all you have to do is talk about this thing." Feiken's remark was made after two friends of the mayor were sued for abuse of affirmative action contracts in the city's Water and Sewage Department. *Detroit Free Press,* 2 May 1986.

50. Joseph Campeau was a major Hamtramck artery which would have been left intact under this design. Parking for the plant would have been across the street.

51. Luther Jackson, "GM Says It Tested Many Plant Sites," *Detroit Free Press,* 4 April 1981, A-3.

52. However, cross-examination revealed that part of the problem was that two of the designs called for moving the power plant to the north which would intrude onto a Conrail holding yard for the Chevrolet Gear and Axle plant. Asked if the Chevrolet plant couldn't be accommodated in some other way, Conn answered that it could, but added that would mean that Grand Trunk Railroad would have to provide the yard. "That's a pretty lucrative contract and I can't see us [giving it up] just because GM wants us to," Conn said.

53. Robert Roach, "GM Plant Granted Tax Break," *Detroit News,* 16 April 1981, B-14; Luther Jackson, "City Destroying History in Poletown, Panel Says," *Detroit Free Press,* 16 April 1981, A-3.

54. On their own, residents printed up a flier offering $2,500 in exchange for information that would convict Poletown's arsonists and thieves.

55. Roach, "GM Plant Granted Tax Break."

56. Jackson, "City Destroying History." Hodas's letter also reported that "Mr. Hal B. Stickney of Star International Enterprises called because he was upset at not being permitted to bid for a subcontract for demolition of houses in Poletown. He spoke with people at Turner Construction Co. and was told that the faster subcontractors knock down houses the more they are paid. Mr. Stickney wanted to knock the houses down in a manner that would save the lumber for future use."

57. Roach, "GM Plant Granted Tax Break."

58. James Ryan dissenting, Poletown Neighborhood Council v. the City of Detroit and the Detroit Economic Development Corp. , 7 March 1981.

59. Luther Jackson, "Judge OKs Large Area in Poletown," *Detroit Free Press,* 23 April 1981, A-3.

60. Moving was a particular hardship for the black churches in Poletown because, unlike the Catholics, they did not have a built-in constituency. The pastors would have to recreate a congregation.

61. Luther Jackson, "GM Breaks Ground in Poletown; A 'Day of Triumph,' Young Says," *Detroit Free Press,* 2 May 1981, A-1.

62. George Bullard, "Blessed Are the Soles at Gucci's," *Detroit Free Press,* 5 May 1981, A-1.

Chapter 7

1. Iver Peterson, "Poletown Vigil Fails to Stop Bulldozers," *New York Times,* 5 May 1981, A-16.

2. Robert Roach, "Court Will Hear New Arguments," *Detroit News,* 1 May 1981, B-1

3. Sandy Livingston, journal, p. 4, Center for the Study of Responsive Law.

4. Donald Postma, GM public relations vice president, to Sigrid Dale, 7 May 1981.

5. Patricia Chargot, "Suburbanites Loot Homes in Poletown," *Detroit Free Press,* 9 May 1981.

6. Jack Etkin, "In GM's Shadow," *Kansas City Times,* 6 June 1981, C-25.

7. George Bullard, "Politics Fails; They Try Prayer," *Detroit News,* 11 May 1981, A-1.

8. Ibid.

9. Joan Walter, Robert Ankeny, "Poletown Church Gets Stay from Judge," *Detroit News,* 12 May 1981.

10. Harry Cook, "Demolition of Poletown Church Delayed by Judge until June 17," *Detroit Free Press,* 12 May 1981, A-6.

11. Joe Stroud, "Pain Is Real, But Can the Church Be Saved?" *Detroit Free Press* editorial, 12 May 1981, A-8.

12. Sandy McClure, "Shock and Hysteria for Pope's Kin in Area," *Detroit Free Press,* 14 May 1981, A-8.

13. "Dearden Declines GM's Offer to Rescue Church," *Detroit Free Press,* 15 May 1981, A-1.

14. Don Tschirhart, "Dearden Stand Dooms Church," *Detroit News*, 15 May 1981, A-1.

15. Harry Cook, "First Tears of Joy; Then a New Anger," *Detroit Free Press*, 15 May 1981, A-1.

16. Don Tschirhart, "Unmoved! Dearden Spurns GM Offer to Shift Church," *Detroit News*, 15 May 1981, A-1.

17. "GM Announces Proposal to Save Poletown Church," *New Center News*, 49, no. 16 (18 May 1981):1.

18. Thomas Ewald, "GM Offers Poletown a Reprieve," *Michigan Catholic*, 22 May 1981, p. 5.

19. "Dearden Declines GM's Offer." Asked by a journalism class, in August 1983, if he would ever lie for General Motors, Postma said the occasion would not arise, but if it did he supposed he'd be a "good soldier."

20. Harry Cook, "Church Doomed Months Ago?" *Detroit Free Press*, 16 May 1981, A-1.

21. Joe Stroud, "A Sad Ending in Fight to Save a Bond to the Past," *Detroit Free Press* editorial, 17 May 1981.

22. Ewald, "GM Offers Poletown a Reprieve."

23. "Dearden Declines GM's Offer."

24. George Bullard, "Defiant Priest Had No Choice," *Detroit News*, 16 May 1981, A-15.

25. Harry Cook, "New Archbishop Firm on Poletown," *Detroit Free Press*, 18 May 1981, A-1.

26. Alan Lenhoff, "GM Pushes for Pay Concessions," *Detroit Free Press*, 23 May 1981, A-3.

27. Ibid.

28. Robert Roach, "Cockrel Hits Council on Poletown Action," *Detroit News*, 28 May 1981.

29. "No Plant Guarantee, Young Admits," *Detroit News*, 31 May 1981, B-8.

30. Luther Jackson, Keith Harriston, "Nader's Poletown Assistance Criticized," *Detroit Free Press*, 30 May 1981, A-3.

31. Keith Richburg, "Polish Resistance, Detroit-style," *Washington Post*, 1 June 1981, A-1.

32. "Poletown Deaths Blamed on GM Project," *Bulletin*, 16 June 1981, p. 14.

33. Ibid.

34. Martha Hindes, "Faithful Place Fate of Church in God's Hands," *Detroit News*, 18 June 1981, B-2.

35. Stanley Stachelski, of the Immaculate Conception Church, to Joseph Karasiewicz, rector, 17 June 1981.

36. Harry Cook, "Fires in Deserted Poletown Up 250% Since February," *Detroit Free Press*, 30 June 1981, A-3.

37. Ann Cohen, "Rash of Arson Blazes Erupts in Poletown," *Detroit News*, 1 July 1981, B-1.

38. Jeanie Wylie, "A Neighborhood Dies So GM Can Live," *Village Voice*, 8 July 1981, p. 1; Marianne Rzepka, "Poletown's Faithful Cling to Their Church," *Detroit Free Press*, 10 July 1981, C-1.

39. It was impossible to preserve the church's outstanding frescoes, be-

cause the paintings had been attached to the church's walls and ceiling with a mixture of wheat paste and black strap molasses—a seal intended to be irrevocable.

Chapter 8

1. Vilandria King, "They Still Yearn for Poletown," *Detroit News*, 11 July 1982, A-11.

2. Ibid.

3. Marianne Rzepka, "They Won't Let Poletown Die," *Detroit Free Press Sunday Magazine*, 18 July 1982, p. 9.

4. Harold Kaczynski died suddenly in 1987 at the age of seventy. On the day that he was buried, the *Free Press* ran a banner headline announcing that the Poletown plant was closing and 2,500 workers were laid off. John Lippert, "GM to Close Poletown 3 Weeks," *Detroit Free Press*, 11 Nov. 1987, A-1. A further irony was that his children chose a cemetery plot at Mount Olivet Cemetery, which may be seized by the city through the power of eminent domain for expansion of the nearby city airport.

5. Rzepka, "They Won't Let Poletown Die," pp. 18-19.

6. Gary Blonston, "Poletown: The Profits, the Loss," *Detroit Free Press Sunday Magazine*, 22 Nov. 1981, p. 38.

7. Laura Berman, "Businessman Fought GM Poletown Plant," *Detroit Free Press*, 19 July 1982, A-5.

8. King, "They Still Yearn."

9. Robert Roach, "GM Delays Poletown Plant," *Detroit News*, 3 Nov. 1981, A-3; Michael Robinson, Ric Bohy, "Poletown Delay Means Layoffs, UAW Warns," *Detroit News*, 29 July 1982, A-1.

10. Roach, "GM Delays Poletown Plant."

11. Christine Kujawski, co-chairperson of the Friends of Father Joe, in a public letter, 17 Dec. 1981.

12. Tim Kiska, "Fiery Poletown Priest Dies at 59," *Detroit Free Press*, 15 Dec. 1981, A-1.

13. *Poletown Lives!* transcript, p. 17.

14. Stuart Elliot, "A Column of Steel Backs GM Promises," *Detroit Free Press*, 26 Jan. 1982, B-8.

15. David Turnley, *Detroit Free Press* photographer, reported this conversation to Jeanie Wylie after Saber's removal from the house. Turnley remained on site, despite police orders that he leave, until Saber was put in the police car.

16. Judy Diebolt, "'Worse than Warsaw,'" *Detroit Free Press*, 23 March 1982, A-3.

17. David Markiewicz, "City Took 130 Lots Wrongly," Detroit News, 25 Feb. 1987, B-1.

18. John Nehman, "Jefferson Proposal Stirs Mixed Feelings for Ratification Vote," *Detroit News*, 10 Aug. 1986, D-1.

19. Bruce Alpert, "Residents Hear Buyout Plan," *Detroit News*, 5 Dec. 1986, B-1.

20. Nicholas Farina to the *Detroit Free Press*, spring 1987. During a 26 April

1988 telephone interview, Farina explained that he had worked in the neighborhood at St. Rose of Lima for five years and was involved in a lot of neighborhood organizations. "I think the city had an idea [for that area] for a long, long time, because we tried to buy land and they wouldn't sell. They'd just say they had a development project in mind." Also, as in Poletown, headlines later announced that the Chrysler plant would be delayed. The land was cleared and the public monies supplied, but employment at the plant would be deferred for at least a year. *Detroit News,* 15 Dec. 1987.

21. Corinne Gilb, director of City Planning Department, in a hearing at the City-County Building, Detroit, 27 April 1983.

22. Peter Gavrilovich, "Talk of Land Sale for Tiger Shrine Troubles Congregation's Conscience," *Detroit Free Press,* 17 July 1985, A-3.

23. Teresa Blossom, "Bridge Area Is Residential Limbo," *Detroit Free Press,* 15 Feb. 1987, B-1.

24. Billy Bowles, "A Neighborhood Past Hope," *Detroit Free Press,* 12 March 1984, E-1.

25. Earle Eldridge, "Council Shifts Grant to Poletown," *Detroit News,* 13 July 1985, A-13.

26. Rosanne Less, Ron Williams, "The Secret Belle Isle Casino Gambling Plan," *Detroit Metro Times,* 10 April 1985, p. 1.

27. Corinne Gilb quit her job as director of city planning partly because "planning in Detroit is the mayor's phone number." Gilb told a trade journal, "I don't believe the mayor's style is compatible with planning." Rick Ratliff, "For Detroit Planning Dial Mayor—Ex-Official," *Detroit Free Press,* 2 Dec. 1986, A-3.

28. George Cantor, "Detroiters Suffer a Sense of Alienation as They Flee the City," *Detroit News,* 10 Aug. 1985, A-8.

29. Chuck Moss, "Save Detroit; Begin with Tiger Stadium," *Detroit News,* 10 Feb. 1988, A-14.

30. Bruce Alpert, "New Center Residents Campaign to Keep Homes," *Detroit News,* 29 Nov. 1984, E-1.

31. Chris Singer, "East Side Activists Urge Tax Strike," *Detroit News,* 7 Feb. 1988, B-1.

32. "Pensions: City Council Members Finally Do the Right Thing," *Detroit Free Press,* 22 Sept. 1988, A-10; Zachare Ball, "Cobo Hall Rejection Debated," *Detroit Free Press,* 4 Aug. 1988, A-15.

33. "Looking for a Fallen Angel," *Detroit News,* 4 Nov., 1985, A-30.

34. "Inside Story—Poletown 4 Years Later," *The Awakening* 2, no. 7 (July 1985), NOAR, P.O. Box 07249, Detroit, Mich. 48207.

35. Neil Shine, "It's Progress Alright, But Poletown Paid Price," *Detroit Free Press,* 26 Feb. 1985, back page.

36. Leon Pastalon, "A Study of Relocation of Elderly Residents: the Detroit Central Industrial Park Project," University of Michigan, pp. 2, 3, 21, 26, 28.

37. Joseph Gorham, *1981-1982 Central Industrial Park Relocation Project,* prepared by the Relocation Unit of the Neighborhood Services Organization, p. 4. Pat Barszenski researched and wrote a Wayne State University master's thesis titled "A Retrospective Study on the Effects of Forced Relocation: Case Study

Poletown." Of 100 people surveyed, 76 percent indicated they wished they could return to Poletown. (Barszenski noted romanticization of the neighborhood.) A full 100 percent said they daydreamed about Poletown. Respondents expressed sadness, loneliness, depression, confusion, and anger, Barszenski reported.

38. *Wall Street Journal*, 13 May 1986, as cited in *Choosing Sides: Unions and the Team Concept*, by Mike Parker and Jane Slaughter (Detroit: Labor Notes/South End Press, 1988), p. 196.

39. Anonymous interview by Jane Slaughter, 12 May 1987, for Parker and Slaughter, *Choosing Sides*.

40. Larry Brown, project planner at CEDD, interview with author, 9 Feb. 1984.

41. Andre McGill, "How Complex Deals Renew City," *Detroit News*, 13 Jan. 1985, A-1.

42. Ibid.

43. AP and UPI, "Educators Fret Over GM Tax Bid," *Detroit News*, 15 July 1985, A-3.

44. David Kushma, "Detroit Sees GM Closings as a $10 Million Tax Loss," *Detroit Free Press*, 25 Feb. 1987, A-1; Teresa Blossom, Helen Fogel, "City Help for Jobless Sought; Fleetwood Employees Sue UAW," *Detroit Free Press*, 11 March 1987, B-9.

45. N. Scott Vance, "GM Workers Facing Layoffs Ask City's Help," *Detroit News*, A-3.

46. Michelle Krebs, "GM Reduces Car-Building Costs," *Automotive News*, 25 May 1987, p. 33.

47. Owen Bieber, UAW president, statement before the subcommittee on labor, Senate Labor and Human Resources Committee, on the Subject of General Motors Plant Closings, 26 Jan. 1987.

48. "Hits Record," *Detroit Free Press*, 8 Jan. 1983, A-1.

49. Bruce Alpert, "Mayor Gives Details on Crime Fight," *Detroit News*, 8 Feb. 1984, A-1.

50. Bruce Alpert, "Gun Law, Slaying Linked by Young," *Detroit News*, 3 Feb. 1985, A-3; Monroe Walker, "Cops, ACLU Back Self-Defense," *Detroit News*, 4 Feb. 1985, A-1.

51. Al Stark, "Vigilante-style Law and Order Can Get Scary," *Detroit News*, 7 Feb. 1985, A-3.

52. David Grant, "Violent Crimes Soar in Detroit," *Detroit News*, 11 Nov. 1983, A-3; Howard Warren, "'Don't Become Paranoid' Chief Gives Cops Talk on Shootings," *Detroit News*, 28 Jan. 1983, A-3; Jim Tittsworth, "Police Team Trains for Crisis Duty," *Detroit News*, 15 Nov. 1987, C-1; Bill McGraw, "Seized Cash to Aid City War on Drugs," *Detroit Free Press*, 27 Sept. 1988, A-3.

53. David Kushma, "$46 Million City Overrun of GM Poletown Project," *Detroit Free Press*, 23 Sept. 1984, A-1.

54. Robert Roach, "Poletown Panel Assails Confiscation Tactics," *Detroit News*, 16 Oct. 1981, B-3.

55. David Kushma, "$46 Million City Overrun."

56. To cover initial attorney fees for Poletown awards, the mayor appropri-

ated $3 million previously designated for neighborhood development. (One of the programs eliminated would have enabled Michigan Legal Services to help identify indigent people who were entitled to, but not receiving, government aid.) In 1985 Young vetoed the city council budget, saying that they erred in foreseeing a $1 million surplus. Then, one month later he announced that there *was* a $1 million surplus, which he allocated to repay a Michigan state loan for the Poletown project (*Detroit News*, 10 July 1985).

57. Robert Roach, "Loss of Coal Firm is Blamed on the City," *Detroit News*, 6 Oct. 1981, A-1.

58. Rebecca Powers, "Poletown's Forgotten Few Sadly Await Settlements," *Detroit News*, 21 April 1985, A-3.

59. Ibid.

60. *Housing and Development Reporter*, 09:1112, 2 July 1979, Bureau of National Affairs, Inc., p. 96.

61. Central Industrial Park Project Citizen's District Council Report, 25 May 1983.

62. Powers, "Poletown's Forgotten Few."

63. Larry Brown, interview with author, 9 Feb. 1984.

Appendices

1. Emily J. Lewis, "Corporate Prerogative; 'Public Use' and a People's Plight: Poletown Neighborhood Council v. City of Detroit," *Detroit College of Law Review* 4 (1982): 914.

2. Laura Mansnerus, "Public Use, Private Use and Judicial Review in Eminent Domain," *New York University Law Review* 58, no. 2 (May1983): 409.

3. Lewis, "Corporate Prerogative," p. 916.

4. Stephen Lefkowitz, quoted in Larry Tell, "Detroit Fray: Progress v. Property," *National Law Journal* 3, no. 38 (1 June 1981): 1.

5. Ibid.

6. Mansnerus, "Public Use, Private Use," p. 409.

7. Jeanie Wylie, "A Neighborhood Dies So GM Can Live," *Village Voice*, 8 July 1981, p. 12.

8. Richard Rosenthal, Piper Area Association, interview with author, Detroit, 14 April 1981.

9. John Carroll, "Decisions Hold Up Many Other Construction Plans, Too," *Kansas City Times*, 30 April 1981, A-1.

10. Donald Woutat, "Oakland Site for GM Plant," *Detroit Free Press*, 1 Feb. 1980, A-1.

11. Alex Taylor, John Castine, "Oakland Auto Plant Expected," *Detroit Free Press*, 31 Jan. 1980, A-1.

12. James Bush, Eastern Michigan Environmental Action Council, interview with author, 14 Dec. 1981.

13. *Pontiac Waterford Times*, 20 March 1980.

14. Colin Covert, "Jobs Don't Salve Their Fears," *Detroit Free Press*, 9 March 1984, B-1.

15. Ibid.

16. Ibid.

Index

Deductions and Adjustments Worksheet

Note: *Use this worksheet only if you plan to itemize deductions or claim adjustments to income on your 1994 tax return.*

1 Enter an estimate of your 1994 itemized deductions. These include: qualifying home mortgage interest, charitable contributions, state and local taxes (but not sales taxes), medical expenses in excess of 7.5% of your income, and miscellaneous deductions. (For 1994, you may have to reduce your itemized deductions if your income is over $111,800 ($55,900 if married filing separately). Get Pub. 919 for details.) ... **1** $ _____

2 Enter:

$6,350 if married filing jointly or qualifying widow(er)
$5,600 if head of household
$3,800 if single
$3,175 if married filing separately
... **2** $ _____

3 **Subtract** line 2 from line 1. If line 2 is greater than line 1, enter -0- ... **3** $ _____

4 Enter an estimate of your 1994 adjustments to income. These include alimony paid and deductible IRA contributions ... **4** $ _____

5 **Add** lines 3 and 4 and enter the total ... **5** $ _____

6 Enter an estimate of your 1994 nonwage income (such as dividends or interest) ... **6** $ _____

7 **Subtract** line 6 from line 5. Enter the result, but not less than -0- ... **7** $ _____

8 **Divide** the amount on line 7 by $2,500 and enter the result here. Drop any fraction ... **8** _____

9 Enter the number from Personal Allowances Worksheet, line G, on page 1 ... **9** _____

10 **Add** lines 8 and 9 and enter the total here. If you plan to use the Two-Earner/Two-Job Worksheet, also enter this total on line 1, below. Otherwise, **stop here** and enter this total on Form W-4, line 5, on page 1. ... **10** _____

Two-Earner/Two-Job Worksheet

Note: *Use this worksheet only if the instructions for line G on page 1 direct you here.*

1 Enter the number from line G on page 1 (or from line 10 above if you used the Deductions and Adjustments Worksheet) ... **1** _____

2 Find the number in **Table 1** below that applies to the **LOWEST** paying job and enter it here ... **2** _____

3 If line 1 is **GREATER THAN OR EQUAL TO** line 2, subtract line 2 from line 1. Enter the result here (if zero, enter -0-) and on Form W-4, line 5, on page 1. **DO NOT** use the rest of this worksheet ... **3** _____

Note: *If line 1 is **LESS THAN** line 2, enter -0- on Form W-4, line 5, on page 1. Complete lines 4-9 to calculate the additional withholding amount necessary to avoid a year-end tax bill.*

4 Enter the number from line 2 of this worksheet ... **4** _____

5 Enter the number from line 1 of this worksheet ... **5** _____

6 **Subtract** line 5 from line 4 ... **6** _____

7 Find the amount in **Table 2** below that applies to the **HIGHEST** paying job and enter it here ... **7** $ _____

8 **Multiply** line 7 by line 6 and enter the result here. This is the additional annual withholding amount needed ... **8** $ _____

9 **Divide** line 8 by the number of pay periods remaining in 1994. (For example, divide by 26 if you are paid every other week and you complete this form in December 1993.) Enter the result here and on Form W-4, line 6, page 1. This is the additional amount to be withheld from each paycheck ... **9** $ _____

Table 1: Two-Earner/Two-Job Worksheet

Married Filing Jointly		All Others	
If wages from **LOWEST** paying job are—	Enter on line 2 above	If wages from **LOWEST** paying job are—	Enter on line 2 above
0 - $3,000	0	0 - $4,000	0
3,001 - 6,000	1	4,001 - 10,000	1
6,001 - 11,000	2	10,001 - 14,000	2
11,001 - 16,000	3	14,001 - 19,000	3
16,001 - 21,000	4	19,001 - 23,000	4
21,001 - 27,000	5	23,001 - 45,000	5
27,001 - 31,000	6	45,001 - 60,000	6
31,001 - 34,000	7	60,001 - 70,000	7
34,001 - 39,000	8	70,001 and over	8

Table 2: Two-Earner/Two-Job Worksheet

Married Filing Jointly		All Others	
If wages from **HIGHEST** paying job are—	Enter on line 7 above	If wages from **HIGHEST** paying job are—	Enter on line 7 above
0 - $ 50,000	$370	0 - $ 30,000	$370
50,001 - 100,000	690	30,001 - 60,000	690
100,001 - 130,000	760	60,001 - 110,000	760
130,001 - 220,000	880	110,001 - 220,000	880
220,001 and over	970	220,001 and over	970

Privacy Act and Paperwork Reduction Act Notice.—We ask for the information on this form to carry out the Internal Revenue laws of the United States. The Internal Revenue Code requires this information under sections 3402(f)(2)(A) and 6109 and their regulations. Failure to provide a completed form will result in your being treated as a single person who claims no withholding allowances; providing fraudulent information may also subject you to penalties. Routine uses of this information include giving it to the Department of Justice for civil and criminal litigation, and to cities, states, and the District of Columbia for use in administering their tax laws.

Form W-4 (1994)

Want More Money in Your Paycheck?

If you expect to be able to take the earned income credit for 1994, you can have part of it added to your take-home pay. For details, get Form W-5 from your employer.

Purpose. Complete Form W-4 so that your employer can withhold the correct amount of Federal income tax from your pay.

Exemption From Withholding. Read line 7 of the certificate below to see if you can claim exempt status. *If exempt, complete line 7; but do not complete lines 5 and 6.* No Federal income tax will be withheld from your pay. Your exemption is good for 1 year only. It expires February 15, 1995.

Note: *You cannot claim exemption from withholding if (1) your income exceeds $600 and includes unearned income (e.g., interest and dividends), and (2) another person can*

claim you as a dependent on their tax return.

Basic Instructions. Employees who are not exempt should complete the Personal Allowances Worksheet. Additional worksheets are provided on page 2 for employees to adjust their withholding allowances based on itemized deductions, adjustments to income, or two-earner/two-job situations. Complete all worksheets that apply to your situation. The worksheets will help you figure the number of withholding allowances you are entitled to claim. However, you may claim fewer allowances than this.

Head of Household. Generally, you may claim head of household filing status on your tax return only if you are unmarried and pay more than 50% of the costs of keeping up a home for yourself and your dependent(s) or other qualifying individuals.

Nonwage Income. If you have a large amount of nonwage income, such as interest or dividends, you should consider making estimated tax payments using Form 1040-ES.

Otherwise, you may find that you owe additional tax at the end of the year.

Two Earners/Two Jobs. If you have a working spouse or more than one job, figure the total number of allowances you are entitled to claim on all jobs using worksheets from only one Form W-4. This total should be divided among all jobs. Your withholding will usually be most accurate when all allowances are claimed on the W-4 filed for the highest paying job and zero allowances are claimed for the others.

Check Your Withholding. After your W-4 takes effect, you can use **Pub. 919**, Is My Withholding Correct for 1994?, to see how the dollar amount you are having withheld compares to your estimated total annual tax. We recommend you get Pub. 919 especially if you used the Two Earner/Two Job Worksheet and your earnings exceed $150,000 (Single) or $200,000 (Married). Call 1-800-829-3676 to order Pub. 919. Check your telephone directory for the IRS assistance number for further help.

Personal Allowances Worksheet

A	Enter "1" for **yourself** if no one else can claim you as a dependent	**A**
B	Enter "1" if: { • You are single and have only one job; or	
	• You are married, have only one job, and your spouse does not work; or }	**B**
	• Your wages from a second job or your spouse's wages (or the total of both) are $1,000 or less.	
C	Enter "1" for your **spouse**. But, you may choose to enter -0- if you are married and have either a working spouse or more than one job (this may help you avoid having too little tax withheld)	**C**
D	Enter number of **dependents** (other than your spouse or yourself) whom you will claim on your tax return . .	**D**
E	Enter "1" if you will file as **head of household** on your tax return (see conditions under **Head of Household** above)	**E**
F	Enter "1" if you have at least $1,500 of **child or dependent care expenses** for which you plan to claim a credit	**F**
G	Add lines A through F and enter total here. **Note:** This amount may be different from the number of exemptions you claim on your return ▶	**G**

For accuracy, do all worksheets that apply.
- If you plan to **itemize** or **claim adjustments to income** and want to reduce your withholding, see the **Deductions and Adjustments Worksheet** on page 2.
- If you are **single** and have **more than one job** and your combined earnings from all jobs exceed $30,000 OR if you are **married** and have **a working spouse or more than one job,** and the combined earnings from all jobs exceed $50,000, see the **Two-Earner/Two-Job Worksheet** on page 2 if you want to avoid having too little tax withheld.
- If **neither** of the above situations applies, **stop here** and enter the number from line G on line 5 of Form W-4 below.

------- Cut here and give the certificate to your employer. Keep the top portion for your records. -------

Form **W-4** Department of the Treasury Internal Revenue Service	**Employee's Withholding Allowance Certificate** ▶ For Privacy Act and Paperwork Reduction Act Notice, see reverse.	OMB No. 1545-0010 **1994**

1 Type or print your first name and middle initial	Last name	2 Your social security number
Michael A	McKee	185 60 1812

Home address (number and street or rural route)	3 ☐ Single ☒ Married ☐ Married, but withhold at higher Single rate.
1216 W Tioga St	Note: *If married, but legally separated, or spouse is a nonresident alien, check the Single box.*
City or town, state, and ZIP code	4 If your last name differs from that on your social security card, check
Phila PA 19140	here and call 1-800-772-1213 for more information ▶ ☐

5	Total number of allowances you are claiming (from line G above or from the worksheets on page 2 if they apply) .	5	0
6	Additional amount, if any, you want withheld from each paycheck	6	$ 0
7	I claim exemption from withholding for 1994 and I certify that I meet **BOTH** of the following conditions for exemption:

The time needed to complete this form will vary depending on individual circumstances. The estimated average time is: **Recordkeeping** 46 min., **Learning about the law or the form** 10 min., **Preparing the form** 69 min. If you have comments concerning the accuracy of these time estimates or suggestions for making this form more simple, we would be happy to hear from you. You can write to both the **Internal Revenue Service, Attention: Reports Clearance Officer, PC:FP, Washington, DC 20224;** and the **Office of Management and Budget, Paperwork Reduction Project (1545-0010), Washington, DC 20503. DO NOT** send the tax form to either of these offices. Instead, give it to your employer.